Broken Record

LEGISLATIVE POLITICS & POLICY MAKING

Series Editors

Jamie L. Carson, University of Georgia

James M. Curry, University of Utah

RECENT TITLES IN THE SERIES:

Broken Record: The Origins and Evolution of Recorded Voting in the U.S. Congress
MICHAEL S. LYNCH AND ANTHONY J. MADONNA

Waves of Discontent: Electoral Volatility, Public Policymaking, and the Health of American Democracy
JACOB F.H. SMITH

Strategic Responsiveness: How Congress Confronts Presidential Power
SCOTT H. AINSWORTH, BRIAN M. HARWARD, AND KENNETH W. MOFFETT

Home Field Advantage: Roots, Reelection, and Representation in the Modern Congress
CHARLES HUNT

The Committee: A Study of Policy, Power, Politics, and Obama's Historic Legislative Agenda on Capitol Hill, Second Edition
BRYAN W. MARSHALL AND BRUCE C. WOLPE

Minority Party Misery: Political Powerlessness and Electoral Disengagement
JACOB F. H. SMITH

The Politics of Herding Cats: When Congressional Leaders Fail
JOHN LOVETT

Committees and the Decline of Lawmaking in Congress
JONATHAN LEWALLEN

Losing to Win: Why Congressional Majorities Play Politics Instead of Make Laws
JEREMY GELMAN

It's Not Personal: Politics and Policy in Lower Court Confirmation Hearings
LOGAN DANCEY, KJERSTEN R. NELSON, AND EVE M. RINGSMUTH

On Parliamentary War: Partisan Conflict and Procedural Change in the U.S. Senate
JAMES I. WALLNER

For a complete list of titles in this series, please see www.press.umich.edu.

BROKEN RECORD

The Origins and Evolution of Recorded Voting in the U.S. Congress

Michael S. Lynch and Anthony J. Madonna

University of Michigan Press
Ann Arbor

Published in the United States of America by the
University of Michigan Press
First published September 2025

A CIP catalog record for this book is available from the British Library.

Library of Congress Cataloging-in-Publication Data

Names: Lynch, Michael S. author | Madonna, Anthony J. author
Title: Broken record : the origins and evolution of recorded voting in the U.S. Congress / Michael S. Lynch and Anthony J. Madonna.
Other titles: Origins and evolution of recorded voting in the United States Congress
Description: Ann Arbor : University of Michigan Press, 2025. | Series: Legislative politics and policy making | Includes bibliographical references (pages 201–223) and index.
Identifiers: LCCN 2025011778 (print) | LCCN 2025011779 (ebook) | ISBN 9780472077472 hardcover alk. paper | ISBN 9780472057474 paper alk. paper | ISBN 9780472905065 OA ebook
Subjects: LCSH: United States. Congress—Voting | United States. Congress—Reform | United States. Congress—History—20th century | United States. Congress—History—21st century
Classification: LCC E743 .L96 2025 (print) | LCC E743 (ebook) | DDC 324.973/0933—dc23/eng/20250610
LC record available at https://lccn.loc.gov/2025011778
LC ebook record available at https://lccn.loc.gov/2025011779

DOI: https://doi.org/10.3998/mpub.14374260

The University of Michigan Press's open access publishing program is made possible thanks to additional funding from the University of Michigan Office of the Provost and the generous support of contributing libraries.

Authorized Representative: Easy Access System Europe, Mustamäe tee 50, 10621 Tallinn, Estonia, gpsr.requests@easproject.com

Contents

Digital materials related to this title can be found on the Fulcrum platform via the following citable URL: https://doi.org/10.3998/mpub.14374260

Figures

Tables

Acknowledgments

This project began when we were still in graduate school at Washington University in St. Louis. We read a recent paper by our professor Matt Gabel and his colleagues on unrecorded voting in the European Parliament. The paper had a line in the introduction that said: "The contemporary US Congress differs from many other legislatures in that almost all legislative votes are by roll call" (Carruba et al. 2006, 691). Thanks to working with Steven S. Smith and having read many volumes of the *Congressional Record* under his tutelage, we were pretty sure that was not quite true. Congress spends a lot of time holding unrecorded votes. In 2009, we began exploring why Congress records some votes but doesn't record others—a mere 15 years later we think we have something to say about recorded and unrecorded voting in the US Congress.

Because we have been working on this project for over a decade, we have accrued many debts of gratitude. This began with the incredible mentors we worked with in graduate school. Steven Smith, Gary Miller, Itai Sened, Randy Calvert, Andrew Martin, Matt Gabel, and Brian Crisp all influenced our work on this project and our views on research and political science more generally.

Colleagues have played an invaluable role, as we have developed this project. We have both had numerous conversations and received excellent advice and feedback from Jason Roberts and Mike Crespin. Discussions with Keith T. Poole and Jamie Carson have also been very fruitful. Colleagues from both the University of Georgia and the University of Kansas, including Keith Dougherty, Erik Herron, Jamie Monogan, Scott Ainsworth, Alexa Bankert, and Geoff Sheagley, have all improved our work.

We presented this project in various forms at lots of conferences and have received a lot of great feedback. We appreciate the comments and suggestions we received from Nathan Kelly, James Wallner, David Karol, Hong Min Park, Frances Lee, Nicholas Howard, Greg Koger, Charles Finocchiaro, Sarah Treul, Richard Valelly, Soren Jordan, Jason Roberts, Larry Evans, Wendy J. Schiller, Adam Dynes, Adam Zelizer, Sarah Binder, Jon Bond, Mark E. Owens, Nolan McCarty, and Christopher Witko. We are especially appreciative of John Wilkerson's invitation to allow us to present this project at his 2017 Poli-Informatics conference and his excellent comments on the project. Similarly, we owe a great deal to John Aldrich and Dave Rohde for allowing us to present the full manuscript at the Annual Book Seminar hosted by the Political Institutions and Public Choice Program at Duke University in 2019. Their comments and those of other conference attendees were invaluable.

We are appreciative of the many people who assisted us on this project. Ed Burmila, Joel Sievert, Ryan Williamson, and Alice Kisaalita all coauthored conference papers with us that influenced this manuscript. Alice's excellent simulation and coding work have greatly improved Chapter 6 of the manuscript. Allison Vick's work editing chapters, and reminding us that most people do not know what a disappearing quorum is, has been invaluable.

The authors would like to thank Keith T. Poole, Joshua Clinton, John Lapinski, David Mayhew, Jed Stiglitz, Scott Adler, John Wilkerson, Mike Crespin, and Jason Roberts for making data available.

This book is ultimately a testament to student research. Since coding on this project began, it was serviced by three high school students, 17 graduate students, and 131 undergraduate students. Without the hard work of these students, this project would not have been possible. We would like to thank Alyssa Achiron, Haidi Al-Shabrawey, Nathaniel Ament-Stone, Rain Ammons, Ari Anderson, Whitney Arp, Matthew Baker, Alice Barker, Carys Behnke, Becca Bennett, Landon Benson, Ethan Boldt, Griffin Braid, Allison Brill, Lauren Corbett Bryant, Destiny Burch, Mark Burkett, Mary Carol Butterfield, Jason Byers, Mathilde Carpet, Maitri Chittidi, Kasey Clark, Aaron Cooperman, Ananda Costa, Shellea Crochet, Christina Chu, Amanda Delaperriere, Sarah Ensley, Michael Evans, James Everson, Patrick Fermia, Christopher Ferguson, Jason Fern, James Floyd, Matthew Fowler, Ryan Freeman, Jacob Frenkel, Catherine Funk, Vinita Gandhi, David Gelman, Sophie Giberga, Heather Globerman, Kunal Goel, Braden Goodgame, Katherine Graham, Hannah Greenberg, Casey Grippando, Cody Hall, Leyall Harb, Spencer Hardin, Jacquelyn Harms, Sharne Haywood, Brittany Helliar, Daniel Helmick, Cameron Henderson, Rory Hibbler, Kyle Hollimon, Lily Holmes, Eileen Hong, Nick Howard, Eric Howell, Elise Hynd, Dory Ille, Brooke Intlekofer,

Taylor Johnston, Sydney Juliano, Elizabeth Jurado, Mariliz Kastberg-Leonard, Da Hae Kim, Caitlyn Kinard, Michael Klein, Cody Knapp, Drew Lance, Haley Lattke, Maggie Little, Jill Maloney, Caleb Masten, Megan Mayfield, Zachary McDowell, Jordan McKissick, Gwen McMillan, Ellie McQuaig, Hayden McRee, Annabel McSpadden, Kayce Mobley, Mikayla Mobley, Amber Morgan, Erin Munger, Susan Murley, Wes Nichols, Katie Nisbet, Charlotte Norsworthy, Rob Oldham, Landon O'Neal, Tiernan O'Neill, Katie Opacity, Mark Owens, Kevin Parker, Caroline Pearson, Matthew Peney, Colin Phillips, Alex Pinckney, Justin Pinkerman, Nathan Pinnell, Spencer Pipkin, Grace Pittman, Elaina Polson, Alex Porter, Maribeth Portier, Kelsey Pruitt, Alexandria Putman, Nathaniel Rice, Scott Riley, Matthew Roberts, Harrison Rogers, Dustin Sammons, Adrien Sandercock, Christian Schoeberl, Laine Shay, Melissa Siegel, Joel Sievert, Veselin Simonov, Rob Smalley, Natalie Speier, Darrian Stacy, Chase Stell, Melissa Strickland, Jessica Suh, Rachel Surminsky, Zach Taylor, Andrew Teal, Kelsey Thomas, Jillian Tracy, Javier Trejo, Maxwell Turner, Katie Umholtz, Abbe Van Gorder, Jaaie Varshney, Adam Veale, Angelina Velaj, Allison Vick, Michael Watson, Hannah Weiss, Ryan Williamson, Simon Williamson, Andrew Wills, Adam Wittenstein, and Sarah Young.

ONE

Recorded Voting in Congress

Powers and Limitations

> [Recorded voting leads to] stuffing the journals with [votes] on frivolous occasions . . . misleading the people who never know the reasons determining the votes.
>
> —Nathaniel Gorham, 1781[1]

> There is no doubt but that [recorded votes] are frequently improper; but as there is no drawing a line, we must submit to the lesser evil for the sake of the greater good. This is almost the only way in which our constituents can be informed of the conduct of their respective delegates which in my opinion is of great importance for them to know.
>
> —John Jay, 1779[2]

The American Health Care Act of 2017

The 2016 election saw Republicans hold their majorities in the House and the Senate and gain control of the White House via Donald J. Trump's presidential election victory. This gave them unified control of the Congress and the presidency for the first time since President George W. Bush left office. Republican Party leaders in the House and Senate declared their top legislative priority for this new 115th Congress would be to repeal the Affordable Care Act (ACA), also known as Obamacare.

Speaker of the House Paul Ryan (R-WI) and House Republicans had already shown they could pass an ACA repeal bill in their chamber without any help from minority-party Democrats. Indeed, during the Obama administration, the Republican-controlled House had cast over 50 roll call votes to repeal the ACA (O'Keefe 2014). While none of these votes ever truly threatened Obamacare—President Obama's veto power gave him the ability to protect the ACA as long as he remained president—they did send a clear message to voters that Republicans strongly opposed Obama's signature healthcare act.

Instead of pursuing a "straight repeal" of the ACA, Republican leaders unveiled a replacement measure, the American Health Care Act (AHCA), on March 6, 2017.[3] It rolled back key provisions of the ACA, such as Medicaid expansion, the "individual mandate" that penalized those that did not purchase health insurance, and requirements forcing large employers to offer health insurance coverage to full-time employees (Pear and Kaplan 2017). On March 23, the House cast two votes on nearly perfect party lines on a special rule that facilitated consideration of the AHCA. The next day, the House cast two more, nearly identical, party-line votes on a special rule that provided for consideration of the bill under a closed rule.[4]

Despite the appearance of unified Republican support for the bill, many news outlets expressed doubts that the AHCA would pass the House—let alone the Senate.[5] The conservative House Freedom Caucus publicly opposed the measure for not going far enough to completely repeal the ACA. Several moderate Republicans had withdrawn their support, arguing that the new bill did not do enough to improve the current state of the healthcare system. While a final passage vote was scheduled for the afternoon of March 24, few were surprised when the bill was pulled from the floor before that vote occurred (DeBonis et al. 2017). The Trump administration initially pushed for a roll call vote on the bill, even if it failed, but Speaker Ryan convinced Trump's team that doing so would have electoral costs. Democrats were sure to attack any Republicans that voted yes on the measure, and what was the point if the measure was destined to fail (Davis and Haberman 2017)?

The House took up the measure again in May. On May 4, the House adopted the previous question motion on another special rule, H.Res. 308, by a vote of 235–193, with only one Republican voting no. The rule then passed by an identical margin. Finally, after six party-line procedural votes, the AHCA passed the House by a much narrower 217–213 margin, with 20 Republican defections (O'Keefe et al. 2017). The bill was eventually abandoned in the Senate after the chamber narrowly rejected a compromise substitute by a single vote (Eilperin et al. 2017).[6]

Why Call the Roll?

The preceding discussion of the AHCA highlights the limitations of the roll call voting record. The record shows near-unified Republican Party support for repealing the ACA. During the Obama administration, Republicans held over 50 recorded votes to roll back parts or all of the ACA. Republican candidates campaigned on these votes, touting their opposition to the ACA in campaign ads and stump speeches. Many of these votes were on proposals that would have much more drastically altered the American healthcare system than did the fairly moderate "repeal and replace" approach taken by the AHCA. Of the 20 Republicans who voted against the bill, 19 of them voted for a previous repeal effort that included none of the moderating language the AHCA did. Moreover, voting on healthcare issues remained highly unified during the first two years of the Trump administration.[7] Accordingly, predicting Republican positions about and future action on the ACA based on these previous roll calls would lead many to think the ACA was doomed. Republicans' failure to demonstrate the same unity on the AHCA that they did on previous repeal efforts is consistent with the view that the roll call record "exaggerate[s] party unity"—at least in the contemporary period (Lee 2018, 1464).

The AHCA also provides insight into how the record gets distorted. Despite Ryan's claims that the Republican Party was "in sync" and working off the "same plan," it was evident that the previous unified Republican votes repealing the ACA were "messaging proposals" (Bade et al. 2017). They had no chance of becoming law due to either a presidential veto or Senate inaction, so members could vote without worry of policy consequences. These messaging amendments were further supplemented by a large number of procedural votes, like the six that were taken in the House prior to the measure's passage. And finally, divisions within the party were further masked by leadership's decision to pull the bill from the floor in March when it became apparent they lacked the votes to pass it.[8] This episode is a reminder that the roll call voting record is *endogenously* generated by Congress. The decision to record votes is frequently done in a way that furthers parties' and members' electoral goals, often at the cost of providing the public with a transparent record of congressional lawmaking.

Despite these limitations, many observers of Congress treat recorded votes as an *exogenous* representation of members' preferences. Journalists use roll call votes to inform the public of member positions on key issues.

Members of Congress, campaign consultants, and political parties use them to promote a positive individual or party "brand" on key issues or to associate a negative brand with political opponents. Political scientists have used the record to generate aggregate measures of ideology for members of Congress (Poole and Rosenthal 2007).

Perhaps even more notably, concerns over recorded voting are frequently used to justify some drastic changes to congressional lawmaking. Potentially "tough" votes have been linked to the leadership decisions to block some legislation from the floor, decisions to delegate policy control to the executive branch, and the increasing usage of omnibus legislation. Major laws are being rushed to the floor in part because bill managers and party leadership believe that will give them a better chance to emerge victorious in the roll call (Curry 2015). Issues stemming from voting on minority messaging amendments have led House leaders to abandon open amending processes on the floor. And they have led Senate majorities to exert more control over the chamber through processes like filling the amendment tree, reconciliation, and others that are generally considered impenetrable to anyone who lacks expertise in congressional rules.

These issues pose challenges for both scholars and Congress itself. Recorded voting is rooted in the Founders' decision to include the yeas and nays clause in the Constitution. The clause provides for a recorded vote to be taken if such a request "at the Desire of one fifth of those Present."[9] If a member asks for a recorded vote, and one-fifth of a quorum agrees to the request, a "sufficient second" is secured and a recorded vote is held.[10] This provision was designed to ensure transparency for the electorate. Constituents can examine their members' recorded votes on important issues, compare those votes to their own policy preferences, and punish members whose votes reveal that they have drifted away from the preferences of their constituents. As John Jay noted during the Continental Congress, recorded voting "is almost the only way in which our constituents can be informed of the conduct of their respective delegates."[11] If the contemporary roll call record is "broken," voters may not be able to hold their elected representatives accountable. It may also introduce significant bias into scholarly measures of ideology and inhibit our ability to track historical change in the institution.

The Roll Call Generating Process

The presence of the sufficient second clause in the Constitution highlights the two-stage process that creates roll call votes. In the first stage, an issue

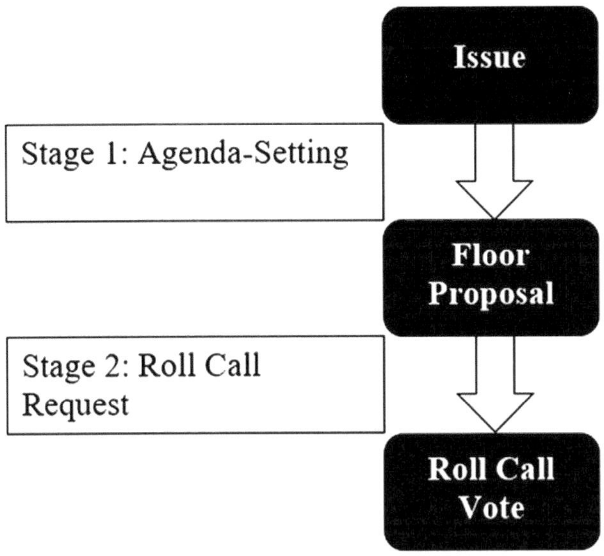

Figure 1.1. The Two-Stage Roll Call Generating Process

is brought to the floor and receives consideration as a proposal. A proposal can take the form of a bill, an amendment, or a host of other motions. Any such proposals are initially considered with an unrecorded voice vote. In the second stage, a recorded vote can be requested by a member. If the request receives a sufficient second, a recorded vote is held. This process is presented in Figure 1.1.

The Framers' decision to require a sufficient second did not resolve the inherent tension between sincere policy transparency and politics. Constituents still need recorded votes to create a transparent record of congressional action—without such a record, monitoring how well members are representing the interests of their districts becomes extremely difficult. Members have incentives to strategically manipulate the recorded voting record to gain a variety of political advantages. They can do this by adding "frivolous" votes to the record—votes that provide a political message to constituents but are not representative of the lawmaking process. They can also omit votes from the roll call record that may send a political message to constituents that members would rather not have them receive. For example, after the failure of the AHCA, Chairman Lamar Alexander (R-TN) and Ranking Member Patty Murray (D-WA) of the Senate Health, Education, Labor, and Pensions Committee, reached a bipartisan agreement on legislation that would help stabilize health insurance markets under the ACA. Concerned the proposal would reveal a split among Republican senators, Senate Majority Leader Mitch McConnell (R-KY) announced he would not hold a recorded vote on the measure (Kaplan and Pear 2017; Morin 2017).

This tension between transparency and politics is clear from Republican attempts to repeal and replace the ACA. The more than 50 votes to eliminate or defund Obamacare that Republicans held while Obama was still in office did not help voters to better understand the lawmaking process—none of those votes had any chance of becoming law due to Obama's ability to veto them. They did allow House Republicans to repeatedly signal to voters their displeasure with the ACA and their commitment to reform healthcare in the future. Republicans were also able to strategically omit votes from the roll call record that would have revealed to the public the inability of the Republican to agree on what exactly should replace the ACA.

Goals of the Book

Despite the primary importance played by the roll call record for scholars of legislative politics and voters, no systematic effort has been made to document its origins and evolution. The Founders provided for the yeas and nays clause in the Constitution because they believed it was necessary for the public to hold their representatives accountable. Its perceived importance is further increased when one considers the sparsity of detail in the Constitution regarding congressional rules more broadly. However, the presence of a sufficient second of one-fifth of a quorum suggests there was also some skepticism regarding its utility.

This is clear when one examines records from the convention. While opposing a provision that sought to ensure recorded votes upon the demand of any single member, Nathaniel Gorham argued that it would lead to "stuffing the journals with [votes] on frivolous occasions . . . misleading the people who never know the reasons determining the votes" (Farrand 1966, 255). The Framers rejected that proposal, and, in an effort to limit potential abuses, instead required the sufficient second provision. Where did the practice of formally recording votes for public consumption originate? What motivated this institutional design choice? What were the consequences of it? How effective was the sufficient second clause? Answering these questions will allow us greater leverage in evaluating the stability of the contemporary roll call voting record. Accordingly, documenting the origins of recorded voting is our first goal.

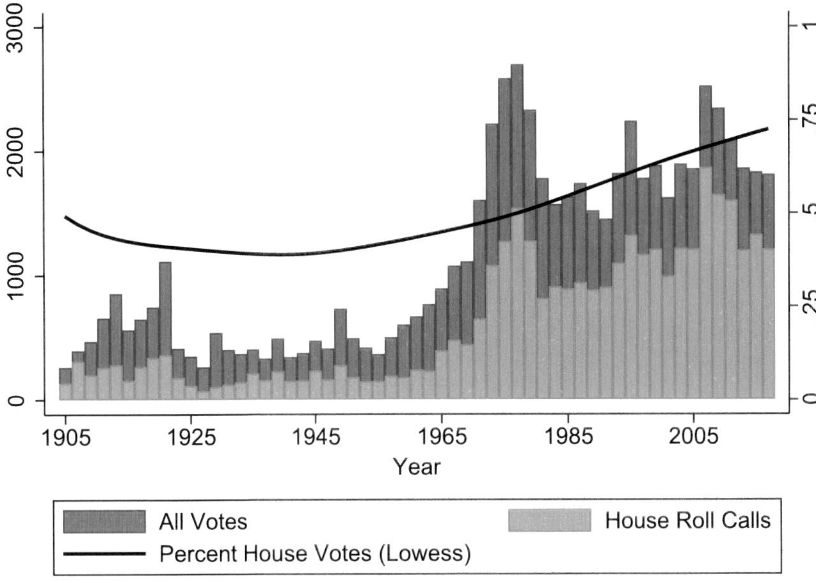

Figure 1.2. Roll Call Votes in Congress, 1905–2014

The ability of the public to transparently monitor its elected representatives through recorded floor voting is predicated on factors governing both Stage 1 and Stage 2 of the roll call generating process depicted in Figure 1.1. Changes to how the agenda is set and to how roll call requests are made have both served to increase the perceived electoral benefit of roll call votes, while simultaneously decreasing the costs of requesting and holding a roll call vote. This has disproportionately benefited more ideologically extreme members, party leaders and the outside groups that support them. This, in turn, has led to a massive increase in recorded voting and substantially mitigated the benefits of transparency that roll calls theoretically provide. This is documented in Figure 1.2, which plots the increase in the number of roll call votes in Congress from the 59th Congress (1905–1907) through the 113th Congress (2013–2014).

The figure plots both the total number of roll call votes per congress and the number of roll call votes in the House and the Senate. The number of votes is reported on the left axis. Figure 1.2 demonstrates a sharp increase in roll calls in the House during recent congresses, with House voting making up almost 75% of total roll call votes. This is consistent with work documenting the increase in the number of roll call votes in the House after the 1971 adoption of recorded voting in the Committee of the Whole and the 1973

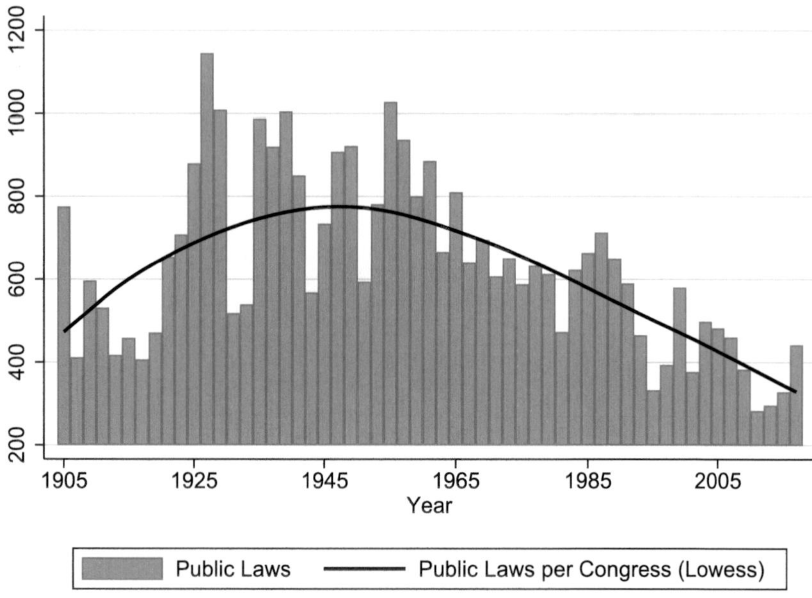

Figure 1.3. Public Laws per Congress, 1905–2014

introduction of electronic voting (Roberts and Smith 2003). However, it also underscores that an increase in recorded voting has occurred in both chambers. The increase in roll call votes documented in Figure 1.2 is even more significant when we consider the decrease in lawmaking productivity during this period. This decrease, depicted in Figure 1.3, has been well documented by scholars and the media (see, e.g., Blake 2016; Ornstein et al. 2019).

If the contemporary roll call record provides a transparent account of lawmaking, then the trend observed in Figure 1.3 suggests we should observe *fewer* roll calls in contemporary congresses. We argue that much of the increase in recorded voting has little to do with sincere roll calls on matters with policy implications. Accordingly, it is perhaps not surprising that the volume of recorded votes has increased, despite a corresponding reduction in the number of public laws generated by Congress. Identifying factors that led to the changes in recorded voting documented in Figures 1.2 and 1.3 will allow us leverage in evaluating the how the utility afforded by the contemporary record has changed. What kinds of members are driving the changing roll call record? How have party leaders and bill managers responded? Are certain types of motions, votes, and proposals more represented in the modern roll call record than in previous eras of Congress? Detailing how the record has changed throughout congressional history is our second goal.

Once our first two goals are met, we move on to our third goal: evaluating the implications of the "broken" roll call record for voters, scholars, and members themselves. Political scientists have not reached a consensus on the degree to which general election voters use recorded voting to monitor their elected members of Congress. Some have argued voters take advantage of the transparency provided by the roll call record to hold members accountable for their votes in Congress (see, e.g., Ansolabehere and Jones 2010; Bovitz and Carson 2006; Canes-Wrone et al. 2002; Carson and Engstrom 2005; Clausen 1973; Crespin 2010; Erikson 1978; Erikson and Wright 2000; Jones 2011; Nyhan et al. 2012; Theriault 2003).[12] Others have challenged this conclusion, arguing that voters frequently lack the ability to interpret roll calls cast in Congress (Dancey and Sheagley 2013; Highton 2019; Matthews and Stimson 1975; Miller and Stokes 1963; Rogers 2017; Sulkin 2009).

The changes to the roll call record we document suggest that, over time, it has gotten more difficult for the public to understand and oversee lawmaking in Congress. There are five to 10 times more recorded votes for the public to track in contemporary congresses than there were in the early 1900s. Moreover, these additional votes overwhelmingly lack any policy relevance. As these "subterfuge" votes make up an ever-increasing percentage of the roll call record, voters find it harder and harder to effectively monitor their representatives' behavior. The recorded votes that should allow the public to demand responsiveness from elected officials instead, as Nathanial Gorham warned, risk "misleading the people who never know the reasons determining the votes" (Farrand 1966, 255).

In previous work, we have argued that these changes in how the roll call record is constructed pose problems for scholars examining policymaking in Congress (Carson et al. 2011; Dougherty et al. 2014; Lynch and Madonna 2013a, 2013b; Madonna 2011; Lynch et al. 2016). We build on that work here. We conclude that the record is no longer an exogenous source of member preferences or ideology for scholars of Congress; rather it represents an endogenously constructed electoral tool used by partisan agenda-setters who know the result of a roll call vote on an outcome before it reaches the floor. For Congress as an institution, concerns over roll call votes have led to a labyrinth of confusing procedural changes, backstage maneuvering, and negative press cover. But despite this painstaking amount of control and attention given to recorded voting, its electoral impact is likely overstated.

Organization

In what follows, we explore the construction and evolution of the roll call record. In Chapter 2, we document the origins and history of the practice. Rules providing for recorded voting were first adopted in colonial state legislative bodies before moving to the Continental Congress and finally the US Congress. Our discussion highlights how the Founders' ideas on recorded voting and legislative transparency more broadly evolved during the period just prior to the development of the US Constitution. Placing a high value on the need for the public to adequately monitor their legislators' behavior, many colonial legislatures, as well as the Continental Congress, adopted rules that provided for decentralized agenda-setting and guaranteed that roll call votes would be taken at the behest of any individual member.[13] We then document how and why politicians during this period lamented the abuse of these rules during the Continental Congress. This led the delegates at the Constitutional Convention to adopt rules they believed would reign in such behavior designed to "mislead the people." With some minor exceptions, these rules were primarily concentrated on the second, floor stage, of the two-stage roll call generating process depicted in Figure 1.1.

We contrast the rules governing recorded voting in the US Congress with those employed by state legislators. Much like the Founders, designers of other legislative bodies also sought to balance the costs and benefits of recorded voting. However, in contrast to the US Congress, many state legislative bodies included exogenous rules in their constitutions that limited the ability of legislators to abuse the roll call record at the first, agenda-setting stage, of the two-stage roll call generating process depicted in Figure 1.1. This includes rules providing for committee autonomy, rules specifying decentralized control over the legislative calendar, rules governing legislative and amendment drafting, and, perhaps most commonly, rules requiring legislation to focus on a single subject. Finally, we conclude by examining the effectiveness of the second-stage rules adopted by the Founders. The most notable of these is the constitutional provision necessitating one-fifth of a quorum to support a call for the yeas and nays. As we demonstrate in later chapters, this provision—interpreted in conjunction with the quorum clause—was effective at dampening recorded voting in early congresses. However, its effectiveness waned as transportation, coordination, and attendance improved throughout the 20th century.

In Chapter 3 we outline our theoretical expectations for how the two parties manipulate the record in the House and the Senate. Using those expectations, we then provide a broad examination of how the record has evolved.

To do so, we extended the Public Institutions and Public Choice Program (PIPC) Roll Call dataset, which codes each roll call vote by vote type, starting with 83rd Congress (1953–1954) in the House and 91st Congress (1969–1970) in the Senate (Crespin and Rohde 2016). Using the coding system established by the PIPC program, we coded vote type for all roll call votes back to the 59th Congress (1905–1907) for both the House and the Senate. We also expanded the data to include the bill on which each vote was taken.[14] These data are explained in greater detail in Appendix A. We observe changes in the roll call record that suggest the record is being increasingly manipulated in a way to mislead voters. This includes a fairly stark decline in votes taken on measures enacted into law, more policies enacted in longer, more complex legislation, more procedural votes, and more votes on failed amendments.

While the data presented in Chapter 3 allows us to explore how the roll call record has evolved, it does not provide leverage to analyze how the roll call generating process has changed. To track how the roll call generating process has changed necessitated data on measures that both did and did *not* receive roll calls. Starting in 2010, we began construction on these datasets by establishing the University of Georgia Congress Project.[15] Our first step involved constructing a dataset of "important" legislation from 1905 to 2014. The decision to focus on important legislation was motivated by several factors, which are discussed in greater detail in Appendix B.[16] Altogether, this left us with a list of 2,086 enactments across 55 congresses.[17]

We tasked teams of coders to read the through *Congressional Record* and collect data on all special rules and amendments related to those enactments. In Chapter 4, we use this special rule dataset to examine the increase in procedural roll calls. As discussed in Appendix C, we use these data to evaluate whether the increase in procedural roll calls was a product of conflict over increasingly restrictive processes. We find that this is not the case, and that rules are substantially more likely to receive one or more recorded votes in recent congresses independent of the restrictiveness of the rule under which a measure is considered. These recorded votes frequently include redundant votes on things like the previous question motion and points of order related to the rule.

As detailed in Chapter 5, and further discussed in Appendix D, we then use our data on nearly 120,000 filed amendments to important legislation to evaluate the rise in messaging amendments. We find that more ideologically extreme members are increasingly more likely to receive recorded votes on their amendments than their centrist colleagues in recent congresses. We argue many of these amendments offered by extremists are drafted by outside interest groups whose support members can cultivate by publicizing these groups' policy goals through a recorded amendment vote. Centrist amendments are more likely to be parochial, leading these members to see a greater benefit from policy change, with or without a recorded vote, than from any political messaging that could be generated via a recorded vote.

We argue the changes documented in Chapters 3 through 5 serve the needs of both parties. They suggest parties can and do force roll calls on votes that will demonstrate nearly perfect party unity. Doing so serves two purposes. First, changes in roll call voting promote unified party brands, which is useful for voters looking for simplified electoral cues. Second, these changes help parties and members meet the needs of their donor class, who financially support members who vote with them (Barber 2016; Barber et al. 2017; Stratmann 2002). In addition to serving the needs of the parties, roll call votes on procedural matters or measures with little chance of enactment serve as subterfuge for members looking to explain votes that might put them at odds with their constituents. Such a tactic is commonly employed by members with some success (Bawn et al. 2012; Grose et al. 2015; Hillygus and Shields 2009).

In Chapter 6, we examine the effects of the changing roll call record on scholarly measures of ideology. Recent scholarship has argued that the increase in polarization apparent in measures derived from roll call votes is not driven solely by ideology (Bateman et al. 2017; Clinton and Lapinski 2008; Egar 2016; Harbridge 2015; Lee 2009, 2016; Lynch and Madonna 2013a). Building on these works, we first employ a mix of case studies that underscore how centralized control over recorded voting has increased in recent congresses. Majority parties in the House and Senate can restrict voting on measures that revealed intraparty divisions, making parties appear more unified than they are. They also have the ability to repeatedly vote on measures that highlight interparty differences, making parties appear more polarized than they are. We then use simulations to assess how sensitive polarization measures are to the inclusion of addition party-line votes and to analyze how different types of votes influence the makeup of ideological and polarization levels in recent congresses. We suggest that roll-call-based measures are likely artificially increasing observed levels of ideological polarization because of changes in how the roll call record is generated.

Finally, in Chapter 7, we revisit our three goals for the manuscript, providing a summary of the finding for the empirical chapters of the manuscript and a detailed discussion of the implication of those findings. We then highlight some of the major problems with the contemporary roll call record. The removal of practical barriers to roll calls, internal changes to legislative procedures, and increased electoral incentives have led to more roll calls on procedural votes, messaging bills, and both amendments and proposals sponsored by more extreme members. Party leaders and bill managers have responded by seeking greater control over recorded voting at the agenda-setting stage, leading to longer enacted legislation and tighter control over the floor. These effects have led some to attribute increased polarization on roll call votes purely to shifts in member ideology. In other words, the record suffers from a combination of "skipped tracks," "endless loops," and "distorted sounds."

While changes in the roll call generating process do not alter the primary products of polarization, namely crippling gridlock on salient issues and anemic legislative productivity, they do suggest alternative means of reform. Specifically, if polarization is partially driven by electoral and institutional factors, then solving the problem requires a more nuanced set of solutions then simply replacing legislators. In the absence of specific procedural reforms and increased public education about how Congress operates, "voting the bums out" will only lead to the creation of new "bums." We conclude Chapter 7 by reexamining the potential electoral benefits of roll call votes and offer some suggested reforms.

TWO

Origins of Recorded Voting

Searching for Balance

> If all legislators were wise and honest, able, and sincere, the Yeas and Nays would be a useless, harmful encumbrance. If all were shift and self-seeking, stupid and dishonest, the Yeas and Nays might be the shield of society.
>
> —Robert Luce (1922, 362)

> What does "denying a second" mean? Denying a recorded vote. Why is that important? When you are breaking the commitments you have made to the men and women who have elected you, the most painful thing in the world is accountability. When you are misleading the men and women who showed up to vote for you, you don't want sunshine making clear that you voted no. A recorded vote means each senator's name is on it.
>
> —Sen. Ted Cruz (R-TX)[1]

Balancing Transparency and Efficiency in Legislative Bodies

It is often taken for granted by political observers that votes cast by members of legislative bodies will be made public. Because of the informational advantages it provides voters, transparency is often viewed as a normative good. It helps ensure lawmakers take voter opinions into consideration before they make decisions. However, transparency comes with substantial costs (Binder and Lee 2016). Accordingly, when designing legislative rules, lawmakers and voters need to remain aware of both the costs and benefits of transparency, and seek to strike a balance between the two. Our primary goal in this chapter is to document the origins of recorded voting. Doing so demonstrates that the Framers were highly skeptical of the long-term impact of the yeas and nays clause on lawmaking. This skepticism, which largely stemmed from lawmakers' experiences in the Continental Congress, led the Framers to adopt a requirement that any request for the yeas and nays be seconded by one-fifth of a quorum.

We contrast the rules governing recorded voting in the US Congress with those employed by state legislatures. Our discussion demonstrates that little consensus exists over how best to balance the costs and benefits of roll call voting and other rules promoting transparency. Finally, we conclude by tracking the impact of the yeas and nays clause throughout the 19th century.

Origins of Recorded Voting

The foundation for legislative transparency in the US Congress is Article 1, Section 5, Clause 3 of the US Constitution. It states:

> Each House shall keep a Journal of its Proceedings, and from time to time publish the same, excepting such Parts as may in their Judgment require Secrecy; and the Yeas and Nays of the Members of either House on any question shall, at the Desire of one fifth of those Present, be entered on the Journal.[2]

This clause ensures that any member who requests the yeas and nays on a question will receive them provided they are supported by a "sufficient second," or one-fifth of the number of members required to make a quorum. Its inclusion suggests the Founders placed a high premium on governmental transparency. The importance of transparency is further highlighted by the fact that this clause represents one of the only references in the Constitution to congressional rules and procedures (Binder 1997). Most questions of legislative procedure are answered by Article 1, Section 5, Clause 2's statement, "Each House may determine the rules of its proceedings."[3] However, a more detailed examination of the history of recorded voting and its evolution suggests the Founders were also aware of the need for balance.

Given its importance today, it is surprising how little information scholars have regarding the origins of recorded voting. The limited scholarly work on the topic suggests that the presence of a formal rule requiring votes of legislators be recorded originated in early American legislatures (Cushing 1856; Luce 1922). It appears to be one of the few parliamentary devices where its regular usage in the United States predated its employment by the British Parliament. The practice of informally publicizing how legislators voted occurred intermittently in 17th- and 18th-century Great Britain. One of the first known instances of this occurred in 1641, after a vote ordering the execution of Thomas Wentworth, the 1st Earl of Strafford. The names of those who voted against the bill of attainder were publicized as "betrayers of their country" (Luce 1922, 355). The vote passed and Strafford was beheaded. These occasions aside, the practice was not regularly employed by the House of Commons until 1836 (Bryce 1889; Luce 1922).

Rules providing for legislative transparency and recorded voting were employed in several early colonial assemblies. This included Pennsylvania, which provided for recorded votes by rule in 1703, and New York, which first took the yeas and nays in 1737 (Luce 1922).[4] Transparency through recorded voting employed in these assemblies likely led to its inclusion in the Articles of Confederation and usage during the Continental Congress. It was usage of the yeas and nays during the Continental Congress that would spark a debate over its inclusion in the Constitution.

Transparency in the Continental Congress

As the Revolutionary War began, delegates to the Continental Congress were understandably wary of empowering a legislative body that could pass policies not supported by citizens and states. Accordingly, the Articles of Confederation assigned a high priority to minority rights and policymaking transparency. Lawmaking in the Continental Congress was governed by rules that inhibited any central agenda-setting, protected minorities through the requirement of supermajority quorums to conduct business, and made it easy to receive a recorded vote. These rules impacted the roll call generating process by completely nullifying any strategic behavior at the agenda-setting stage and making the roll call requesting stage pro forma. As a result, the Continental Congress was a legislative body beset by inefficiency and gridlock (Miller 1948; Jillson and Wilson 1994). We discuss these issues and their impact on the Constitutional Convention below.

In May 1778, Article IX of the Articles of Confederation specified that "the yeas and nays of the delegates of each state on any question shall be entered on the Journal, when it is desired by any delegate."[5] This provision allowed any individual member to ask for the yeas and nays *without* a second. While this highlights the value placed on transparency, the experiences of delegates to the Continental Congress both before and after the adoption of the yeas and nays provision suggests they understood the potential limitations of the practice. The initial draft of the rules provided by the Articles in July 1777 contained no mention of the yeas and nays in Congress.[6] It seems likely that this was due to benefits provided by secrecy. Miller (1948, 434), for example, argued recorded votes were abandoned early on during the war "on the ground that the enemy learned from them that Congress were not so unanimous as it was politic in us to make them believe."

A number of observers of early American politics have argued that the lack of a sufficient second clause led to an abuse of calls for the yeas and nays in the Continental Congress. Joseph Story (1833, 303), for example, argued it had been "used to excess" by members of a "dissatisfied minority, to retard the passage of measures, which are sanctioned by the approbation of a strong majority." In a letter published under the pseudonym "Leonidas," Benjamin Rush assailed the Congress for taking far too many "yea and nay" votes, which he suggested led to them failing the people on substantive issues (Butterfield 1951).[7] Former Connecticut Delegate Jesse Root wrote to John Jay asserting that "the frequency of the yeas and nays, on questions not of the greatest importance, appearing in your Journals, adds not to the dignity [and] reputation of Congress in the view of the people."[8] Finally, in an attempt to rein in its abuse, a committee led by James Madison recommended revising the rules to require the yeas and nays to be requested *before* voting commenced. This was adopted in 1781.[9]

Despite criticism, recorded voting had a good number of supporters as well. Story argued that despite its abuses, recorded voting enlightened the public mind by providing definitive facts instead of "vague conjecture." He concluded by warning, "When the people become indifferent to the acts of their representatives, they will have ceased to take much interest in the preservation of their liberties" (Story 1933, 302). In his response to Root, Jay agreed that too many roll calls were being taken, but asserted that Congress was submitting "to the lesser evil for the sake of the greater good" and that recorded voting was "almost the only way in which our constituents can be informed of the conduct of their representatives."[10] When a presiding officer balked at his request for the yeas and nays, Delegate Henry Laurens of South Carolina claimed that "nothing less than violence could deprive him of his right to a roll call."[11]

Arguments over recorded voting grew so heated that a 1780 dispute over a recorded vote led Elbridge Gerry of Massachusetts to refuse to attend any sessions of Congress for the next three years.[12] In addition to a liberal sufficient second clause, the Continental Congress struggled with other rules related to minority rights and policymaking transparency. Perhaps the most significant of these related to the absence of agenda-setting mechanisms. The office of the president of the Continental Congress was famously weak. Presidential terms were short in duration and limited. They had only limited authority to recognize members during debate, no authority to control the order and manner in which legislative proposals would be brought to the floor, and no control over the committee appointment process. As a result, the office was not popular among delegates to the Continental Congress, and several members actively avoided it (Jillson and Wilson 1994; Wilson and Jillson 1989).[13]

Legislation and committee reports were largely considered in the order they were reported. In instances where conflict over this arose, consideration was determined by a majority vote of the states. Once on the floor, rules allowed members to divide any questions if they "contained several points" (Hinds 1907, 578). This was liberally interpreted. Questions would be divided on the basis of the words employed, as opposed to their substantive meaning, and one sentence could be divided into three separate provisions (Cushing 1856).[14] Such a provision made it impossible for delegates and committees to package proposals into a larger, omnibus provision (Jillson and Wilson 1987, 1994). This lack of any agenda-setting mechanisms led members to frequently complain that too much time was spent on unimportant issues.[15] Because of this inefficiency, Laurens stated that he "wish[ed] to be anywhere but in Congress" (Jillson and Wilson 1994, 151). Miller (1948, 433–434) equated being elected to the Continental Congress to being sentenced to "hard labor."

Another, and perhaps better-documented, issue in the Continental Congress related to quorum requirements.[16] The Articles specified that each of the 13 states would send between two to seven delegates to the Continental Congress and that voting was to be done by state bloc. States paid the costs of their delegates, so they had an incentive to keep costs down by limiting the number of delegates (Luce 1922). In 1776 and 1778, the rules also specified the assent of nine states was needed on important matters. This was done in response to concerns regarding the passage of legislation by minorities during sparsely attended sessions. Regardless of its intent, it appeared to be rarely enforced until 1781 (Jillson and Wilson 1994). Few rules governing debate and frequent recorded votes exacerbated the issue. This led a number of instances of "disappearing quorum" tactics being employed. A "disappearing quorum" is when a minority group of legislators intentionally leave the chamber or refuse to answer quorum calls, forcing the majority to form a quorum solely from their own members. Minority members can therefore defeat legislative matters not by winning a vote but rather by disappearing, preventing a quorum from forming, and stopping a vote from ever occurring.

An early example of the disappearing quorum being utilized occurred in 1778. Delegate Thomas Burke of North Carolina took issue with a letter being drafted that was critical of General George Washington. After a lengthy debate and sensing his side might lose, Burke left the chamber. After a messenger arrived at his room requesting his attendance so that a quorum could be formed, Burke informed him that the "Devil take him if he would come." The issue boiled over into a committee investigation into Burke's conduct (Burnett 1941; Douglass 1949). The committee, which was considering expelling or potentially jailing Burke, demanded he acknowledge his errors. Burke declined and took leave of the Congress. This left the committee with little recourse, as any disciplining of Burke would first necessitate his attendance so a quorum could be met (Burnett 1941).

Problems maintaining quorums worsened over time. In 1781, after the Articles were ratified, provisions requiring nine states to support any important matters and seven states to be present for other business to be conducted were more strictly enforced. This occurred despite objections by Madison and others that a majority of the nine states should be sufficient. The decision led to a downturn in the passage of successful motions (Jillson and Wilson 1994). Attendance also greatly dropped off in final years of the Continental Congress. As Dougherty (2001, 176) notes, "The proportion of working days that Congress had a quorum of seven or more states declined by more than 40 percent from the period of 1783–1785 to the period of 1786–87."

Balance and the Constitutional Convention

Their lawmaking experiences during the Continental Congress clearly impacted the Framers attitudes toward congressional rules during the Constitutional Convention. This was evident at the start of the convention when delegates grappled with rules governing the convention. The initial draft of the rules followed the Articles by allowing any member of the body to call for the yeas and nays (Cushing 1856). On May 28, Rufus King of Massachusetts and George Mason of Virginia rose in opposition to that rule. King argued that "it was unnecessary to exhibit this evidence of the votes; and improper as changes of opinion would be frequent in the course of the business and would fill the minutes with contradictions" (Farrand 1966, 10). Mason concurred with King's objection and added that such a provision would provide weapons to the enemies of the convention. The removal of the yeas and nays rule—combined with rules allowing questions to be revisited at any point and requiring secrecy regarding the nature of the debate—mitigated the influence of public opinion and allowed the delegates more freedom to act. Madison would later argue that the Constitution would not "have been adopted by the convention if the debates had been public" (Beeman 2010, 83).

Debate on the journal clause that sets the rules for recorded voting commenced on August 10, 1781.[17] Upon its introduction, Gouverneur Morris of Pennsylvania, supported by Edmund Randolph of Virginia, proposed amending it to allow any one member to call for the yeas and nays. This proposal would do away with the requirement that one-fifth support the motion and essentially return to the clause as provided under the Articles. Morris "urged that if the yeas and nays were proper at all, any individual ought to be authorized to call for them" (Farrand 1966, 255). He then professed concern about the ability of small states to reach the one-fifth threshold.

Morris's motion was quickly countered by Roger Sherman of Rhode Island, Oliver Ellsworth of Connecticut, and Nathaniel Gorham of Massachusetts, who proposed eliminating the requirement altogether (Farrand 1966; Binder 1997). Sherman argued that roll call votes had "done much mischief" and that they were "not proper as the reasons governing the [vote] never appear along with them." Gorham worried about the practice of "stuffing the Journals with [votes] on frivolous occasions" and "misleading the people, who never know the reasons determining the votes" (Farrand 1966, 255). Morris's motion was rejected.

This was followed by a motion by Daniel Carroll of Maryland and Randolph that sought to insert a provision that confined the clause to the House and allowed senators to enter explanations for their dissent on a question.[18] This proposal was rejected by an 8 to 3 vote. Gerry then proposed to strike the words "when [Congress] shall be acting in its legislative capacity" from the clause and insert "except such parts thereof as in their judgment require secrecy" (Farrand 1966, 256). Gerry worried that, as written, senators would be able to avoid publicizing their positions on executive business, such as treaties and nominations.[19] This proposal was adopted 7 to 3.

On August 11 debate continued. Proposals by Madison (and John Rutledge of South Carolina) and Gerry (and Sherman) that sought to give Congress more discretion on the publishing of the journals were defeated. Ellsworth then expressed his support for deleting the clause altogether, suggesting that voters would pull the chamber in line if it wasn't publishing its proceedings and votes. James Wilson of Pennsylvania disagreed, arguing that the "people have a right to know what their agents are doing or have done." Wilson added that the provision was already in the Articles of Confederation and that removing it would "furnish the adversaries of reform with a pretext by which weak and suspicious minds may be easily misled" (Farrand 1966, 256). All three parts of the clause were then adopted.

The journal clause was the subject of some attention during ratification. During the Virginia ratifying convention, both Mason and Patrick Henry took issue with the qualifying language that the journal must be published "from time to time" and that Congress may use its judgment on matters that "require secrecy." Mason asserted this would allow Congress to "conceal what they please" (Elliot 1888, 3:367–368). Henry took this further, arguing the yeas and nays "will avail nothing" as they will "be locked up in their chests and concealed forever from the people" (Elliot 1888, 2:60).

Their experiences during the Continental Congress led delegates to seek to balance the goals of transparency and efficiency in other areas as well. Recalling difficulties from disappearing quorums, some delegates pushed for a less than majority quorum requirement. Gorham and John Francis Mercer of Maryland specifically pointed to the delays caused by high quorum requirements in other legislative bodies. Mercer went so far as to assert that enforcing large quorum rules may "endanger the government" (Farrand 1966, 251). They argued for omitting a formal quorum rule in the Constitution and allowing the legislature to fix it themselves, as was done in Great Britain.[20]

In opposition, Mason argued travel problems could lead to representational problems for the more distant states. No changes were enacted to the original provision, which specified that a majority of each chamber shall "constitute a quorum to do business," though it also provided "a smaller number may adjourn from day to day."[21] As we discuss later, the Constitution did not specify how a quorum was to be counted, nor did it formally define "business."

Comparatively less attention was given to rules related to agenda setting. This is unsurprising given the absence of it during the Continental Congress. Each chamber was left to determine agenda-setting procedures when the House and Senate adopted their own rules. On this point, the delegates adopted Clause 2, which specified that "Each House may determine the rules of its proceedings," with minimal debate.[22] The First Congress did address the issues stemming from "dividing the question" that occurred in the Continental Congress by including the qualifying clause that divisions may be granted "where the sense will admit of it" (Hinds 1907). It was amended several more times in the early 19th century to make divisions more difficult (Fink 2000; Hinds 1907).

There was also little discussion over the power of leadership positions at the Constitutional Convention. Apart from an unsuccessful push by John Dickinson of Pennsylvania to make the House Speaker subject to recall from the states, there was almost no dissent on the provision allowing the House of Representatives to select its own Speaker. There was more disagreement over making the vice president the president of the Senate, with some delegates expressing concern that the Senate's presiding officer would not be electorally accountable to the chamber. They suggested this might provide the executive branch with agenda-setting authority in the Senate (Lynch et al. 2018). Ultimately, these concerns were ignored.[23]

Formal and Informal Rules Governing Recorded Voting

The origins of recorded voting in the United States highlight the pivotal role played by formal legislative rules in balancing transparency and efficiency. As discussed in Chapter 1, the ability of the public to monitor its elected representatives' voting behavior in a legislative body is dependent on a two-stage roll call generating process. This process is governed by the motivations of agents to put issues on the floor and to request recorded votes on those issues. Those motivations are often conditioned by formal and informal rules governing both stages of the process.

Perhaps the most important decision a legislative body can make regarding its rules is the source from which they are derived. Exogenous rules specified by a constitution are more difficult to alter and serve as more significant constraints on legislators. Those who ignore them invite intervention on behalf of other political actors, frequently courts, that can invalidate legislative actions that violate them. For example, in 2008, the Virginia Supreme Court struck down a legislative provision that allowed the state's transportation authority to impose regional taxes in part because it was not adopted by a recorded vote, as specified by the state's constitution (Dinan 2014).[24] In contrast, when rules are endogenously determined by majorities in a given legislative body "doubts are legitimately raised about how effective those rules can be" (Cox 2000, 170).

The Founders reacted to problems stemming from transparency under the Articles of Confederation primarily by including rules designed to restrict abuses during Stage 2 of the roll call generating process. By virtue of their inclusion in the Constitution, Stage 2 rules like the sufficient second clause place exogenous restrictions on contemporary members of Congress. In contrast, they largely allowed factors governing Stage 1, like the agenda-setting powers of leaders, to be altered endogenously. Employing formal rules to balance efficiency concerns in legislative bodies is a difficult endeavor, and there is substantial variance in the content of rules across countries and state legislative bodies. This variance exists in both Stage 1 rules (e.g., quorum sizes and agenda powers) and Stage 2 (e.g., the types of motions and measures subjected to recorded votes and the size of a sufficient second required).[25] As we discuss below, there is also some variance in the source of these rules. While many are specified in written constitutions, especially in US state legislatures, others are not.

Measures Subjected to Recorded Votes

The necessity of requesting a recorded vote is not uniform across all legislatures and issues. Most legislative bodies mandate recorded votes on specific types of questions.[26] Such an approach was taken in the Constitution for veto overrides. Required roll call votes are especially common in state legislative bodies on votes requiring a supermajority for passage, like amending a state constitution, impeachment, or veto overrides. Similarly, a number of state legislatures require recorded votes on other specific types of proposals. For example, Delaware, Alaska, Alabama, Illinois, Colorado, Louisiana, Minnesota, and Montana require recorded votes on all final passage votes (Vermeule 2004). Requiring roll call votes is frequently done in other countries' legislatures as well (Carey 2007; Crisp and Driscoll 2012).

Throughout the 19th century, a number of states altered their constitutions to require recorded votes on fiscal matters (Luce 1922). Some, like Colorado and Wisconsin, have maintained those rules through the contemporary era. Both chambers of the Missouri state legislature require recorded votes on third reading, final passage, concurrence, and conference reports.[27] Slightly less common are rules providing for mandatory roll call votes on all questions. In a study of voting rules in 92 countries, Hug (2010, 226–227) finds that 20 parliaments require the publishing of all votes. Conversely, 23 require no roll call votes at all, 43 mandate roll calls on specific votes, and 28 require recorded voting upon request.

At the state level, mandatory recorded voting provisions were included in state constitutions to ensure responsiveness from legislators (Luce 1922). However, these constitutions are often dated, and legislators frequently find these mandatory voting provisions burdensome. Accordingly, many have adapted their behavior to get around them. For instance, discussing mandatory roll calls on financial legislation, Luce (1922, 360) asserted, "Many bills are of a routine nature; many appropriations are perfunctory. It was absurd to expect that any assembly would waste from ten to twenty minutes in a genuine roll call on each of such things. The result has been a widespread evasion of the rule that has thrown the rule itself into disrepute." Other common tactics include having legislators vote for absent colleagues. In Alabama, lawmakers will often cast votes for "an entire row of fellow legislators" (Doudna 2018).

Sufficient Seconds

Another common source of variance in Stage 2 recorded voting rules is the necessity of a sufficient second. As the debate during the Constitutional Convention suggests, recorded voting rules are generally viewed as protections for the minority, and, accordingly, the size of a sufficient second is generally less than a majority (Cushing 1856). Some legislatures require no sufficient second and specify that any one member can request the yeas and nays. Others, like the US Congress, set a one-fifth threshold.[28] While there is high variance among state and foreign legislative bodies on sufficient second requirements, the one-fifth of quorum threshold rates as one of the most demanding. This further highlights the Framers' skepticism of recorded voting. However, unlike most state and foreign legislatures, the sufficient second clause is not accompanied by any restrictions on Stage 1 processes. Table 2.1 highlights this variation among US state legislatures.

The source of the recorded voting rule also varies. Nearly all state legislatures have a journal clause in their state constitution that sets the size of a sufficient second for the yeas and nays on all questions. For example, the Maryland Constitution specifies, "Each House shall keep a Journal of its proceedings, and cause the same to be published. The yeas and nays of members on any question, shall at the call of any five of them in the House of Delegates, or one in the Senate, be entered on the Journal." The Nebraska Constitution states, "The Legislature shall keep a journal of its proceedings and publish them, except such parts as may require secrecy, and the yeas and nays of the members on any question shall at the desire of any one of them be entered on the journal."

TABLE 2.1. States per Sufficient Second Required for Recorded Votes

Sufficient Second Required	Total States
Minimum Proportion	
One-Fifteenth Quorum	1
One-Tenth Quorum	7
One-Sixth Quorum	8
One-Fifth Quorum	25
Minimum Number	
One Member	14
Two Members	20
Three Members	8
Five Members	11
Ten Members	1
Fifteen Members	2

Note: Data collected by the authors.

Some state legislatures do not set a sufficient second in their state constitutions, however. For example, the Kansas Constitution mandates the yeas and nays on final passage of every bill and amendments to the state and US Constitution, but makes no reference to the yeas and nays on other questions.

Quorum Rules

Quorum rules can impact both Stage 1 and Stage 2 of the roll call generating process and are closely linked to broader transparency goals in legislatures in a number of ways. First and foremost, certain types of business cannot be conducted if a quorum is not present. Ergo, no information can be presented on member behavior to voters if no business is occurring. Second, legislatures that necessitate a percentage of its membership to second a call for a recorded vote generally operate under the presumption of a quorum. Thus, determining the precise number of members needed for a recorded vote is done by multiplying the percentage required by the minimal number needed for a quorum. For example, 11 votes are required for a recorded vote in the Senate, as the Constitution specifies a "majority" is needed for a quorum (50 senators) and one-fifth is needed for a roll call (Oleszek et al. 2016).

Third, recorded votes are frequently used by minorities to demonstrate the lack of a quorum and negate legislative action. The incident with Thomas Burke during the Continental Congress is a nice example of this. As they are commonly known, "disappearing quorum" tactics have been employed even in the absence of recorded voting (Koger 2010). However, history demonstrates they are particularly effective when sufficient seconds are low and quorum requirements are greater than a majority. Accordingly, while most state constitutions specify a majority to conduct legislative business, some states do require supermajorities for specific issues and a few require supermajority quorums for all business.[29] This has led to a number of high-profile usages of the "disappearing quorum" in contemporary politics.

For example, the Wisconsin Constitution requires voting on fiscal bills to be conducted by a recorded vote and also that "three-fifths of all the members elected to such house shall in all such cases be required to constitute a quorum."[30] In 2011, Wisconsin Democrats took advantage of this rule by leaving the state to prevent a vote on a bill that cut collective bargaining rights for public workers (Davey 2011). While the disappearing quorum maneuver delayed passage of the bill, it did so temporarily. Three weeks later, Senate Republicans, who held a 19–14 majority in the chamber, stripped all fiscal provisions from the measure and passed the measure by a vote of 18 to 1 in the Democrats' absence (Fletcher and Cha 2011).

Agenda Control Powers

Whether issues reach the floor—and in what capacity—is dictated by agenda control powers. Scholars of congressional politics often distinguish between negative agenda powers that allow actors to block proposals from the floor and positive powers that allow them to influence the content of proposals and pressure members for support (Cox and McCubbins 2005; Finocchiaro and Rohde 2008). Of these, a great deal more attention has been given to negative agenda powers. The bulk of this work has found that the majority party's negative powers stemming from its control over the Rules Committee has translated to success on the floor (Cox and McCubbins 2005; Jenkins and Monroe 2012a).

While the Constitution establishes that the House will be presided over by an elected Speaker and the Senate by the vice president, it is largely silent on the topic of agenda powers in Congress. In the absence of an exogenous rule, the House of Representatives was largely free to centralize agenda-setting powers in the Speaker.[31] Senators have been less willing to follow suit, in part because their president is unelected by the chamber (Lynch et al. 2018). While much of the scholarship on House agenda powers has focused on formal, endogenously determined chamber rules, the sources of agenda powers are far more varied, and many are informal. This is especially true of positive agenda influence, which can stem from informational advantages (Curry 2015), informal caucuses that increase coordination (Crespin et al. 2015), and partisan peer group pressures (Lee 2008b; Smith 2007). Additionally, there is substantial variation in agenda control powers at the state and comparative levels, a great deal of which comes from exogenously set provisions. Variance in formal agenda-setting powers largely centers on three issues: (1) the degree to which committees operate autonomously; (2) the amount of control the majority party exerts over the legislative calendar; and (3) the level of freedom members have in the drafting of legislation.

When committees lack autonomy from the majority party, the party can use them as a way both to screen out bills that could embarrass them on the floor and to package unpopular proposals in a more palatable way. Thus, they can effectively decide the proposals that will receive recorded votes on the floor. This can substantially mitigate the benefits of transparency. Measuring committee autonomy is difficult. However, many chambers have rules governing how committees are appointed, how legislation is drafted and amended, and how hearings are controlled. Generally, these rules are endogenous, though language mandating committees hold hearings on bills referred to them can be found in some state constitutions. For example, Massachusetts specifies that certain initiatives "shall be referred to a committee thereof, and the petitioners and all parties in interest shall be heard, and the measure shall be considered and reported upon to the general court with the committee's recommendations." In 27 of 99 US state legislative bodies, committees are required to hold hearings on bills referred to them (Anzia and Jackman 2013).[32]

Control over the legislative calendar is also not absolute. And while the US Constitution does not provide exogenous rules dictating how bills get to the floor, some states have constitutions that do. For example, in 1988, Colorado adopted a constitutional amendment requiring that bills passed out of a committee be considered on the floor in the order they are reported (Cox et al. 2010). This decentralization of agenda-setting power led to an increase in the majority party's roll rate. Other work at the state level and comparative level has reported similar findings linking negative agenda-setting institutions with party roll rates (Anzia and Jackman 2013; Chandler et al. 2006; Cox et al. 2010; Crosson 2019). Anzia and Jackman (2013) report that there are 35 state chambers where bills are considered on the floor in the order in which they are reported.

Finally, while negative agenda-setting institutions have received a great deal of attention, rules governing how legislation is drafted substantially influence the value afforded voters by recorded votes. Whether through control of the amending process within the committee or through other procedures that allow them to package multiple issues together on the floor, centralized bill drafters have substantial resources to either provide members "cover" on certain issues or pass legislation that might not pass separately (Hanson 2014). For example, in 1994, President Clinton worked with Democratic leaders in the House to quash an effort to force a separate vote on the assault weapons ban included in the Violent Crime Control and Law Enforcement Act. They felt a separate vote would likely kill the provision (Devroy 1994). In contrast, exogenous rules limiting centralized control over bill drafting are common in state legislatures.

The most common exogenous restriction on bill drafting at the state level is the presence of a single-subject rule. For example, the Ohio Constitution states, "No bill shall contain more than one subject, which shall be clearly expressed in its title." Justified in part on the basis of ensuring transparency to voters, over 40 states have some type of single-subject rule in their constitutions (Gilbert 2006). Its presence has had a significant impact on policy, as courts have frequently relied on it to strike down measures related to immigration, gay marriage, and reapportionment (Cooter and Gilbert 2010). While single-subject rules are the subject of some controversy for legal scholars, it seems likely they would limit the ability of centralized party leaders to control the roll call record. Similarly, Ryan (2014) found that rules ensuring the minority party could offer an alternative conference report on the floor led to larger, more bipartisan coalitions on final passage votes.

Omnibus lawmaking and control over floor and committee amendments provide legislative leaders with tools for dealing with potentially "tough votes." However, an even more commonly used tool relates to the well-documented rise of the "messaging vote" (Lee 2016). While commonly associated with amendments, messaging votes on bills with little to no chance of enactment are also frequently employed. This tactic, discussed in greater detail in Chapter 3, allows members to dilute the impact of any one specific vote by building up a broader legislative track record on policies perceived to be more popular.

Early Abuses of Recorded Voting

Debate during the Constitutional Convention demonstrated that delegates worried about balancing the need for Congress to be transparent to constituents and the fear that recorded voting would be abused and the public misled. To do so, the Founders primarily established a majority quorum rule (which influences both stages of the roll call generating process) and by instituting an exogenous sufficient second clause (which influences Stage 2). The goal of the former was to prevent minorities from hijacking the legislative process through disappearing quorums. The goal of the sufficient second clause was to make recorded voting more difficult, in an effort to ensure it would only be used on the most salient votes. Both approaches were met with mixed results during the 19th century.

Reed's Rules and the Disappearing Quorum

Roll call voting in the 19th and early 20th centuries was primarily used by the minority party as a tool to obstruct the majority's agenda. It allowed the minority to slow down the majority party's agenda in two primary ways. First, roll call voting takes time—especially in chambers that do not employ electronic voting. The possibility of electronic voting dates back to 1869, when Thomas Edison filed a patent on a vote recorder machine and demonstrated its usage to Congress (Straus 2008). However, it was not adopted in the House until 1972 and is still not employed in the Senate. In the 63rd Congress (1913–1915), Rep. Allan Walsh (D-NJ) estimated the average time consumed in a roll call was 45 minutes. Despite this, members were reticent to adopt electronic voting, expressing concerns both regarding the price and that it would shorten vote times, leading Congress to "flood the country with legislation" (Straus 2008, 3).

Second, recorded votes allow minorities to demonstrate the lack of quorum. By the late 19th century, disappearing quorum tactics had plagued the House (Koger 2010). Arguing that the yeas and nays clause had been hijacked to force disappearing quorum votes, future Speaker Thomas Brackett Reed (R-ME) asserted he would "not be surprised to find that double the number of pages of the House journal had been wasted in the record of yeas and nays on frivolous motions than had been used to record all the votes on serious questions." He added, "The flagrant abuse of [the yeas and nays clause] of the Constitution goes far to justify Roger Sherman's desire to have it stricken out altogether" (Reed 1889, 423).

When Republicans took control of the House in the 51st Congress, Reed was elected Speaker and the implementation of "Reed's Rules" shortly followed. The rules empowered the Speaker to count members present but not voting for the purpose of making a quorum, lowered the threshold of members necessary to form the Committee of the Whole, and prohibited the offering of certain dilatory motions (Binder 1997; Roberts 2010).[33] Such a centralization of authority was available in the House due to lax constitutional restrictions on leadership and agenda setting, as well as the Founders' decisions to not specify how a quorum would be counted.

The implementation of Reed's Rules began in January with a ruling by Reed during consideration of a contested election case in West Virginia.[34] Rep. John Dalzell (R-PA) brought up a resolution dealing with the case, and the Democrats, under the leadership of Rep. Charles Crisp (D-GA), raised a question of consideration against it (Binder 1997). The initial division vote revealed 136 votes in favor of considering the resolution and 124 against. Crisp then called for the yeas and nays. Democrats refused to vote and the final tally revealed 162 yeas and three nays, one vote shy of a quorum.

After announcing the result, Reed directed the clerk to record the names of members present but not voting. The Democrats were outraged. Crisp immediately appealed. To the applause of his fellow partisans, Rep. William Breckinridge (D-KY) declared, "I deny the power of the Speaker and denounce it as revolutionary" (*Congressional Record*, 51st Congress, January 29, 1890, 949). Rep. James Bright Morgan (D-MS) declared it unconstitutional. Rep. James Outhwaite (D-OH) argued that it was not for the chair to decide whether or not he should vote. Their complaints continued for nearly three days (Binder 1997).

The Republicans followed up Reed's ruling with a formal proposal revis-

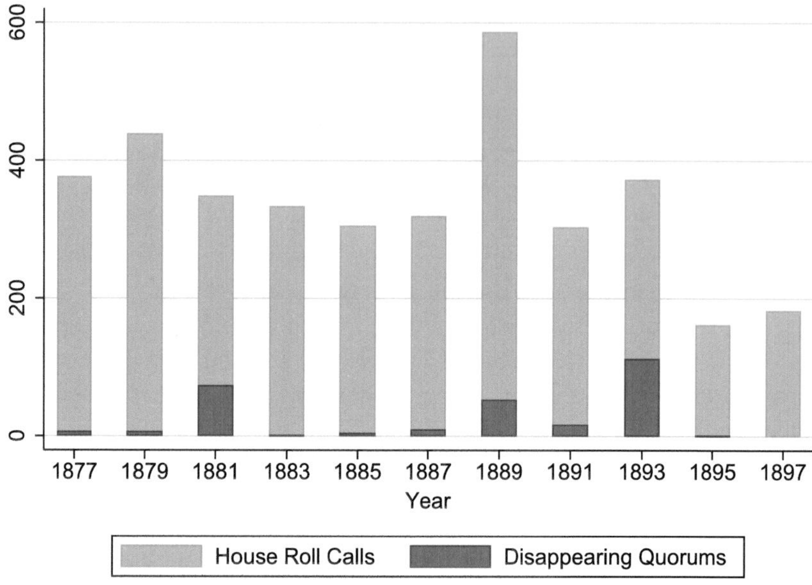

Figure 2.1. Disappearing Quorum Roll Calls, 1877–1897

ing the chamber's rules. The measure, introduced by future Speaker Joseph Cannon (R-IL), gave the speaker the ability to bar dilatory motions and a great deal of discretion to determine what constituted a dilatory motion. The Democrats attempted to water down the effect of Cannon's resolution with a series of amendments, but Binder (1997) notes that the Republicans maintained perfect voting cohesion against them. The formal Reed's Rules proposal passed 163 to 147. Democrats repealed Reed's Rules the following Congress after winning the majority. However, usage of disappearing quorums became so common that the rules were reinstituted during the 53rd Congress. Figure 2.1 plots the total number of House roll call votes where less than 10% of the minority party voted in the congresses before and after Reed's Rules.

The Insufficient "Sufficient Second" Clause

As James Galloway argued during the North Carolina ratifying convention, the lack of a sufficient second during the Continental Congress led to abuse of the yeas and nays and their repeated usage on "trifling occasions." Galloway went on to note he had "no doubt one-fifth would require them on every occasion of importance" (Elliot 1888, 4:72–73). The Founders had ample reason to believe this. They mandated the yeas and nays on only veto override votes, Senate votes confirming treaties, votes expelling a member, and votes on adopting a constitutional amendment. As Table 2.1 demonstrates, one-fifth of a quorum is a substantial number compared to most US state legislatures. Indeed, as we argue below, the clause was effective at curbing the number of roll call vote requests throughout the 19th and early 20th centuries. However, roll call vote requests have become largely pro forma in the contemporary Congress.[35] Members being denied sufficient seconds occurs so rarely that when it does happen it generates substantial media attention.

For instance, in 2015, Sen. Ted Cruz (R-TX) was denied a sufficient second on a request to table an amendment so he could offer one himself that dealt with defunding Planned Parenthood (Everett 2015a). Outraged, he dubbed the denial "an unprecedented procedural trick" and accused senators of seeking to "avoid accountability" (*Congressional Record,* 114th Congress, September 28, 2015, H6376).[36] Sen. John McCain (R-AZ) noted that he had "never before seen a senator who couldn't get even one other person in the Senate to raise his hand to help him get a [recorded] vote" (Hawkings 2015).[37]

But cases like this are very unusual in the modern Congress. In recent years, leaders have found far more success avoiding uncomfortable roll call votes by blocking bills and amendments before they reached the floor stage. Generally, this is done through restrictive special rules in the House (Lynch et al. 2016) or filling the amendment tree in the Senate (Madonna and Kosar 2015). But as we have discussed, such tactics have limitations and once a proposal reaches the floor, a roll call vote is almost a certainty if a member requests one. When roll call requests are denied, it is usually for deliberate, strategic reasons, as was the case with Cruz.

Historically, sufficient seconds were denied far more frequently, and often for practical reasons. The most common explanation for the denial of a sufficient second was attendance. During periods of low attendance, it was difficult to generate the necessary one-fifth of a quorum needed for a sufficient second. Moreover, presiding officers frequently enforced the one-fifth requirement. Figure 2.2 plots the average attendance in the House on roll call votes from the 59th Congress (1905–1907) to the 113th Congress (2013–2014). The figure also includes a simple lowess smoothing line to indicate the general trend in the data.[38] Figure 2.2 demonstrates that it was not until the second half of the 20th century that average attendance surpassed 80%.

This low attendance was due to a variety of factors, with travel issues being the most notable of them. For much of American history, travel to and from Washington, DC, was difficult. As Mason argued in his opposition to sub-majority quorums, this posed problems for members from more distant states. Because of this, members would frequently form "vote pairs" with a

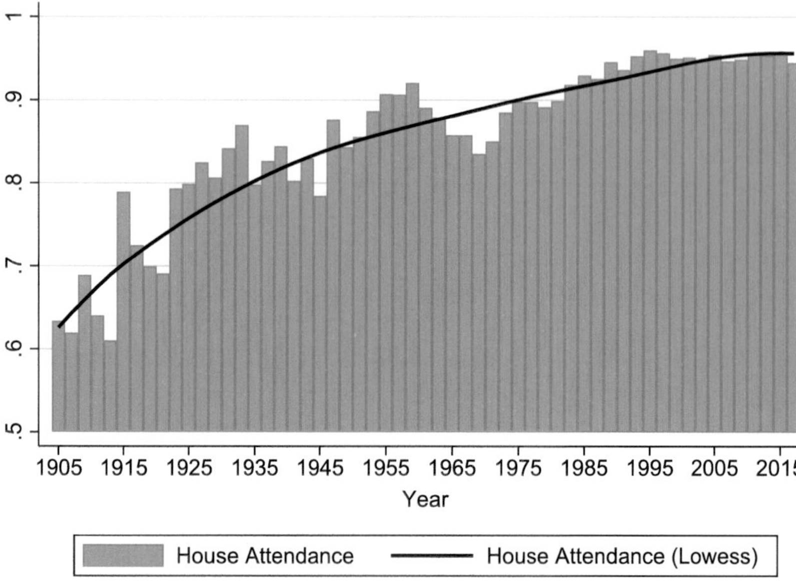

Figure 2.2. Average Attendance on Roll Call Votes per House, 1905–2014

member of the opposing parties. Pairs would agree to abstain on key votes when one or the other was absent. Members tended to keep their pairs for extensive periods and tried to make them with opposing partisans that they disagreed with frequently.[39] As Figure 2.2 demonstrates, technological advances—including the opening of Washington National Airport in 1941—made travel to and from the district easier (Fenno 1978).

In addition to attendance and travel issues, staffing changes likely represent an additional practical barrier to roll call requests. Staffing levels in Congress were low in the 19th and early 20th centuries. Personal staff, as well as staffers for Congressional Member Organizations, play an important role in drafting amendments and advocating for or against certain proposals (Malbin 1980). In the absence of competent and committed staff, members would be unlikely to propose and press as many measures for electorally driven roll calls. Staffing changes also led to increased party coordination, allowing leaders and rank-and-file members of both the majority and minority parties to better coordinate their roll call generating behavior in Congress with electoral priorities (Crespin et al. 2015).

As a result, sufficient seconds were difficult for many members to muster in earlier congresses. This was especially true for members who had a reputation for extreme policy views. For example, Rep. Thomas Lindsey Blanton (D-TX) was a very conservative member first elected to the House in 1917. He was loathed for his aggressive manner, frequent usage of points of order, and repeated requests for recorded votes. In 1921, during consideration of a naval appropriation bill, Blanton moved to recommit the measure with instructions that sought to cut funding for construction from $90 million to $10 million.[40] After the Speaker announced the "noes appeared to have it," Blanton requested a roll call vote (*Congressional Record*, 67th Congress, April 28, 1921, 765–766). The Speaker announced that just over a quorum was present. However, he then noted an insufficient number supported Blanton's call for the yeas and nays. Blanton was frequently denied sufficient seconds, and his unpopularity would be further solidified later in that same Congress when a motion to expel him from the chamber failed by a mere eight votes.[41]

Leaders, especially in the House, would often use a lack of support for a sufficient second as a way to avoid difficult roll calls. Such an approach was often taken on measures that increased benefits for members of Congress, either through salary or staff compensation. Member reticence to go "on the record" on salary increases and funding for legislative staffing is well-established and occurred throughout the 19th and 20th centuries (Madonna and Ostrander 2019; Alston et al. 2006; Theriault 2004). For example, during debate over a resolution providing compensation to committee clerks for work already completed, Rep. William Samford (D-AL) complained that it was "impossible" to get enough men to "call the yeas and nays" in many cases on these questions (*Congressional Record*, 46th Congress, June 6, 1877, 1879).

In sum, in earlier eras, there were not only fewer members available to provide sufficient seconds, but many members were reticent to do so because of efficiency concerns. This combination should result in not only fewer roll calls overall, but in more roll call requests that fail to generate sufficient seconds. To examine this, we tracked failed requests for division, teller, and roll call votes on amendments to important bills in the House and Senate from the 59th Congress (1905–1906) to the 96th Congress (1979–1980).[42] These are plotted in Figure 2.3, which plots the percentage of amendments coded with a failed vote request. The figure also includes a simple lowess smoothing line to indicate the general trend in the data. While Figure 2.3 demonstrates failed requests are decreasing sharply over the time series, it highlights that failures were common in the 19th-century Congress.

Figure 2.3 suggests the sufficient second clause has become increasingly insufficient as a mechanism for deterring roll call votes. In the contemporary Congress, it is widely assumed that a recorded vote will be granted if it is requested. In addition to improved attendance, other institutional changes further undercut the effectiveness of the sufficient second clause. In the Sen-

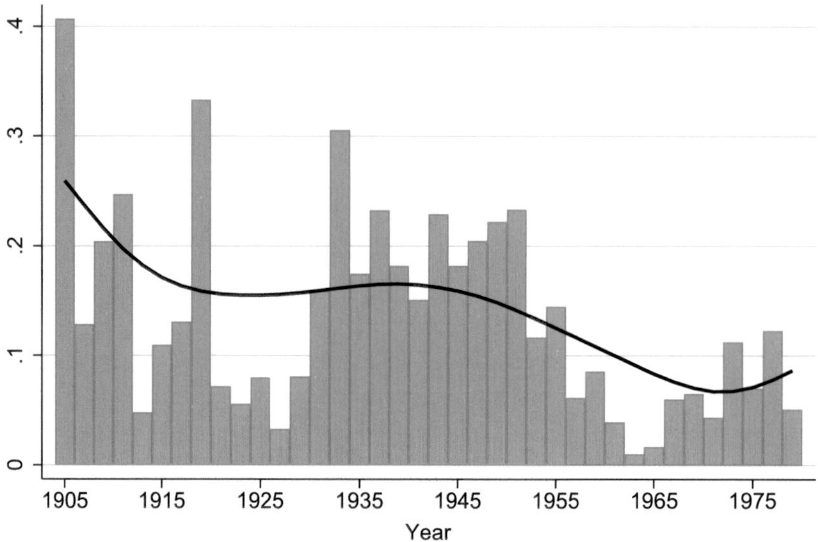

Figure 2.3. Percentage of Amendments Subjected to Failed Vote Requests, 1905–1980

ate, increasing obstruction and the threat of delay was often enough to secure the yeas and nays on a question if a member was determined enough. For example, in the 75th Congress (1937–1938), Sen. George Vandenberg's (R-MI) request for a roll call on a committee amendment was denied. He then informed the Senate that he "shall be very frank about the matter": The Senate would "simply save some time if [a roll call was granted]" (*Congressional Record*, 75th Congress, December 15, 1937, 1528–1529). After a quorum call, the Senate capitulated and provided a sufficient second to Vandenberg's request.

Both chambers also adopted changes to their standing rules that increased the number of automatic roll call votes. The Senate adopted a formal cloture rule to end debate in 1919. This rule included a provision mandating the yeas and nays.[43] As detailed in Chapter 4, usage of cloture motions, and recorded votes on them, have increased sharply in recent congresses. In the 104th Congress, the House followed many states by adopting automatic recorded votes on the adoption of bills and conference reports that dealt with appropriations, tax, and budgetary measures.[44]

The most salient change in the House was the adoption of recorded voting in the Committee of the Whole (Roberts and Smith 2003; Rohde 1991). The Committee of the Whole is a parliamentary mechanism employed by legislative bodies to conduct business under committee rules, as opposed to rules binding the full chamber. The use of such a committee predates the Constitution. For much of the House's history, its usage ensured that nearly all floor amendments would be dispensed with by an unrecorded vote (Alexander 1916). This changed in the House after the adoption of the Legislative Reorganization Act of 1970 (first applied in the 92nd Congress). The reform led to an explosion in roll call votes on minority-sponsored amendments, most of which failed (Roberts and Smith 2003). This reform and others adopted in the early 1970s were motivated by a desire to make Congress more transparent but were quickly regretted by many reformers. As Rep. George Miller (D-CA) put it, "We destroyed the institution by turning the lights on" (Lawrence 2018, 5).

Conclusion

Transparency in legislative bodies is not costless. These costs are frequently paid for through efficiency loss. As we discuss in the next chapter, rules promoting transparency also provide minorities with an avenue to put their opponents "on the record" by taking legislative behavior out of context. While legislative bodies frequently try to balance the costs and benefits of transparency, the preceding discussion demonstrates that doing so can be difficult.

There is substantial variance in factors governing transparency across legislative bodies by examining Stage 1 (quorum rules and agenda powers) and Stage 2 (direct roll call rules and sufficient second requirements). The Founders believed the Constitution would successfully strike such a balance. However, as we have argued, their approach was initially limited in a number of ways. Moreover, technological changes they could never have foreseen further weakened the system. As a result, the sufficient second clause is largely irrelevant in contemporary congresses.

In the next chapter, we build on this discussion by examining how majorities have used positive and negative agenda-setting powers to respond to increased requests for roll call votes. We provide a more detailed theoretical discussion for "calling the roll," arguing that in contrast to sincere policy transparency, contemporary congresses are more likely to use recorded voting as a way to signal to their donor class. This is a function of increased electoral competitiveness, the perceived effectiveness of attack ads, a desire to promote a unified party brand and the rising importance of money in campaigns. We examine our theoretical discussion using an expanded dataset on roll call vote types from the 59th (1905–1907) to the 113th Congresses (2013–2014).

THREE

The Evolving Roll Call Record

> There is a need to know how we vote in order that an honest evaluation of our effectiveness as a Representative may be made by the voters in the election.
>
> —Rep. John Emerson Moss (D-CA), 1970

> I don't think it makes much sense to allow our rules on roll calls in effect to be used as a filibuster.
>
> —Former Rep. David Obey, quoted in Lawrence (2018, 238)

The Helping Sick Americans Now Act of 2013

Four years before the failure of the American Health Care Act of 2017, Republicans attempted a comparable healthcare reform effort. The Helping Sick Americans Now Act was introduced by Rep. Joseph Pitts (R-PA) to the Republican-controlled House on April 15, 2013 (Dougherty et al. 2014). The measure sought to shift nearly $4 billion allocated primarily to the Affordable Care Act's Prevention and Public Health Fund and move the funds to pay for an extension of the Federal High-Risk Pool Program—a program designed to subsidize health insurance costs for individuals with preexisting conditions. House Republican leaders sought to use the legislation to highlight pieces of Obamacare they disagreed with and spotlight alternatives. Press accounts suggested it was part of Majority Leader Eric Cantor's (R-VA) broader effort to "rebrand" the party for the 2014 elections (Drucker 2013; Weisman 2013a). The bill was referred to the House Committee on Energy and Commerce, amended, and reported out of committee on a party-line vote on April 17 (Ethridge 2013b).[1]

The next week, on April 23, Republican leaders moved forward with H.Res. 175, a special rule that provided for consideration of the Helping Sick Americans Now Act under a structured rule.[2] In arguing for the rule, Republicans criticized the ACA, claiming the Federal High-Risk Pool Program was a more efficient allocation of funds and that the bill would reduce the deficit. Democrats, knowing this bill would never pass the Democratic-controlled Senate or receive the support of President Obama, panned the Republican effort. Minority Whip Steny Hoyer (D-MD) accused the majority of "wasting our time here" for the purposes of political messaging (*Congressional Record*, 113th Congress, April 24, 2013, H2270).[3] The rule was adopted after two nearly perfect party-line votes.[4]

Despite their near unanimity in support for the rule, it was clear the bill lacked broad support among Republicans. Two prominent conservative groups, the Club for Growth and Heritage Action, came out against it. In a statement, the Club for Growth argued that "fiscal conservatives should be squarely focused on repealing ObamaCare, not strengthening it by supporting the parts that are politically attractive" (Ethridge 2013a). Press accounts suggested final passage on the bill would expose deep divisions within the Republican Party.[5] In what would become a precursor to the American Health Care Act of 2017, Republicans opted to pull the bill from the floor before a passage vote was cast.

One month after pulling the Helping Sick Americans Now Act, the House went forward with a different healthcare bill, H.R. 45. This bill, sponsored by Rep. Michele Bachmann (R-MN), would implement a full repeal of the ACA. The measure was considered under a closed rule that barred any amendments and passed 229–195, with two Democrats joining all voting Republicans in support.[6] As expected, the Democratic-controlled Senate took no action on Bachmann's bill, just as the Senate had failed to take up previous House measures that weakened or repealed the ACA. In addition to these many failed attempts to change Obamacare that filled the roll call record, such votes also filled the voter guides of conservative interest groups. Both the Heritage Foundation and the Club for Growth used member votes on H.R. 45 in their annual congressional scorecards, as they had done on 14 other separate measures that would either have fully or partially repealed the ACA had they become law. These scorecards allow conservative interest groups to highlight how members of Congress vote on measures determined to be some of the most important votes of 112th and 113th Congresses. Of all the "important" measures that sought to repeal or weaken the ACA, only one was ever enacted into law.[7]

Like the American Health Care Act of 2017, the Helping Sick Americans Now Act provides a good example of how the roll call record is manipulated in the contemporary Congress. The Pitts bill featured two party-line roll calls on the rule. Fear that interest group scoring would have led to members defections and shown internal party divisions led leadership to pull the measure before a roll call was taken. Instead, three nearly party-line votes on the Bachmann bill and closed rule were cast and the measure was not considered again. The case also demonstrates that even if the public is unconcerned about a member's roll call behavior, members themselves certainly are. The mere threat an interest group would include a vote in its score led to the bill being taken off the agenda. It seems likely such concerns have contributed to the high levels of policy gridlock frequently reported. We argue cases like this are indicative of how the record has shifted. While it could previously be considered a nearly exogenous tool that could provide voters with transparent insight into the policy positions of their elected members, it has evolved into an endogenously constructed mechanism used by parties seeking to win elections. This is significant, as changes in the roll call generating process significantly undercut the utility of roll call voting for both the general public and scholars of political science. As Carroll and Poole (2014, 116) have argued, "Roll-call votes are only as useful as the underlying process by which they are generated."

In Chapter 2, we documented the origins behind the Framers' decision to codify recorded voting in the United States and noted the lack of consensus around their institutional design choices. In this chapter, we focus on our second goal for the manuscript: documenting how the roll call voting record has changed. To do so, we first revisit the scholarly literature on recorded voting, highlighting divergent conclusions over the degree roll call votes are monitored by constituents. Building off this literature, we argue that changes to the way roll calls are generated have made it even more difficult for voters to use these votes to monitor the behavior of their representatives. We conclude by introducing a new dataset and using it to document changing patterns of roll call generation from the 59th Congress (1905–1907) to the 113th Congress (2013–2014).

Generating the Record

A member's roll call voting record is the product of his or her individual roll call votes. As we discuss below, there are a number of reasons why individuals or groups of legislators might want a recorded vote (or want to avoid one). But regardless of members' motivations, the utility of roll call votes is drawn from their perceived ease of interpretation. Unlike political speeches and campaign promises, roll call votes are "hard data" that "represent discrete acts the fact of whose occurrence is not subject to dispute" (Truman 1951, 12). Or as Stuart Rice (1925, 60) put it in his seminal study on measuring group behavior, votes are "simple and precise." Recorded votes, especially those on the final passage of an enactment "seem to be particularly easy to understand back home, and political missteps can be costly" (Mayhew 1991, 121). As we discuss below, there is some evidence suggesting roll calls still provide "simple and precise" policy transparency, but more reasons to believe recorded votes are primarily a tool of electoral manipulation.

Policy Transparency

As we have discussed, roll call voting was instituted to provide policy transparency for voters. Knowing how a legislator voted on a given issue or aggregate set of issues allows voters to decide whether that legislator is adequately representing their views. If voters decide the legislator is not doing so, they may opt to support someone else in the next election. Scholars have argued that legislators, aware that recorded votes will be observed by their constituents, will adapt their voting behavior on recorded votes so that it is in line with a majority of the voters in their district. The implication from this argument is that recorded voting helps ensure median policy outcomes will occur (Black 1948; Downs 1957). For example, Kingdon (1989, 42) highlights a quote from a congressman justifying his support for the House Un-American Activities Committee:

> It doesn't take too many votes like this before you've got several groups against you, all for different reasons, and they all care about that one issue that you were wrong on. A congressman can only afford two or three votes like that in a session. You get a string of them, then watch out.

This transparency thesis has long been countered by work demonstrating that voters are woefully uninformed about the voting behavior of their elected members. This position is put succinctly by Miller and Stokes (1963, 47): "Far from looking over the shoulder of their Congressmen at the legislative game, most Americans are almost totally uninformed about legislative issues in Washington." Reporting results from a survey of 100 members of Congress, Matthews and Stimson (1975, 28) report that "79 percent said their constituents seldom knew or cared how they voted." Other research has echoed this, demonstrating that voters are poorly informed about their representative's votes on even the most highly visible legislation (Alvarez and Gronke 1996; Ansolabehere and Jones 2010).

Despite this lack of information, the view that roll call votes help voters hold members electorally accountable has some broad support within the literature (Bovitz and Carson 2006; Canes-Wrone et al. 2002; Carson and Engstrom 2005; Erikson 1978). For example, Nyhan et al. (2012) find that Democratic roll call votes on the Affordable Care Act, Economic Stimulus, and Cap and Trade during the 111th Congress may have cost Democrats their majority in the House. Other work has reported that ideological extremity is associated with lower incumbent vote share and an increased likelihood of defeat (Ansolabehere et al. 2001; Brady et al. 2000; Erikson and Wright 2000).

Scholars generally highlight several mechanisms that allow the general public to hold members accountable for their votes. First, political campaigns provide valuable information about members' voting records. Even if voters are not closely monitoring the work of Congress, members and their political opponents both have incentives to report voting activity to the public as part of electoral campaigns. Members believe they can inform voters of their positions on popular issues by emphasizing their voting record through advertising, campaigning, and constituent communications (Lipinski 2001). Political opponents are likely to draw attention to votes where members' views are out of step with the views of their districts. Indeed, the threat of opponents advertising such votes may be enough to encourage members to vote in accordance with the desires of their districts.

Second, parties and partisan cues can provide the public with information that helps hold members accountable (Ansolabehere and Jones 2010; Jones 2011). Voters may not know much about the individual voting patterns of their representative, but can much more easily monitor and assess the performance of political parties. By knowing the voting behavior of a party, voters can punish and reward a political party and, in turn, the individual members that make up that party.

Finally, some have argued that member roll call behavior closely tracks voters' preferences primarily because members incorrectly believe their constituents monitor their voting behavior. As Erikson and Tedin (2015, 300) put it, "[Congress] sometimes [does] what they think the public wants because they mistakenly believe the public is paying attention!" Thus, the electoral transparency argument implies that not only should members alter their positions on roll call votes to reflect their district's preferences, they should seek to publicize their positions that are supported by the district by requesting recorded votes.

Electoral Manipulation

Conversely, there are reasons to believe that members do not need to be very concerned about their district's preferences when they are casting recorded votes. First, there is evidence members have a difficult time even ascertaining their voters' preferences on key issues. Matthews and Stimson (1975, 28) suggest the impact of constituency is limited by the inability of members to anticipate "the views of the folks back home."[8] This finding is bolstered by work that reports that members of Congress, regardless of their party, view their district as more conservative than it actually is (Broockman and Skovron 2018). Knowing voters' desires on whether they should vote yea or nay becomes even more difficult when votes are held on complex bills that include multiple key issues (Bianco et al. 1996).

Second, a number of studies report little to no evidence that voters hold members accountable for their votes in Congress. Achen and Bartels (2017), for instance, report only a modest correlation between district ideology and the roll call voting records of their members of Congress.[9] Using survey data, Highton (2019) reports little evidence linking roll call votes, voter preferences, and member vote share. Given this, it is perhaps not surprising a number of studies find members often vote in ways that are inconsistent with the preferences of their district (Carson and Engstrom 2005; Clinton 2006).

Sulkin (2009) argues that voters have a difficult time using roll call votes to monitor whether members are acting according to their campaign promises, since candidates do not campaign using the type of specific policy proposals that are found in legislation. Sulkin argues that "they more often make claims along the lines that they are 'champions for education' or are 'tough on crime'" (2009, 1095). Dancey and Sheagley (2013) find most voters cannot correctly identify how senators voted on important roll call votes when they adopt positions contrary to their party and the type of broad party slogans highlighted by Sulkin. Ansolabehere and Jones (2010) report a similar finding for House members.

Finally, the public is frequently presented with information about roll call voting that obfuscates the true record of members, making it even harder for members to feel bound by the views of their constituents. Since voters have a difficult time using votes to accurately assess their representatives' record, politicians, their political opponents, and outside groups are all anxious to tell the public what to think about roll call votes. Members highlight votes when it serves their political purposes and avoid mentioning votes when it does not.[10] Campaigns often discuss roll call votes in a way that misrepresents the true underlying substantive issues the votes considered. This results in the general public being bombarded with ads that provide conflicting information on how members voted on certain issues.

Campaigns have a great deal of leeway when it comes to tying the substance of a vote to an issue, and, not surprisingly, campaigns frequently take advantage of this. For example, in the 2014 Georgia Republican Senate primary race, businessman David Perdue's campaign ran advertisements that featured an attack on his opponent, 11-term Rep. Jack Kingston (R-GA), that accused Kingston of voting to raise his own pay seven times. The seven votes were not direct votes on pay increases. Rather, they were votes to order the previous question on a special rule. Had the rule been voted down, a minority Democratic Party member announced his intention to offer an amendment to deny an annual pay raise. Majority party members rarely vote against special rules, as doing so would significantly interrupt their agenda. The minority is aware of this and will make such declarations for electoral posturing (Badertscher 2014; Bluestein 2014).[11]

Outside groups, such as interest groups, think tanks, and campaign donors, monitor member actions more carefully than does the general public. In the contemporary US Congress, there are over a hundred different interest groups that track and often score member votes (Davidson et al. 2013). In the Helping Sick Americans Now Act case we began this chapter with, the threat that an interest group would score the vote was enough for the bill to get dropped. As the number of outside groups monitoring votes and reporting their "meaning" to the public has increased, so has the number of roll call votes prominently featured in political attack ads. A common tactic is to feature how often a member voted with an unpopular national figure, like a president or the Speaker of the House (Carson et al. 2014). For example, in 2014, Republicans put out an advertisement asserting that Rep. John Barrow (D-GA) voted with President Barack Obama 85% of the time. Barrow did vote with Obama 85% of the time in 2009, a fact the ad noted in a footnote with very small print, but he only voted with Obama 28% and 35% in the two years preceding the 2014 election, a fact the ad failed to report (Jacobson 2014). Although Rep. Gene Taylor (D-MS) supported Republican John McCain during the 2008 presidential election, he was still attacked in campaign ads for voting with former House Speaker Nancy Pelosi (D-CA) 82% of the time (Taylor 2010).[12]

Scholars have demonstrated these outside groups tend to be more ideologically extreme than the general electorate (Bafumi and Herron 2010; Miller and Schofield 2003). Consistent with this, outside groups are also more supportive of ideologically extreme legislators who vote with them on roll call votes (Barber 2016; Barber et al. 2017; Stratmann 2002).[13] While there is some disagreement on this point, it is consistent with the reported influence of conservative groups in recent congresses. For example, in addition to the Helping Sick Americans Now Act, the Club for Growth and Heritage Action announced they would "key vote" several votes related to the passage of the Farm Bill that same year. This included several controversial amendments allowed under the special rule. Press accounts suggested that this interest group scrutiny of the Farm Bill tempered Republican support for the bill and eventually led to its defeat (Dumain 2013).

This kind of activity occasionally puts interest groups in conflict with party leaders. The Farm Bill episode was one of several that led House Speaker John Boehner (R-OH) to declare these conservative advocacy groups had "lost all credibility" (Everett 2014; Kane and Gold 2013).[14] Others accused the groups of taking increasingly conservative positions in an effort to generate headlines and fundraising dollars (Ball 2013; Walsh 2013). The Senate Conservatives Fund, a political action committee headed by former senator and later Heritage Foundation President Jim DeMint (R-SC), took in $1.5 million in August 2013 primarily on the strength of its public efforts to repeal the ACA (Palmer 2013). Despite the occasional conflict, party leaders recognize these outside groups play an influential role in their ability to raise money and keep vulnerable members from being defeated in primary races. So they will pull bills from the floor the groups oppose and press for votes on measures doomed for failure to appease them. All of this serves to weaken the roll call record's ability to be used by the public to monitor the legislative behavior of their representatives.

Transparency or Electoral Manipulation?

To evaluate changes to the roll call voting record, we first employ an expanded dataset on roll call voting. As documented in Appendix A, we extended the PIPC Roll Call dataset, which codes each roll call vote by vote type starting with 83rd Congress (1953–1954) in the House and 91st Congress (1969–1970) in the Senate (Crespin and Rohde 2016). The PIPC data uses 110 different categories of vote type. These include common types of roll call votes such as votes on final passage and amendment votes. The data also include rarely used vote types, such as recorded votes on the rules of evidence during an impeachment. Using the coding system established by the PIPC project, we coded vote type for all roll call votes back to the 59th Congress (1905–1907) for both the House and the Senate. We also expanded the data to include the bill the vote was taken on.[15]

For votes to provide transparency to the voters, roll call votes should be on interpretable, substantive proposals. As scholars have argued, final passage votes are the easiest of congressional votes for the public to interpret. Consistent with other scholarship, we observe increases in final passage votes in both chambers. However, both increases in amendment and procedure votes in the House, and increases in amendment, procedure, and nomination votes in the Senate, appear more pronounced. This is presented below in Figures 3.1 and 3.2. We discuss these trends in the sections below.

The increase in the raw number of procedural votes appears more problematic when we break the vote types down by partisanship. Figure 3.3 plots raw counts of vote types across three eras for reference purposes: Era 1, from the start of our data in the 59th Congress (1905–1907) through the end of the 78th Congress (1943–1944), when attendance levels stabilized; Era 2, from the 79th Congress (1945–1946) through the 91st Congress (1969–1970), marking the beginning of the post-reform House; and Era 3, from the 92nd Congress (1972–1973) to the 113th Congress (2013–2014). For each era, the vote types (which are pooled across chambers) are characterized as either party votes or nonparty votes. We adopt the standard approach by classifying votes as a party vote if a majority of the two parties are on opposite sides of a roll call.

Procedural Coverage

Despite procedural votes being ostensibly nonideological, scholars have argued that partisan conflict on them has increased sharply (Lee 2009; Theriault 2008). Party unity on procedural votes tends to be substantially higher than on substantive votes (Cox and Poole 2002; Crespin 2010; Jessee and Theriault 2014). Roll calls on procedural issues are frequently requested by minority-party members, often to make the parties appear more polarized (Egar 2016). However, Figures 3.1 and 3.2 demonstrate that the increase in procedural roll calls was accompanied by increases in not only amendment and nomination roll calls, but also final passage votes. Using the extended time series, procedural votes do not appear to be a more substantial percentage of the contemporary roll call record than in other eras.

Two important points can be drawn from Figure 3.3. First, the increase in final passage votes observed in the post-reform congresses is driven by nonpartisan votes. Many, though certainly not all, of these votes are passage of trivial issues like renaming public buildings. Of the 12,490 final passage votes

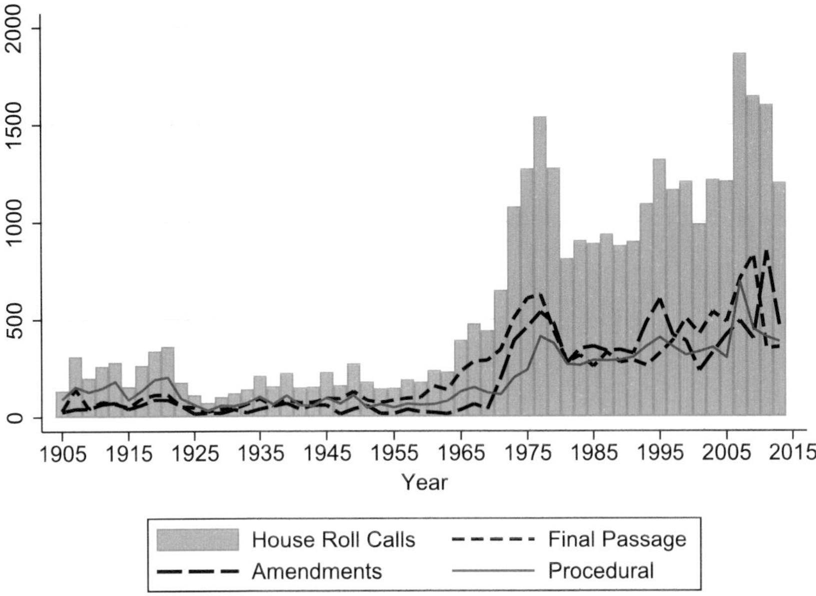

Figure 3.1. House Roll Call Votes by Type, 1905–2014

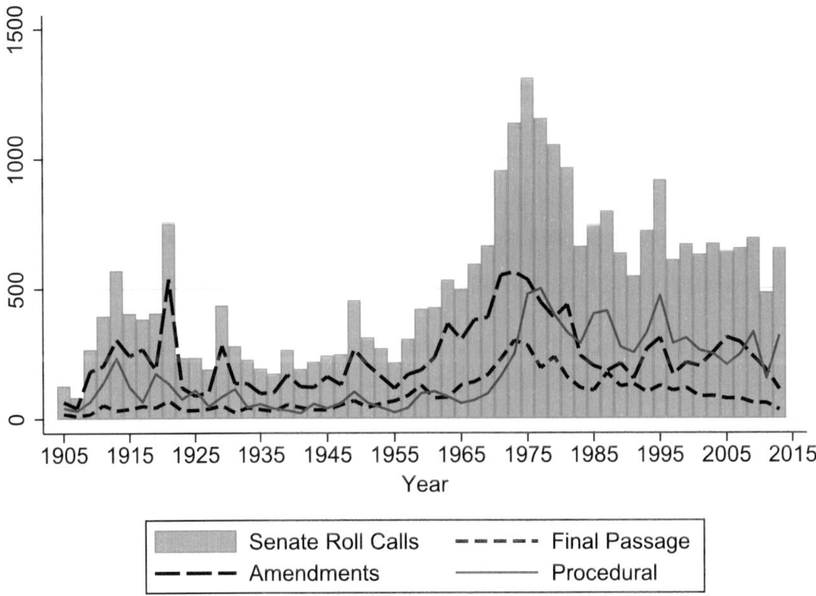

Figure 3.2. Senate Roll Call Votes by Type, 1905–2014

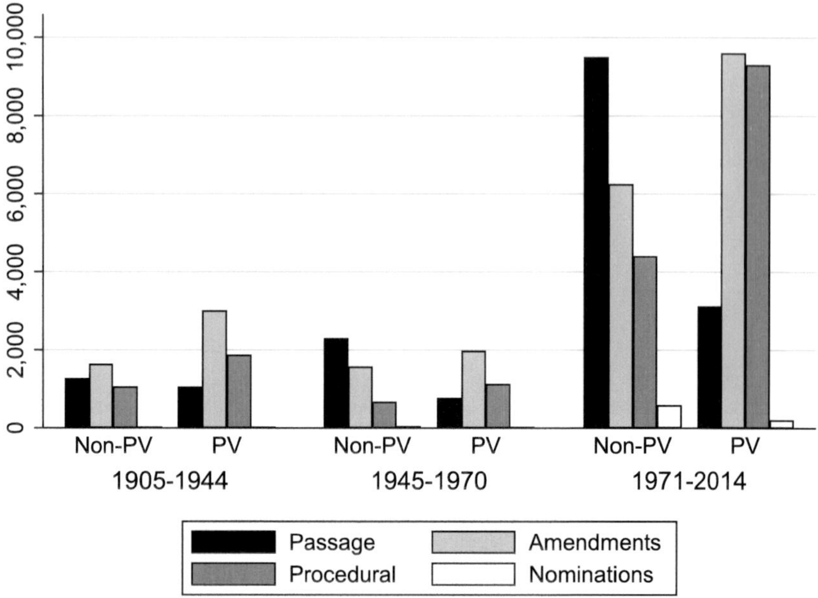

Figure 3.3. Party Votes in Congress Across Vote Type, 1905–2014

observed in the most recent era of our data, just under 25% of them were party votes. Moreover, of the nonparty final passage votes, over 60% of them were lopsided (i.e., the enacting coalition was greater than 95%). Despite this, there are still substantially more party votes on final passage per congress in the most recent era. Party votes on final passage increased from 49.35 per congress in Era 1 to 59.3 in Era 2, and 141.4 in the most recent Era 3. However, a closer examination of the outcome of these votes in the next section suggests this increase may be more reflective of changes in party centralization than an increase in policy transparency.

Second, the percentage of party votes on procedural matters has remained fairly stable across our different eras. It moved from 64% in our first era to 63% in the second and just under 68% in the third. However, changes in party voting patterns on procedural matters are more evident when the data is examined at the Congress level.

Figure 3.4 plots the total number of non-lopsided procedural roll call votes in Congress. The light gray notes the total number of procedural roll call votes, and the dark gray notes the number of those votes that were party votes. The raw number of procedural roll call votes is displayed on the left axis. A lowess smoothing line was added to illustrate percentage of all procedural roll call votes that are party votes.

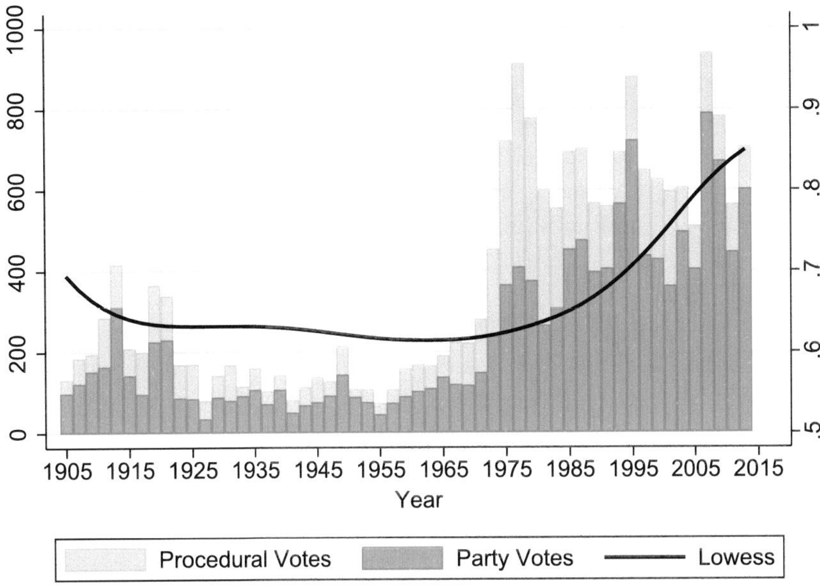

Figure 3.4. Party Votes on Procedural Roll Calls, 1905–2014

The figure suggests that procedural votes were not always effective for parties trying to promote a unified party brand. In the 1960s the average percentage of procedural votes that were party votes dipped below 70%. However, as the perceived value of recorded votes increased, so did both the quantity of procedural votes and the percentage of them that yielded party votes. In recent congresses, virtually all roll call votes on procedure have led to party votes. Consistent with recent work on procedural roll calls, they appear to operate as "*de facto* declarations of partisan identification" (Jessee and Theriault 2014, 845).

While the rise in procedural roll calls is consistent with the argument that members of Congress are trying to differentiate themselves from their partisan opponents for electoral purposes, it could also simply reflect changes in lawmaking. Restrictive rules have been increasingly used on major and minor legislation. Members have consistently objected to their usage. Thus, more procedural votes may reflect sincere disagreement over the type of procedure employed.[16] In Chapter 4, we investigate this by examining the types of procedures employed over time and evaluating how roll call vote patterns have changed using data not drawn from the roll call record. We find recorded voting is more common even on open rules in the contemporary era.

Winning by Losing

For the record to provide transparency for voters, it should be reflective of Congress's legislative output. This is not to suggest negative outcomes are not valuable to voters. As former Speaker Thomas Reed (R-ME) put it, "A negative decision by a legislative body is of as much value to the community as a law" (1889, 424). Roll calls rejecting a bill or an amendment can provide the public with valuable information regarding the positions of their members. But many issues that may be of interest to the general public are not considered on the House or Senate floor. Additionally, cases of House speakers following the "Hastert Rule," refusing to bring up legislation opposed by a majority of their party, are quite common. For instance, shortly after the Senate passed comprehensive immigration reform in 2013, Speaker John Boehner (R-OH) announced the House had no intention of considering the measure (Gibson 2013).

In the event public pressure or a distant status quo point renders negative agenda-setting untenable, leaders can rely on their positive powers to provide coverage. It is now common for agenda setters to allow large numbers of votes on bills and amendments that both leaders and sponsors know will fail. The increase in so-called messaging amendments has been well documented (Lee 2009; Madonna and Kosar 2015; Roberts and Smith 2003). Figures 3.1 and 3.2 demonstrate large increases in the number of amendments that receive recorded votes across more recent congresses. Moreover, as depicted in Figure 3.5, these amendment votes have become increasingly party votes.

Figure 3.5 reports the total number of non-lopsided amendment roll call votes in Congress. The light gray references the total number of amendment roll call votes, and the dark gray notes the number of those votes that were party votes. The raw number of amendment roll call votes is displayed on the left axis. A lowess smoothing line was added to illustrate the percentage of all amendment roll call votes that are party votes. The figure demonstrates that roll call votes on amendments are increasingly likely to be party votes.

This is consistent with claims that leaders have been increasingly using their procedural powers to screen and manage amendments and that more ideological members working with outside groups are offering greater numbers of ideological amendments. However, without knowing the universe of amendments that could receive recorded votes on the floor, we are unable to properly analyze the roll call generating process. One senator's "messaging amendment" may be another senator's sincere policy goal. We evaluate this in Chapter 5 using a new dataset on nearly 120,000 filed amendments to important legislation.

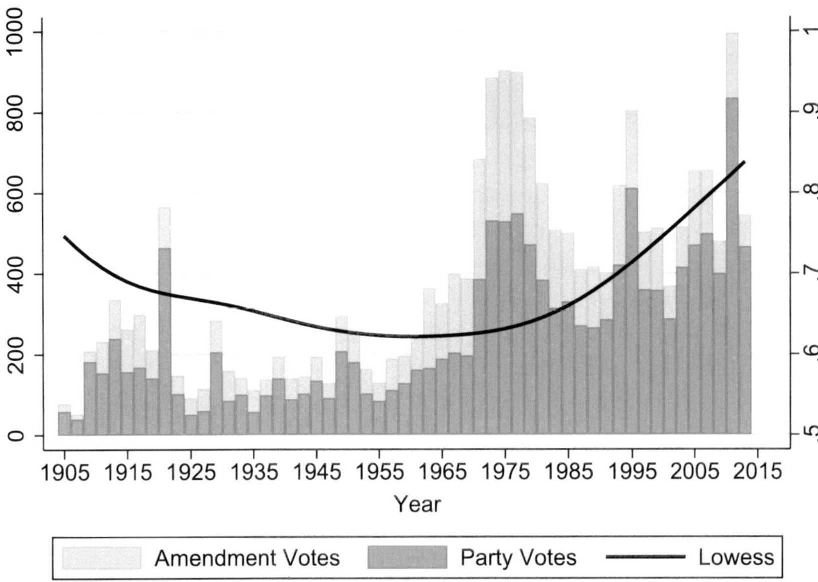

Figure 3.5.: Party Votes on Amendment Roll Calls, 1905–2014

Additionally, in recent years, leaders in both the House and the Senate have used their procedural powers to block many amendments before they reach the floor. This is evident in Figures 3.1 and 3.2 as amendment roll calls dropped sharply in the last two congresses in our dataset. As we discuss in Chapter 5, House leaders were greatly aided by the development of the structured rule. Structured rules not only allow leaders to bar divisive amendments that might damage the parties' brand, but also allow them to select amendments offered by minority-party extremists that could force them to take difficult votes. On the Senate side, leaders have significantly ramped up their usage of filling the amendment tree, preventing other senators from offering their own amendments.

We should note that while controlling the floor can help leaders protect the party from divisive roll calls, some have argued it can be too effective. For example, in the 113th Congress, Senate Majority Leader Harry Reid (D-NV) filled the tree so frequently the Senate cast only 107 non-lopsided roll calls on amendments. This was the lowest number since the 75th Congress (1937–1938). As a result, vulnerable Senate Democrats had few votes to distinguish themselves from President Obama and the party's liberal wing during the midterm election. Republicans then hammered vulnerable Democratic senators like Mark Udall (D-CO) for having high presidential support scores. These support scores are calculated by determining the number of times a member votes with the president on proposals he has taken a public stance on. Because of tight floor control, in the 2014 midterm elections these support scores were based largely on nomination votes (Lesniewski 2014a, 2014b).

While votes on "messaging amendments" have received substantial attention in recent years, less focus has been given to whether the roll call record is actually representative of lawmaking. Failed roll calls are to be expected, and measures may pass one chamber and fail in the other for a variety of reasons, but it has been increasingly common for leaders to force failed votes on identical or very similar proposals in the same Congress. Similarly, one chamber may pass a bill (often multiple times) knowing it will fail in the other. House Republicans treatment of the ACA is a clear example. Democrats have engaged this tactic as well. In the 111th Congress, the House passed the Development, Relief, and Education for Alien Minors Act (DREAM Act). Senate Democrats forced four roll calls on the proposal, none of which were successful, before the Congress adjourned.[17]

For the roll call voting record to provide transparency to the electorate, a stable portion of it should be composed of votes on the legislation Congress enacted into law. While congress-to-congress variance is expected, we observe a fairly stark decline in votes taken on measures enacted into law. Specifically, Figure 3.6 documents the percentage of roll call votes taken on bills enacted into public law. The raw number of roll calls is on the left axis. The percentage of those roll calls taken on measures enacted into law is on the right.

Figure 3.6 demonstrates that the percentage of roll calls on enacted measures has dropped sharply in recent congresses. In the 113th Congress (2013–2014), a mere 15.4% of roll calls were on enacted measures. That means approximately 85% of recorded votes in this Congress were on measures that do not become law. As the raw number of votes has increased across the time series, the percentage of them that report actual lawmaking has greatly decreased. The figure tracks the underlying bill on which each roll call was taken. It accounts for votes on bills that became public law and not companion or related measures. While companions and vehicles have been increasingly common in recent congresses, it is worth noting that vehicles can work both ways. This is an admittedly imperfect measure of position-taking, though we believe it provides a good proxy. Congress may take a law passed for position-taking purposes and use it later in that same Congress for a measure enacted into law. For example, in the 113th Congress, House Republicans passed H.J.R. 59, a continuing resolution that fully repealed the ACA. The Senate ignored it initially, eventually passing it as a separate vehicle for another continuing resolution, but without the ACA repeal included.

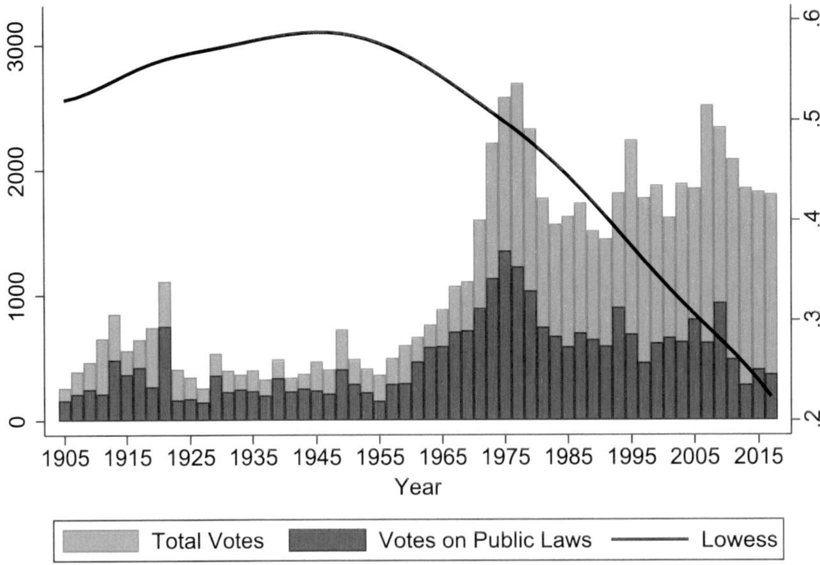

Figure 3.6. Percentage of Roll Call Votes on Bills Enacted into Public Law

Moreover, our data demonstrate that roll calls on bills not enacted into law are significantly more likely to yield party votes than those on bills that become public laws. Excluding lopsided votes, 68.6% of roll call votes on bills not enacted into public law were party votes. For bills enacted into public law, party votes occurred 10% less often. This is not surprising. While the agenda-setting powers enjoyed by US congressional leaders do not allow them to strong-arm proposals into becoming public laws, they do allow them ample leeway in controlling what gets to the floor. In state and international legislative bodies, scholars have demonstrated that when agenda-setting powers are not centralized, majority parties suffer more frequent legislative defeats. In the contemporary Congress, leaders are rarely surprised. As with procedural votes, if they want to demonstrate the party is unified, they have a wide range of issues they can bring to the floor to demonstrate that. We discuss this in greater detail in Chapter 6.

Political Cover Through Omnibus Lawmaking

Finally, even when "must-pass" policies come up, leaders can employ their positive agenda-setting powers to draft legislation in a way to minimize defections on the floor. Party leaders enjoy greater informational advantages over rank-and-file members and committees via staffing resources (Curry 2015;

Lee 2016). This, combined with increased legislative complexity, allows them substantial leverage in lawmaking. Leaders will frequently work with committee chairs to draft major legislation quickly. They will then quickly rush the measure to the floor in an effort to pressure their rank-and-file members to support it.

This approach allows them to move the bill before interest groups and their members have an opportunity to digest it and mount an opposition. As Drutman (2017) noted in an article on the Republican effort to repeal Obamacare in the 115th Congress, "[This is] by far the most effective way to get a bill passed. . . . The longer [Republicans] wait, the more likely it is that fellow Republicans get cold feet on a repeal, as they hear from more and more constituents and various interests that didn't get the influence they wanted in the early drafting stages."

This approach is consistent with scholarship on omnibus lawmaking. For example, Hanson (2014) convincingly argues that when they are confronted with an issue they might lose on, party leaders include it in broad, omnibus legislation, precluding dissident fellow partisans from voting directly on it. Omnibus lawmaking, especially when used in conjunction with must-pass deadlines like reauthorizations, government shutdowns, and debt ceiling increases, frequently work to deter amendments. This provides bill drafters with substantial leverage.

While the number of public laws enacted has dropped substantially (see Figure 1.3), enacted bills are getting substantially longer. The average number of pages per public law was between two and three for congresses in the prereform House. For the last five congresses in our data, it was just under 18. In Chapter 4, we investigate this in more detail using our dataset on important legislation. We find that roll calls on measures not enacted into law are significantly shorter in the contemporary era than their successful counterparts.

Conclusion: An Inconsistent Roll Call Generating Mechanism

This chapter sought to more theoretically establish why the two parties manipulate the record in the House and the Senate and provide a broad examination of how recorded voting has changed using an extended roll call dataset. The data demonstrate that the increase in recorded voting is marked by more procedural votes and more votes on amendments. Moreover, we have observed a fairly sharp decline in votes taken on measures enacted into law and more policies enacted in longer, more complex legislation. Leaders in both the House and the Senate have increasingly exploited institutions, informal powers, and procedural votes to craft the record in a way they believe better serves their policy goals. This is consistent with our argument that the contemporary roll call record is no longer a tool for transparent insight into members' policy positions.

However, it is impossible to adequately evaluate changes in the roll call generating process using only recorded votes. As we have argued, doing so leaves us unable to observe the two-stage selection mechanism behind each vote. In what follows, we employ several new datasets that track proposals that did and did not receive recorded votes. Building on Figures 3.3 and 3.4, in Chapter 4 we examine a set of procedures using our important legislation data and data on House special rules. In Chapter 5, we examine amendments in both the House and the Senate. Once we have better established the selection mechanism, we use simulations to examine its effect on polarization scores in Chapter 6.

Finally, we have argued in this chapter that changes in the roll call generating process are partially motivated by the *perceived* electoral value of roll calls. Roll calls likely help members raise campaign funds. However, there is little evidence to suggest that maintaining tight control over the roll call generating process helps members with primary and constituency voters. Members put a great deal of time and effort into using roll call votes to position themselves electorally. We argue they have drastically overthought roll call voting, and their efforts could be better used elsewhere.

FOUR

Legislative Transparency

A Casualty of Procedural Warfare

> You know, here in Washington, there are a couple of different ways you can kill a bill. One is the honest way—you vote no. . . . Another way you can kill legislation in this town is by offering up amendments or offering up procedures and offering up confusion about the bill, that it goes down for that reason and you don't quite have your fingerprints on it.
>
> —Rep. Anthony Weiner (D-NY)[1]

> I'll let you write the substance on a statute and you let me write the procedure, and I'll screw you every time.
>
> —Rep. John Dingell (D-MI)[2]

James Zadroga 9/11 Health and Compensation Act of 2010

On February 4, 2009, Rep. Carolyn B. Maloney (D-NY) introduced H.R. 847, the James Zadroga 9/11 Health and Compensation Act of 2010. The bill sought to provide funds to a new program designed to treat individuals with medical conditions stemming from the attacks on September 11, 2001.[3] It was cosponsored by 100 Democrats and 15 Republicans and supported by comedian Jon Stewart and prominent politicians like New York City Mayor Michael Bloomberg and former Republican presidential candidate Mike Huckabee (Shapiro 2010). The bill was opposed by a number of Republicans who took issue with the total cost of the measure, the bill's consideration late in the congressional session, and the inclusion of an offset provision in the bill that altered how foreign-based companies can use tax treaties to avoid higher rates (Scholtes 2010). A motion to suspend the rules and pass the bill failed 255–159 on July 29, 2010 (Simon 2010).

Two months later, the House tried again. This time supporters sought to bring the bill to the floor under H.Res. 1674, a special rule that provided for consideration of H.R. 847 under a closed rule.[4] Prior to voting on the special rule, minority-party Republicans mounted a spirited fight against the previous question motion. The previous question motion requires a simple majority to enact and serves to terminate debate. Defeating the previous question motion allows the minority to amend a rule, and such a defeat is devastating to majority-party agenda control. Accordingly, majority-party voting on previous question motions is almost always unanimous.

If the rule were defeated, Rep. Erik Paulsen (R-MN) announced, he would offer an amendment that would have cut "$80 billion in funds" not yet dispersed by the Troubled Asset Relief Program.[5] Paulsen's proposed amendment had been selected as the "YouCut" winner of the week. "YouCut" was a Republican program pioneered by House Minority Whip Eric Cantor (R-VA) that selected a weekly proposal to cut spending (Fahrenthold 2013). The Troubled Asset Relief Program (TARP) was not popular with the public. Because they were in the minority, Republicans generally offered the proposal to cut TARP as either a proposed amendment to a special rule or as part of a motion to recommit with instructions.

Despite support from 12 electorally vulnerable Democrats and a unified Republican Party, the previous question motion was adopted 235 to 183. H.Res. 1674 was then adopted by a nearly identical vote of 234 to 183. Prior to passing H.R. 857, Rep. Christopher Lee (R-NY) offered a motion to recommit the bill with instructions that would have stripped the bill of most of its funding by dropping the offset provision. Lee's motion would also have set additional restrictions on medical lawsuits (Scholtes 2010). A motion to recommit with instructions essentially provides the minority with a final opportunity to offer an amendment of its choosing before a bill receives a final passage vote. It has a long procedural history as a tool used for partisan messaging (Roberts 2005).[6]

In opposing the motion, Rep. Anthony Weiner (D-NY) characterized two different ways you can kill a bill in Washington. First, you could do it "the honest way–you vote no." A second way is by "offering up amendments or offering up procedures and offering up confusion about the bill that it goes down for that reason and you don't quite have your fingerprints on it" (*Congressional Record*, 111th Congress, September 29, 2010, 17030). Lee's motion to recommit, Weiner argued, represented the second way. The motion to recommit with instructions was rejected on a nearly perfect party-line vote, 244–185.[7] The bill then passed 268–160, with 17 Republicans voting in favor.[8] The three prior procedural votes only mustered a total of five Republican "yea" votes. Both parties featured votes on the measure and the procedural motions in electoral attacks in 2010.[9]

The Zadroga 9/11 Health and Compensation Act of 2010 highlights the potential pitfalls caused by procedural roll call votes in the contemporary Congress. Procedural votes are highly partisan, and their usage has risen sharply over time. This can cause difficulties for parties trying to balance their policy and electoral goals. Additionally, the increasingly complex nature of legislative rules has made interpreting procedural votes impossible for voters.

Weiner's comment about Lee's motion to recommit is illustrative in two ways of many politicians' cynical views on congressional rules. First, by noting the use of procedures to kill bills, Weiner acknowledges the enormous impact rules can have on policy output. Former Rep. John Dingell (D-MI) famously said, "I'll let you write the substance on a statute and you let me write the procedure, and I'll screw you every time" (Oleszek and Oleszek 2012, 261). As we discuss below, this view and the notion that rules impact policy outcomes more broadly is generally well accepted by congressional scholars.

Second, Weiner notes that procedures like the motion to recommit allow members to kill legislation without putting their "fingerprints on it." He argued earlier in the debate that the first responders that filled up the House galleries to watch the bill pass "don't know a motion to recommit from a suspension" or "what the rule is." Instead, they care about the policies contained in the bill.[10] This point is also accepted by many congressional observers (Arnold 1990; Den Hartog and Monroe 2010). While procedural roll calls do not present voters with transparent insight into lawmaking, some scholars disagree that they lack electoral implications (Smith et al. 2013).

In the rest of this chapter, we explain the increase in procedural votes by first highlighting the perceived electoral benefit of these votes and then detailing how minorities employ and majorities respond to procedural votes. More procedural roll calls are consistent with our argument that the contemporary record has become an endogenously constructed mechanism used to further partisan electoral goals. Moreover, an increase in procedural roll call votes can distort roll-call-based measures of ideology. However, as we note in Chapter 3, this could also reflect an objection to increasingly restrictive lawmaking processes. In this chapter we utilize two new datasets to (1) determine what types of votes are driving the increase in procedural votes and (2) evaluate how roll call vote patterns have changed using data drawn from outside the roll call record.

Escalating Procedural Warfare

Procedural rules are necessary to minimally ensure an orderly legislative process. They play a crucial role in balancing two competing interests in lawmaking: transparency and efficiency. They provide guidelines to legislators that allow the contentious process of lawmaking to be carried out in a calm and professional manner. Clearly specified rules that are consistently enforced can help mitigate the passions of representatives and senators. As sports fans who feel their team has been cheated can attest, the utility of consistently enforced rules in this respect extends beyond the legislative realm. Conversely, when rules lack clarity or are unintuitive and arbitrarily applied, their usage can seem like procedural warfare and further enflame the opinions of voters and politicians (Smith 2014).

An example of how the arbitrary use of rules can polarize a legislature occurred during the 100th Congress. In October 1987, minority-party Republicans picked up enough support from conservative Democrats to defeat H.Res. 296, which provided for consideration of H.R. 3545, the Omnibus Budget Reconciliation Act, under a restrictive rule. H.R. 3545 included a tax increase, which was not popular with many conservatives. In the wake of the victory, Rep. Newt Gingrich (R-GA) took to the floor and chastised Speaker Jim Wright (D-TX) and fellow Democratic leaders for bringing the rule to the floor after "a significant number of Democrats told them [it] was unacceptable."[11]

House rules barred Wright from bringing a second rule to the floor that same "legislative day" without a two-thirds majority. Wright opted to have the House formally adjourn at 3:00 p.m. and reconvene 10 minutes later, which technically created a new "legislative day" despite it being the same calendar day. A second rule, H.Res. 298, was then brought to the floor and passed 242 to 186, despite Republican outrage.[12] H.R. 3545 was considered shortly afterward. The bill was losing, with 205 in favor and 206 against, when time for the roll call expired. However, Wright used his powers as speaker to delay the vote several minutes so Rep. Jim Chapman (D-TX) could come to the floor and change his vote. The bill passed by a final tally of 206 to 205.[13]

Republicans were outraged. Minority Whip Trent Lott (R-MS) argued the "unfairness of it all caused me to lose control" and pound "the rostrum in the well of the House until it bent" (Lott 2005, 99).[14] Even centrist Republicans took exception to the maneuver. Rep. Connie Mack (R-FL) claimed it broke down all "cooperation between Democrats and Republicans," adding he had "absolutely no respect for Jim Wright" (Fuerbringer 1987). And Rep. Bill Gradison (R-OH) asserted, "It takes a lot to politicize me. Wright's done it. I'm partisan as hell now" (Barry 2015, 2).

Coverage or in the Line of Fire?

Legislative rules frequently have significant impact on policy output. Even when parties are weak, usage of chamber rules can serve to facilitate non-median policies (Cox and McCubbins 2005). A consequence of this is moderate majority-party members incur policy loss under this arrangement (Cox and McCubbins 2005; Jenkins and Monroe 2012a, 2012b; Lynch et al. 2016; Monroe and Robinson 2008; Young and Wilkins 2007). Moreover, by extension, this can lead to policy loss for their supporters in the electorate. This is somewhat paradoxical, as party leaders need the support of their centrists on procedural votes (Finocchiaro and Rohde 2008).

As noted in Chapter 3, majority-party leaders typically get the support of majority-party centrists. Even members who oppose a bill on final passage frequently support the party's position on the procedural votes that precede it (Carson et al. 2014). Scholars have shown party unity is substantially higher on procedural than substantive votes (Cox and Poole 2002; Crespin 2010; Jessee and Theriault 2014; Lee 2009).[15] This potential for policy loss highlights a key question for scholars of legislative politics: How do legislative entrepreneurs convince enough members to form a winning coalition if it is hard to imagine a situation where a member is punished for being on the losing side of an issue?

The existing literature appears to have coalesced around an argument about procedural vote traceability (Arnold 1990).[16] Specifically, restrictive and complex special rules provide political coverage for moderate members. As Monroe and Robinson (2008, 218) note, "Instead of requiring majority-party members to make difficult choices on highly visible substantive final passage votes, restrictive rules allow for less costly acts of loyalty by voting with the party on much less visibly (and less widely understood) "procedural" votes." Moreover, partisan theorists note that centrists are not being asked to vote against their ideological interests, but rather forgo opportunities to pull status quos to their ideal points (Jenkins and Monroe 2012a).[17]

There are reasons to be skeptical of the traceability thesis. As we have argued, interest groups and campaigns will utilize votes on procedural matters to attack incumbents. Focusing on the usage of tabling motions in the US Senate, Smith, Ostrander and Pope (2013) find that interest group scores are as likely to include procedural votes like the motion to table as other "substantive votes." Sievert (2015) reports similar findings, noting that interest groups frequently use procedural votes to portray incumbent members as being either supportive or opposed to their substantive issues. This does not mean such attacks are effective, only that campaigns believe them to be. In the next section, we highlight how minorities use procedural votes for electoral purposes and how majorities respond. We argue that the "stickiness" of rules leads majorities to primarily respond to minority tactics through their agenda-setting powers, as opposed to changing formal rules.

Minority Messaging Through Procedural Votes

As the Jack Kingston example from Chapter 3 demonstrates, campaigns have wide latitude when it comes to claiming what issue a roll call vote was actually about. Unsurprisingly, campaigns frequently employ procedural votes to take advantage of this. Like the Kingston case, attack ads featuring charges that incumbent members of Congress have voted to raise their own pay are particularly common. For incumbent House members, these ads generally rely on roll call votes against ordering the previous question motion on a special rule under the assumption that if that vote were successful, a minority-party member would offer an amendment cutting legislative pay. It is exceptionally rare for majority-party members to defect on a motion to order the previous question motion, so these claims are highly dubious.

In the Senate, the ads are generally based on votes against appropriation bills or amendments that would freeze member pay. Typically, these bills and amendments feature other legislative proposals the member opposes, leading to the no vote. An example of this occurred in the 2016 Arizona Senate race when Sen. John McCain (R-AZ) attacked Rep. Ann Kirkpatrick (D-AZ) for voting to increase her own salary. This was based on a vote against H.R. 5325, a continuing appropriations bill that included a provision freezing the pay for representatives. As Kirkpatrick's campaign pointed out, McCain had voted against a similar bill, H.R. 2029, the previous year (Ung 2016).[18]

Usage of motions to recommit like Lee's in the Zadroga case have long played a role in minority-party messaging strategies (Roberts 2005). In 2014, the Democratic Congressional Campaign Committee used both previous question motion votes and motion to recommit votes to justify attacks against three vulnerable Republican House members. Their press release asserted the members—Rep. Ileana Ros-Lehtinen (R-FL), Rep. Sean Duffy (R-WI), and Rep. Erik Paulsen (R-MN)—voted against fixing the wait times at Veterans Administration health centers. Nearly all of the votes cited were purely procedural (Sherman 2014).

The Senate is no different. An early example of this occurred in 1980, when Sen. Robert Morgan (D-NC), who was recently defeated, called attention to the issue after the Senate voted to overturn a ruling of the chair on the germaneness of an amendment. Morgan noted that he wanted to "enlighten some of my colleagues, especially some here who are targeted for next year, as to what can happen to us on these so-called parliamentary votes." Morgan claimed his opponent's campaign was distributing leaflets accusing him of voting against limiting the bureaucracy. He later found out the vote was a vote upholding the ruling of the presiding officer that an amendment was out of order for procedural reasons. He concluded by noting:

> I just want to caution my colleagues that when you are playing with parliamentary moves, you are giving potential opposition ammunition to throw at you; because in a one-line excerpt—and I say to Sen. McGovern that I had his picture and Sen. Kennedy's picture at the top of it. We distributed their pictures quite frequently in North Carolina. [Laughter.]
>
> Some of my friends down there were surprised to know how close we were. [Laughter.]
>
> Nevertheless, this one line generated an impression that was directly contrary to what my own opinion was and what I had supported and had voted for and had even introduced. Once that impression is created, it takes an awful lot of explaining to try to explain it or to make it understood (*Congressional Record*, 96th Congress, November 25, 1980, 31063–31064).

Perhaps even more common than taking individual votes out of context for attack ads is using those votes to inflate member support scores. These are frequently used in ads when opponents seek to portray a member as being ideologically supportive of an unpopular national figure (Carson et al. 2014). For example, during the 2010 midterm elections, Rep. Scott Rigell (R-VA) put out an advertisement alleging that incumbent Rep. Glenn Nye (D-VA) "voted lockstep with Nancy Pelosi 83% of the time." The ad was comparable to many ads run by Republicans en route to their taking control of the House of Representatives. In explaining his decision to challenge Pelosi as party leader, Rep. Heath Shuler (D-NC) pointed to the effectiveness of these ads. He said, "I just want you to understand that every single Blue Dog who lost, one hundred percent of the attack ads that were run associated you with them. You have a very low approval rating in our districts" (Draper 2012, 59).[19]

To be certain, minorities have long sought to use procedural votes for messaging purposes. However, recent work has demonstrated that electorally driven behavior in Congress has been on the rise in recent decades as campaigns have become more nationalized and expensive television attack ads more common. Lee (2016) argues that key changes occurred in 1980, when

Republicans ousted the long-serving Senate Democratic majority, and 1994, when the long-serving Democratic House majority was defeated. Accordingly, she suggests that when either party is in the minority, members think the next election has the potential to move them back into majority status, leading to an increase in things like messaging amendments and roll call votes.

Majority-Party Counterattacks

In some cases, majorities will respond to minority messaging success by formally changing the rules (Binder 1997). For example, minority-party Republicans were particularly effective at employing the motion to recommit in the 110th Congress (2009–2010). In the first five months of that Congress they successfully altered 11 bills with it (Layton 2007). This led Democrats to alter rules governing the motion at the start of the 111th Congress.[20] However, formally changing rules is often more costly than mitigating their effect through agenda setting.[21]

As discussed in Chapter 2, the Founders sought to balance transparency with efficiency goals through the establishment of the sufficient second clause. While this solved some of the Stage 2 problems with the roll call generating process that occurred during the Continental Congress and early state legislative bodies, it did not address Stage 1. The implementation of Reed's Rules documented in Chapter 2 demonstrates how majorities can use centralized Stage 1 powers in combination with formal rules changes in response to perceived abuses by the minority. In another early example of this, majority-party Republicans responded to dilatory roll call vote requests in the 60th Congress (1907–1909) by employing both more special rules and crafting more omnibus laws (Sala 2002).

Centralization of both negative and positive agenda-setting powers has increased throughout the past few decades. Leaders can use negative powers to block potentially divisive issues and content from receiving recorded votes. This has been well documented by scholars of the House (Cox and McCubbins 2007; Binder 1997; Monroe and Robinson 2008; Rohde 1991). Positive agenda-setting powers allow leaders influence in selecting and drafting unifying issues. As we discuss below, these powers are not always formalized.

Leaders in both chambers have enjoyed pronounced increases in their informal agenda-setting powers. Technological advances improved travel and communication. This made it easier for leaders to understand how members felt on certain issues and helped them better coordinate legislative schedules (Meinke 2016). Groups like the Democratic Policy Committee could be used by leaders to better determine what bills, procedures, and amendments they had consensuses on and bring those to the floor (Crespin et al. 2015). Other partisan peer groups meet more frequently, increasing pressure on members to "go along to get along" (Lee 2008a; Smith 2007).

Improved coordination further enhances leadership's influence when considered in conjunction with their informational advantages. House and Senate leaders enjoy substantial staffing resources over rank-and-file members (Lee 2008a). Policy staff resources for member offices have been stagnant for nearly 30 years, whereas leadership has seen stark increases. The informational disparity is further increased during the construction and scheduling of legislation (Curry 2015). Working with committee chairs and other partisans, leaders design larger, more complex legislation in ways to entice the support of members who might be considering defecting and supporting a minority proposal. By giving members a short window to analyze the bill, they can pass it before potentially negative information is disseminated to members by outside groups.

Finally, in cases we describe below, majorities might simply reply to a minority's messaging strategy through the usage of other procedures or rules. By covering multiple bills, bifurcated and multi-measure (or "grab-bag") special rules can decrease the number of opportunities the minority has to force previous question votes. The usage of vehicles allows parties that control both houses of Congress to bypass motions to recommit and obstruction on the motion to proceed in the Senate. And as we demonstrate below, tabling motions are increasingly employed to counter messaging amendments. The end result is a drastic increase in recorded votes on certain types of procedural matters that obfuscate the public's ability to monitor and assess congressional lawmaking. In sum, rather than change the rules in a way that better suits their transparent policymaking goals, majorities have responded to minority messaging by making the roll call record even more confusing. In the next section we employ two different datasets to examine the tools of procedural warfare.

The Dogs of Procedural War

To evaluate how procedural roll calls have influenced the roll call record, we first take a more detailed look at data from our extended roll call dataset discussed in Appendix A. Later in the section, we supplement that analysis with enactment-level data detailed in Appendix B. As the preceding discussion suggests, not all procedural votes are created equal. Votes on motions to recommit and ordering the previous question have substantial messaging

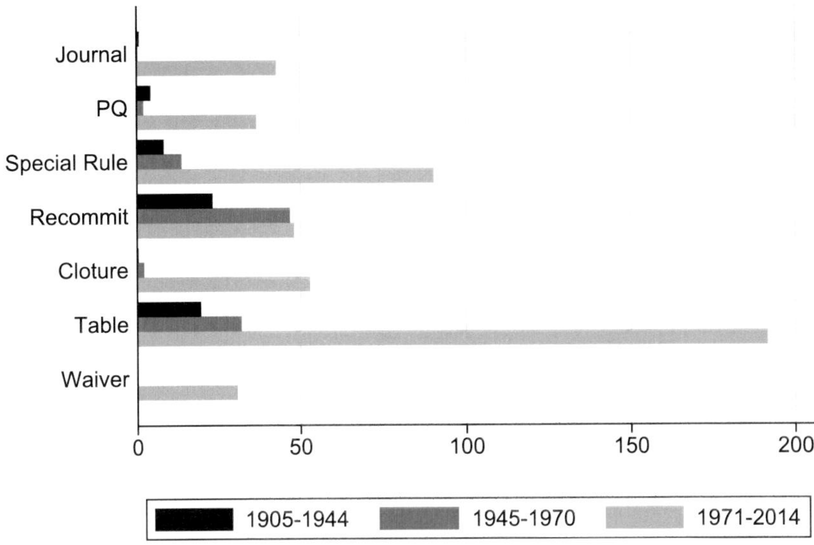

Figure 4.1. Average Procedural Votes per Congress by Era, 1905–2014

implications for minorities. Other procedural motions, like tabling motions in the Senate, help majorities combat minority messaging. Finally, there are other procedural motions, like journal votes, that purely obfuscate the roll call record.

Procedural roll calls are increasingly common in the contemporary era, both in terms of raw roll call numbers and as a percentage of the record (see Figures 3.1 and 3.2). Breaking the broad procedural category down to specific motions demonstrates the procedural category is dominated by seven motions. The first four of these are almost exclusively found in the House: motions to recommit, motions to approve the House journal, ordering the previous question motion on special rules, and adopting special rules. The next three almost exclusively can be found in the Senate: cloture motions, tabling motions, and motions to waive.

Figure 4.1 plots the average number of roll calls on each motion across three eras for reference purposes: first, from the start of our data in the 59th Congress (1905–1907) through the end of the 78th Congress (1943–1944), when attendance levels stabilized; second, from the 79th Congress (1945–1946) through the 91st Congress (1969–1970), marking the beginning of the post-reform House; and third, from the 92nd Congress (1972–1973) to the 113th Congress (2013–2014).

Figure 4.1 demonstrates that for most of these motions, their representation in the roll call record has increased across eras. Specifically, these motions composed 30% of all procedural roll calls in Era 1, 63% in Era 2, and 79% in Era 3. With the notable exception of journal votes, most are also reliably partisan votes regardless of the Congress. Looking across the three eras, 75% of the 1,116 votes in Era 1 were party votes, 66% of the 1,259 votes in Era 2 were party votes, and 76% of the 9,914 Era 3 votes were. Just over 5% of roll calls on these motions yielded lopsided coalitions. We discuss these motions and their roles in procedural warfare in the rest of the section.

Motions to Recommit

Under House rules, a motion to recommit the bill, either with or without instructions, to the committee that originally reported it is almost always in order. A motion to recommit without instructions sends the bill back to committee from which it originated, essentially killing it. Because the motion is not provided in advance, the majority party has limited opportunities to signal its opposition or support of it (Carson et al. 2014). While the motion often includes an amendment that may be difficult for majority-party members to oppose, oftentimes motions to recommit include substantive or technical amendments majority-party leaders may support.[22] Usage of the motion as a tool of the minority dates back to 1909 (Ornstein 2010).

The motion to recommit has been a reliable messaging tool for the minority throughout the 20th century. As Figure 4.1 demonstrates, it is the only one of these motions whose usage did not increase dramatically across eras. One potential reason for this is the majority party minimizing opportunities for the minority to offer it through a number of ways.[23] As the previous cases demonstrated, votes on motions to recommit are often used in campaign ads.[24]

Journal Votes

The increase in roll calls approving the House journal is perhaps the most glaring example of the "broken" roll call voting record. As detailed in Chapter 2, the US Constitution specifies that each chamber must publish a journal of its proceedings. House rules further specify the speaker must announce the chamber's approval of the journal at the start of each legislative day. Members can call for a vote on approving the journal and can request a roll call on it (Hudiburg 2018). Defeat of a motion to approve the journal can leave it open to amendment.

Given its relative lack of any substantive implications, it is not surprising roll calls on approving the journal were rare historically. When they were called for, it was primarily done in conjunction with a broader minority-party strategy to delay business. For example, in the 60th Congress, minority-party Democrats under the leadership of Rep. John Sharp Williams (D-MS) forced recorded votes on all motions dispensed with on the floor (Osborn 1943). This included journal votes. The action frustrated Rep. John Dalzell (R-PA), who by 1908 had served in the chamber for over 20 years and was the "Dean of the House." He declared:

> Does [the minority leader] believe that the people in this country can be persuaded that any principle is involved in a demand for the yeas and nays on the approval of the Journal and then voting for the approval of the Journal? Can any man conceive of a more asinine performance than that? (*Congressional Record*, 60th Congress, April 4, 1908, 4367)[25]

The House recorded a mere 16 journal votes from the 59th Congress (1905–1907) to the 94th Congress (1975–1976). Dalzell would be disappointed to learn they have recorded over 1,000 since then. The most common reason given for contemporary roll call requests on motions to approve the journal is it allows members to cast votes distancing themselves from leadership (Hudiburg 2018). They are just as likely to be requested by majority-party members as minority-party members (Patty 2010). In sum, journal votes serve no substantive purpose other than lowering a member's leader support scores.[26]

Previous Questions, Special Rules, and Martial Law

Previous question motions, and to a lesser extent, votes on the rule itself, provide clear partisan messaging opportunities.[27] While it is possible increased roll calls on previous questions motions reflect changes to legislative process, increased usage as well as procedural innovations by the majority party have also likely expanded their role. Special rules are now common for most House business. This includes initial consideration, as well as secondary consideration of bills altered by the Senate.

Additionally, as the Jim Wright case suggests, House rules require special rules lay over for one day before they can be considered unless the rule is waived by two-thirds of the chamber (Rybicki 2017). Most majorities are unlikely to have two-thirds support.[28] Rather than alter standing rules, they have resorted to passing special rules waiving the same-day rule. These "martial law" rules are exceptionally common on major legislation, as Chapter 3's American Health Care Act case suggests. As a result, many bills are considered after four recorded votes on special rules: previous question motion on the martial law rule, passage of the martial law rule, previous question motion on the rule, and passage of the rule.

During a speech chastising the majority's use of a martial law rule, one member asserted its usage indicated a "state of war" existed in the House. This is certainly an over-dramatization. However, if the general public finds roll calls on procedures that govern the consideration of substantive legislation untraceable, roll calls on procedures that govern the consideration of future procedures are likely to be even less transparent.[29]

Cloture Votes

The Senate adopted its first formal cloture rule for ending debate in 1917. While today, three-fifths of the chamber can vote to invoke cloture to end debate, the process is fairly time consuming. A cloture petition must lie over for two calendar days before it is voted on. Because of the time-consuming nature of cloture motions, senators would rarely use them if they thought they were going to fail. In recent years, the number of roll calls on cloture motions, both successful and failed, has skyrocketed (Smith 2014).[30] Many of these are majority-party messaging strategies. In other cases, these cloture motions are filed to facilitate a leader's filling of the amendment tree or to provide them leverage during negotiations.[31]

Tabling Motions

While tabling motions are used in both chambers, they are more common in the Senate. It is one of the rare, non-debatable motions in the chamber subject to a simple majority vote. Measures that are successfully tabled are almost always killed.[32] They are typically used by senators looking to quickly dispose of a pending question. Senators whose amendments are subject to tabling motions often complain the motion deprives them of a direct vote on their amendment as well as debate and discussion (Carson et al. 2016; Den Hartog and Monroe 2011).

Early in its history, many felt tabling motions were employed primarily to allow cover for members who might be inclined to support the underlying proposal. For example, in 1957, Sen. Clinton Anderson (D-NM) introduced a resolution that would change Senate rules to allow a simple majority to end debate. The proposal was part of a broader strategy by liberals to pass civil rights legislation. Majority Leader Lyndon Johnson (D-TX) moved to table the resolution. This allowed moderates to block Anderson's resolution without directly voting on it. Sen. Wayne Morse (D-OR) argued that "the Senate will not face up to the question [of its rules] directly," and instead will deal with "the parliamentary diversionary tact of the motion to lay on the table" (*Congressional Record*, 95th Congress, January 3, 1957, 11). The tabling motion passed 55 to 38.

While coverage may play a role in its contemporary usage, it also provides leaders with an efficiency tool.[33] During a 2015 debate over the Keystone Pipeline, Senate Majority Leader Mitch McConnell (R-KY) was confronted with over 300 filed amendments. This led him to table a number of amendments sponsored by minority-party Democrats. Democrats accused him of violating his pledge to maintain "regular order," noting that McConnell used the motion to table to cut off any debate and block direct votes on their amendments (Barron-Lopez 2015).[34]

Motions to Waive

The Congressional Budget Act of 1974, in addition to several other rules and statutes, sets various restrictions on lawmaking that affects legislation that deals with finance (Saturno 2015). In the event a bill or amendment violates those restrictions, members will raise budgetary points of order against them. As is the case with the motion to table, budgetary points of order provide majorities with a tool to dispose of amendments that might be substantively difficult for some members to oppose (King et al. 2012). While the House often waives these points of order ahead of time through special rules, the Senate lacks this alternative.

Either in response to or in anticipation of a budgetary point of order, Senate amendment sponsors will make a motion to waive the Budget Act. This motion is subject to a three-fifths vote. Figure 4.1 highlights the lack of motions to waive in our first two eras due to the motion being used only after the passage of the 1974 CBA. The motion to waive is generally employed before a tabling motion can be offered.

Enactment-Level Change

While the roll call dataset suggests usage of these tools of procedural warfare has increased, we cannot tell if this reflects a change in the roll call generating process or in the legislative process more broadly. To gain leverage on that question, in this section, we employ a new dataset and examine procedural votes at the enactment level. This helps mitigate potential biases stemming from changes in the lawmaking process, as well as chamber workload. It also allows us to control for legislative substance. As described in Appendix B, our important enactment-level data contains 2,036 enactments over 55 congresses from the 59th Congress (1905–1907) to the 113th Congress (2013–2014). It also includes 3,199 total bills corresponding with all enactments, including enacted bills, related and companion measures.

Figure 4.2 plots the average number of non-lopsided votes by type per enactment by Congress in a stacked bar graph.[35] The figure pools House and Senate roll calls together.[36] For the 111th Congress, enactments in our dataset averaged just under 20 non-lopsided roll call votes per enactment. Of these, 10.4 were procedural votes, 7.3 were amendment votes, and 2.1 were on passage. A lowess smoothing line was added to illustrate the percentage roll call votes on procedural motions in a given Congress. The percentage varies from a low of 10.8% in the 70th Congress (1927–1928) to a high of 52.6% in the 111th Congress (2009–2010).

Figure 4.2 further suggests that procedural votes are on the rise in Congress. For example, enactments in the first five congresses in our dataset averaged 2.72 procedural roll calls per enactment. For the last five, this number jumps to 7.89 roll calls per enactment.[37] Another way to demonstrate how the process has changed is provided by Figure 4.3. Figure 4.3 plots our important legislation by how they were initially considered on the House floor. We plot the total number of enactments and whether they were considered under a special rule or a restrictive special rule.

As expected, the figure demonstrates a huge increase in both the percentage of measures receiving any rule on the House floor and the percentage of those measures that were considered under restrictive rules.[38] "Restrictive rules" are defined to include closed rules, modified-closed rules, and structured rules. Measures not granted a special rule were typically considered on the House floor either by unanimous consent or suspension of the rules. Additional information on the coding of rule types can be found in Appendix C.

Cover Through Positive Agenda-Setting

In addition to demonstrating the drastic change in lawmaking processes, our enactment-level data confirms that majorities are drafting longer legislation. Scholars have documented that enacted bills are longer on average than in historical periods (Ornstein et al. 2019). Consistent with this, we find the average page length of important legislation has increased fourfold, from the 59th Congress to the 113th.

This stands in contrast to measures leaders know are doomed to fail and are used for position-taking votes. Our important legislation dataset tracks a

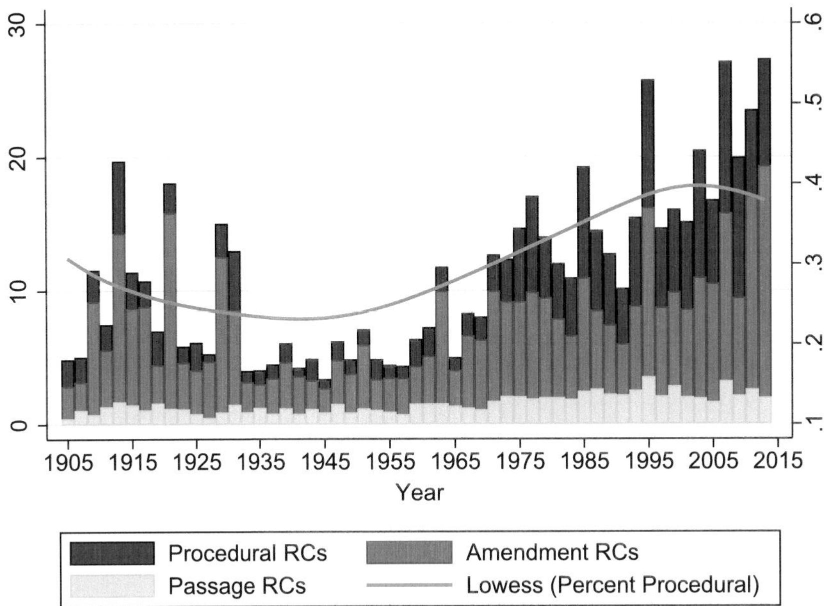

Figure 4.2. Average Votes per Enactment by Type, 1905–2014

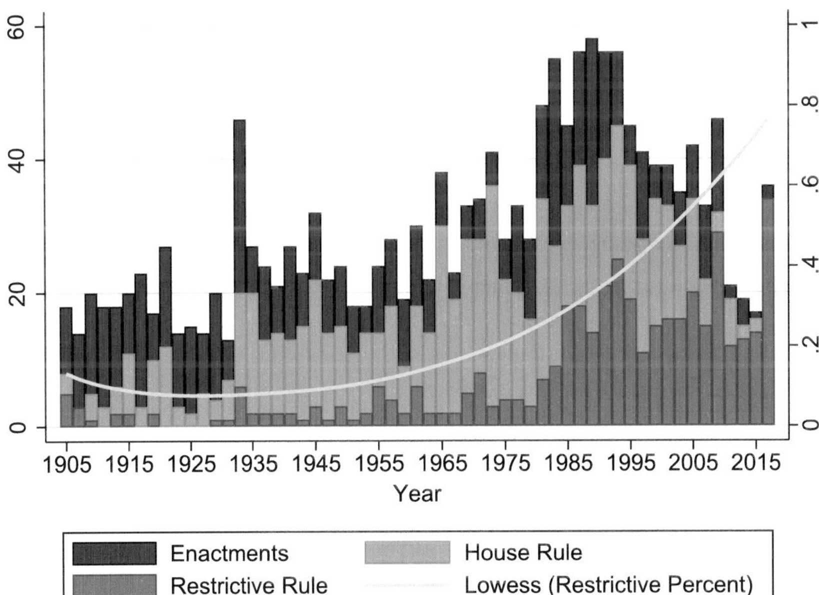

Figure 4.3. Important Enactments by House Floor Consideration

number of major, failed enactments starting in the 97th Congress. The average page length of the 189 failed measures from the 97th to 113th Congress was 159.05 pages. The 419 enacted important measures considered during the same period were on average over 100 pages longer.[39] This is consistent with arguments made in this chapter and Chapter 3 that party leaders can use their influence in legislative drafting to provide coverage for their members.

Examining Procedural Votes per Enactment

In order to more systematically examine how the likelihood of a procedural roll call vote has changed in the contemporary period, we fit a negative binomial model. Our dependent variable is the number of procedural roll calls on a given enactment. The data are at the enactment-chamber level. The number of procedural roll calls ranges from 0 to 96 with a mean of just under 2.

Given the changes in legislative process, substantive content, and omnibus lawmaking, we included controls for a variety of factors. Even when narrowing a dataset to only important or landmark legislation, certain issues are likely to generate more controversy than others. Accordingly, we include controls for four of these: tariff legislation, civil rights bills, immigration, and revenue bills (Madonna 2011). The dataset also includes a subset of routine appropriation bills, in addition to landmark measures, so we control for those, anticipating fewer roll calls. We also separate routine appropriation bills from continuing appropriation bills, the latter of which are rarely subjected to amendments in either chamber. In order to control for omnibus lawmaking, we included variables denoting the total number of bills included in an enactment and the total number of pages. We included controls for processes like vetoes, the presence of a restrictive House rule, and suspension of the rules. Finally, we included controls for attendance, majority seat share, and divided government. The results are presented in Table 4.1.

Table 4.1 presents models pooling the House and Senate, as well as each chamber separately. We can see from Table 4.1 that, even after controlling for content, changes in legislative process, and omnibus lawmaking, procedural roll calls are significantly more likely to occur on enactments considered in the contemporary era (Era 3). Most of our control variables operate as expected. While the results from our admittedly simple models conform to our theoretical claims that procedural warfare roll call votes are increasingly used to mislead the general public, we examine the robustness of this finding using one final alternative dataset below.

TABLE 4.1. Negative Binomial Models of Procedural Roll Calls by Enactments, 1905–2014

Variable	Model 1 (Pooled)	Model 2 (House)	Model 3 (Senate)
Attendance	−1.812	−1.339	−2.754
	(1.379)	(1.057)	(2.271)
Majority Seat Share	−1.482	−1.104	−1.355
	(0.772)	(0.648)	(1.587)
Divided Government	−0.252*	−0.295*	−0.197
	(0.119)	(0.120)	(0.158)
Suspension of the Rules	−1.022*	−1.088*	−0.943*
	(0.153)	(0.204)	(0.191)
Restrictive House Rule	0.341*	0.582*	0.085
	(0.078)	(0.075)	(0.111)
Chamber	0.290*	-	-
	(0.085)	(-)	(-)
Tariff	1.363*	1.267*	1.512*
	(0.317)	(0.218)	(0.459)
Revenue	0.590*	0.517*	0.658*
	(0.120)	(0.133)	(0.178)
Civil Rights	1.269*	0.706*	1.620*
	(0.376)	(0.291)	(0.444)
Immigration	0.127	−0.103	0.347
	(0.342)	(0.307)	(0.432)
Total Bills	0.191*	0.218*	0.178*
	(0.026)	(0.035)	(0.034)
Pages	0.001*	0.001*	0.001*
	(0.000)	(0.000)	(0.000)
Appropriations	0.365*	0.431*	0.319
	(0.127)	(0.127)	(0.165)
Continuing Appropriations	−1.216*	−0.981*	−1.607*
	(0.340)	(0.260)	(0.578)
Landmark	0.155	−0.111	0.381*
	(0.146)	(0.137)	(0.181)
Veto	0.607*	0.652*	0.558*
	(0.170)	(0.180)	(0.180)
Era 1 (1905–1944)	0.061	0.229	−0.226
	(0.241)	(0.161)	(0.479)
Era 3 (1971–2013)	1.232*	0.983*	1.470*
	(0.179)	(0.138)	(0.290)
Constant	1.371	0.911	2.255
	(1.306)	(0.959)	(2.090)
Observations	3,426	1,713	1,713
Pseudo R^2	0.094	0.123	0.081

$^*p < .05$. Robust standard errors are presented below estimates. Both models are fit with standard errors clustered on Congress.

Process or Posture?

If the rise of roll calls on procedural votes is simply a reflection of the changing legislative process, we should expect to find elevated numbers of procedural roll calls when restrictive House rules are employed. Indeed, Table 4.1 suggests as much. The presence of a restrictive House rule on a bill results in more procedural roll calls in the House, but not in the Senate. To more systematically evaluate this, we employ a new dataset that tracks recorded voting on special rules from 1905 to 2018.

Discussed in Appendix C, we built off data from Roberts (2010) and coded rule types for all special rules and orders from 1905 to 2018. This amounted to 7,329 House special resolutions, or 8,027 rule-bill level observations. Using the same restrictive rule dummy variable employed in our important enactment data, we compare the recorded voting rates between bills considered under restrictive and nonrestrictive rules. We further compare these differences between the five most recent congresses in these data (2009–2018) and older congresses (1905–2008). If increased recorded voting on procedural matters was purely reflective of changes in process, we should expect roll call voting percentages to fluctuate only with the status of the rule type. Put more bluntly, we should not expect to see roll calls ordering the previous question motion and adopting the rule when the rule is nonrestrictive. The data demonstrate this is not the case.

From 1905 to 2008, recorded voting on the previous question motion and special rules was quite rare when the rule in question was nonrestrictive. Of the 5,147 nonrestrictive rules voted on during that period, 1,330 received roll calls on the rule (25.8%). Just 312 of them (6.1%) featured a recorded vote on the previous question motion. As expected, roll calls on restrictive rules were more common, with 847 of 1,547 restrictive rules (55.6%) receiving recorded votes and 463 (30.3%) featuring a previous question roll call. In contrast, from 2009 to 2018, the last five congresses in our data, 94.2% of 547 restrictive rules were subject to recorded votes, and 73.3% featured recorded votes ordering the previous question motion. Of the 77 nonrestrictive rules, 83.1% were subject to a recorded vote on the rule, and 55.9% included a recorded vote on the previous question motion. This suggests that the motivation behind forcing the recorded vote stems from the messaging incentives from the previous question motion as opposed to highlighting disagreements over floor procedures between the two parties.

Procedural War: What Is It Good For? Electoral Position-Taking

Several conclusions can be drawn from our analysis here. First, the increase in procedural roll calls is a consequence of increased procedural warfare. It appears to be a product of *both* changes in the legislative process and a perceived increase in the value of messaging votes. Determining causality is not feasible, but we have argued majorities have responded to increased minority messaging through procedural votes primarily by employing other procedures (i.e., through procedural changes). This includes tabling motions, motions to waive, more restrictive special rules, and martial law rules. In other cases, like cloture votes, the procedural vote provides majorities with messaging opportunities.

Second, despite the changes to the process, it is clear that the perceived increase in messaging has led to elevated roll call vote numbers on procedural issues. Votes on motions like adopting the House journal are straightforward attempts to obfuscate the record for electoral purposes. Employing enactment-level data, we control for process issues, enactment size, and content and still find roll calls are more common in the contemporary period. Data from our special rules dataset demonstrate a sharp jump in the likelihood a roll call vote occurs on previous question motions and special rules regardless of the rule is restrictive or not.

The findings presented here are broadly consistent with our argument in Chapter 2 that institutional reforms, electronic voting in the House, and increased attendance have rendered the sufficient second clause ineffective at preventing roll calls on matters of low salience. The contemporary era features far more roll calls yielding party votes but also far more roll calls yielding lopsided coalitions.[40] This is consistent with the view that roll call votes requests have become pro forma in recent decades. For example, in 2016, Rep. Tim Huelskamp (R-KS) forced recorded votes on 19 bills on the suspension calendar that were widely supported. He justified this by a desire to promote a "transparent, open process" (McPherson 2016).

However, if voters do not understand the substance of the vote, the presence of a roll call does not provide transparency. Procedural roll calls are not transparent for voters. They merely provide campaigns with fodder to tie to the substantive issue of their choosing. Meanwhile, these votes have real consequences for policies.[41] Given this, it seems the first casualty of procedural warfare might be the American voter.

FIVE

Viagra for Ideologues

The Rise of Messaging Amendments

We believe secrecy undermines the democratic process and saps public confidence in the House as a responsive and legislative body.

—Rep. Barber Conable (R-NY) and Rep. Sam Gibbons (D-FL), 1970[1]

[I]f this bill goes through without this amendment, your tax dollars are going to be paying for Viagra for child molesters.

—Sen. Tom Coburn (R-OK), 2010[2]

Jeff Flake and the Defense Appropriations Act of 2010

On July 27, 2009, US House members received a letter from Rules Committee Chair Louise Slaughter (D-NY). The Department of Defense Appropriations Act of 2010 (H.R. 3326) would be considered under a structured rule, and any member wishing to offer an amendment to the act would need to pre-submit the amendment to the Rules Committee. The Rules Committee would consider all submitted amendments and issue a rule that would outline which of the amendments, if any, would be allowed consideration on the House floor.

Rep. Jeff Flake (R-AZ) submitted a staggering 596 potential amendments to the committee. Most of these amendments were sought by the fiscally conservative Flake to remove no-bid contracting provisions from the over $600 billion spending bill. The Rules Committee reported a rule allowing consideration of 10 Flake amendments, including an en bloc amendment that combined 553 of Flake's amendments into a new single amendment. During consideration of the bill, each of Flake's 10 amendments was defeated on the floor. For nine of these failed amendments, Flake requested a recorded roll call vote after his amendment failed to pass by voice vote. The roll call record now contains vote totals for each of these amendments, providing a durable record of Flake's defeats.[3] Altogether, there were 606 proposed amendments to H.R. 3326 submitted to the House Rules Committee, and the structured rule allowed consideration for 16 of those. There were 74 amendments considered on the Senate floor, 10 of which received recorded votes. In total, there were 36 roll call votes: 20 in the House and 16 in the Senate.[4]

This stands in stark contrast to House amending activity on the 1909 Naval Appropriations Act. The House considered 12 amendments to this bill, none of which received a roll call vote. The fact that these amendments did not receive a roll call vote does not mean that they were unimportant—one amendment attempted to increase the number of "first-class battleships" funded by the bill from two to four. Nor does it mean that these amendments were unanimously supported. Six of the 12 amendments received division votes after an initial voice vote, and the battleship amendment received a voice vote, a division vote, and finally a teller vote where it failed by an 83 to 199 margin. While the Senate considered 108 amendments on the same bill, only four of these amendments received recorded votes.[5]

As the above examples show, the manner in which Congress generates the roll call voting record, the central tool used to ensure congressional transparency and responsiveness, has drastically changed over the history of the House and Senate. We have argued that because of the changes in what does and does not get a recorded vote, the modern record is "broken" such that it does not provide a transparent look at the legislative process in the same way that recorded votes of past eras once provided. This broken record has important implications for evaluating key features of Congress, such as polarization, the effectiveness of institutions and rules, and the chamber's ability to formulate policy.

In this chapter, we argue that changes in the roll call generating process have largely been driven by extreme members. We test our argument using a new dataset of 117,269 amendments to 2,087 important legislative enactments from the 59th Congress (1905–1906) to the 113th Congress (2013–2014). Our results demonstrate that more ideologically extreme amendment sponsors are positively related with the likelihood of a roll call vote, but only for more recent eras in our dataset. We also find a positive relationship between a roll call vote on an amendment and several member-specific and content-specific factors. Our findings suggest that contemporary claims of increased ideological polarization may be artificially driven in comparison to previous congresses, a concept we examine in greater detail in Chapter 6.

Congressional Floor Amendments

Conflict over the floor amending process in Congress is not surprising. Floor amending plays an important role in both legislative policymaking and electoral position-taking. From a policy standpoint, floor amendments "provide the crucial linkage between procedural mechanisms and final passage votes and have the ability to fundamentally shift the substantive content of bill proposals in Congress" (Carson et al. 2013, 108). Formal theoretic models of legislative politics highlight the important role of the floor amending process in checking the preferences of committees (Weingast 1989). In its absence, majority-party and committee leaders can produce non-median policies (Cox and McCubbins 2005, 2007; Jenkins and Monroe 2012a, 2012b; Monroe and Robinson 2008).

For members who lack influence with leadership or with the underlying committee, the floor amending process can represent their last opportunity to pass a policy they (or at least their constituents) care about. As detailed in Appendix D, most rank-and-file members have greater opportunities to influence lawmaking through amending than through legislative drafting. This is especially true for more junior members. The erosion of the apprenticeship norm in the Senate in the 1970s was marked by an increase in floor amending by junior members (Sinclair 1989).

As the Flake example has highlighted, however, the amending process also provides clear electoral position-taking opportunities for members as well. Roll calls on floor amendments have increased sharply throughout congressional history. Further, these roll calls were increasingly likely to be party votes. This finding was consistent with other scholarship that has documented the rise in so-called messaging amendments (Lee 2009; Madonna and Kosar 2015; Roberts and Smith 2003). However, as was the case with the rise of procedural votes, the increase in amendment roll calls could simply reflect a change in the lawmaking process. In order to better evaluate the link between messaging amendments and extremity, we employ a dataset of amendments that did and did not receive recorded votes. Prior to that, we highlight conflict over the amending process, detail the growth in floor amendments and expand on why we believe changes in the amending process benefit extremists.

Congressional Leaders and the Myth of "Regular Order"

In the 2014 midterm election, Republicans took control of the Senate for the first time since 2006. Sen. Mitch McConnell (R-KY), the new majority leader, announced that his first order of business would be to return the chamber to "regular order." What McConnell meant was that he planned on allowing a more "open floor" and would not block senators from offering amendments. Offering floor amendments, he suggested, was "the job of a senator" (Hulse 2014). McConnell and Senate Republicans had hammered the outgoing majority leader, Sen. Harry Reid (D-NV), for barring floor amendments by filling the amendment tree.[6]

For example, Sen. Orrin Hatch (R-UT) referred to the Senate under Reid as "a sham" and argued that under his "heavy hand, the twin pillars of the Senate's careful deliberation—unlimited debate and an open amendment process—have been almost entirely curtailed" (Hatch 2014). McConnell claimed Reid and the Democrats "have turned the Senate into a graveyard of good ideas and good democratic debate" (Hulse 2014).[7] Republican candidates featured Reid's control of the chamber in attack ads on their opponents in virtually all competitive races, including North Carolina, Alaska, Kansas, Kentucky, Louisiana, and Georgia (Alpert 2014; McLaughlin 2014). The criticism was not limited to Republicans. Sen. Christopher Murphy (D-CT) noted that he "got more substance on the floor of the House in the minority than I have as a member of the Senate majority" (Raju and Everett 2014). Sen. Mark Begich (D-AK) lambasted the majority leader in a formal statement and was one of several Democratic candidates that did not endorse Reid as majority leader (Everett 2014).

Despite the Republican criticism of Reid, members from both parties would later concede that blocking amendments was not surprising given the increase in messaging amendments. Perhaps the most well known of these was Sen. Tom Coburn's (R-OK) proposed amendment that sought to bar insurance coverage of Viagra for child molesters and rapists. Specifically, Coburn's amendment was offered to H.R. 4872, a reconciliation bill that amended and made corrections to the Affordable Care Act (111 PL 148). Democrats wanted to pass the measure without alterations so it would not have to be considered a second time by the House. Recognizing this, Coburn and other Republicans, introduced over 164 floor amendments, forcing recorded votes on 34, during the Senate's vote-a-rama. As the *New York Times* noted, these "amendments will be constructed in an artful way in hopes of making them politically difficult for senators to oppose" (Herszenhorn 2010).[8]

Coburn argued that his amendment was not a messaging amendment, rather a sincere attempt to impact policy. He asserted it was a "constructive amendment that saves millions and millions of dollars in Medicare," and added that voting against his amendment constituted providing "active aid to help those who would hurt our children" (*Congressional Record*, 111th Congress, March 24, 2010, S1942–S1943). Senate Democrats disagreed. The bill manager, Sen. Max Baucus (D-MT) asserted Coburn's amendment was "not a serious amendment" and it made "a mockery of this Senate." Baucus added that it was "a crass political stunt aimed at making 30 second commercials, not public policy" (*Congressional Record*, 111th Congress, March 24, 2010, S1998). Baucus's motion to table the Coburn amendment was adopted 57–42, and the amendment was defeated.[9]

As Baucus anticipated, the amendment was prominently featured in a number of electoral attack ads. For example, an ad targeting Majority Leader Reid asserted "Reid actually voted to use taxpayer dollars to pay for Viagra for convicted child molesters and sex offenders" (Barr 2010). Coburn would point to a Congressional Research Service report to defend his claims. The report noted that the law did "not appear to prohibit a qualified health plan in a health insurance exchange from providing coverage for drugs prescribed to treat ED for a non-incarcerated beneficiary who was previously convicted of rape, child molestation, or another sex offense" (Stanton 2010).

Fact-checkers like PolitiFact still rated the ad as "mostly false" for a multitude of reasons, including the procedural context and the fact that Reid's vote was against Coburn's amendment and not for any specific policy (Jacobson 2010).[10] Others pointed out that the Coburn amendment also included language restricting access to the "morning after" pill (Kiely 2010). Members of both parties would later criticize the "Viagra" amendment as being emblematic of the kind of messaging amendments that led leadership to limit floor amending. For example, Sen. Angus King (I-ME) quoted a member up for reelection, noting the member claimed he didn't "mind taking hard votes" on "crazy, gotcha amendments—Viagra for sex offenders or whatever." But the member argued there was no point in doing that if the bill was not going to pass the House. Likewise, Sen. Saxby Chambliss (R-GA) argued it was easy for members of his party to blame Reid but that they deserved some of the blame for the "crazy [and] purely political amendments" they were offering instead of "doing the business [they] were sent here to do in a very serious way" (Warren 2015).

In the face of increasing usage of messaging amendments, political observers were skeptical of McConnell's pledge for a more open Senate—such a pledge gets made virtually every time a new House or Senate leader takes over their respective chamber. When Reid became the Senate majority leader in 2007, he pledged a more inclusive process, asserting that "majorities must work with minorities to make that lasting change" (Mimms 2015).[11]

These pledges are even more common in the House, where leaders have increasingly employed restrictive rules to curtail floor amendments. Upon his election as speaker in 2011, Rep. John Boehner (R-OH) offered a "commitment [of] openness." He criticized outgoing Speaker Nancy Pelosi (D-CA), adding, "There were no open rules in the House in the last Congress. In this one there will be many" (James 2011). But Boehner quickly began employing more restrictive rules. This decision was criticized by conservative Republicans of the House Freedom Caucus, who attempted to oust Boehner on several occasions in part because of his use of the Rules Committee to bar amendments (Drutman 2015a; French and Sherman 2015).[12] When Rep. Paul Ryan (R-WI) was elected to replace him, he called for more amendments and a return to regular order (DeBonis 2015; McPherson 2015).[13] During his speakership, Ryan would go on to break the record for most closed rules in a session (Bade 2017).[14] The circle was completed in January 2019, when Pelosi was again elected speaker. She criticized Ryan and the Republicans and pledged to seek a more open process (Willis 2019).[15]

Pledges to return to regular order are appealing to members and the general public even though the concept is ambiguous. Or at least, in the words of Walter Oleszek (2014), it represents a "flexible construct." More cynically, Sen. Mike Lee (R-UT) argued that calls to return to regular order are made only "when it serves [members'] interests" (Lee 2015). As the preceding discussion suggests, open amending processes rarely serve leader interests.

Transparency, Reforms, and the Rise of Floor Amendments

As we argue in Chapter 6, the reticence of leaders to allow an open amending process is not baseless. Whether offered by minority-party members or fellow partisans, floor amendments have the potential to surprise and break leaders' carefully assembled coalitions. Procedural innovations like filling the amendment tree in the Senate and structured rules in the House allow leaders to screen amendments and negotiate before they arrive on the floor. They also provide leaders with an opportunity to make ex post adjustments to legislation if they determine they need the support (Lynch et al. 2015).

The increase in floor amending observed in recent decades is due to a multitude of factors, including diminished practical barriers rendering the sufficient second clause toothless and increased partisan coordination. Internal changes to legislative procedures have also played a major role in explaining the sharp increase in floor amending. The most notable of these was the decision to allow recorded voting in the Committee of the Whole (Roberts and Smith 2003).

Prior to adoption of the Legislative Reorganization Act (LRA) in 1970, recorded voting was not permitted in the Committee of the Whole.[16] Instead, members would receive a voice vote, and if requested and supported by a sufficient second, an unrecorded division or teller vote. If a division vote was granted, members would rise to take the affirmative on a question, and then be counted by the chair. This process is repeated for those in opposition. During a teller vote, members file past appointed tellers and are counted as either for or against a measure. While it is likely to yield more accurate vote totals than either voice or division votes, its usage led to accusations of manipulation and high absenteeism (Smith 1989). Liberals felt teller voting was particularly biased against them, as centrists would vote against the desires of their constituents, who would not know how the member voted, to appease conservative committee chairs, who would (Rohde 1991). Accordingly, they pressed for recorded voting in the Committee of the Whole to be included in the LRA. However, earlier in the year, such a measure was defeated in committee.

This led liberals to form an alliance with minority-party Republicans. They believed recorded voting in the Committee of the Whole would increase their chances of enacting favored policies and would provide them more influence in the chamber. Republicans felt a more open floor process would better serve their electoral and policymaking interests as well (Schickler 2001). Prior to floor consideration of the LRA, a bipartisan group of 45 reformers waged a public war against "secrecy" in the House. The group, led by Rep. Barber Conable (R-NY) and Rep. Sam Gibbons (D-FL), put out a statement asserting, "We believe secrecy undermines the democratic process and saps public confidence in the House as a responsive and legislative body" (Quirk and Hinchcliffe 1998, 31). Gibbons would go on to state he did not "think democracy can work in secret."

On July 29, 1970, an amendment by Rep. Thomas "Tip" O'Neill (D-MA) providing for recorded teller voting was adopted by voice vote. O'Neill argued the presence of recorded voting likely would have changed the outcomes of some previous votes and he added that "there were 15 really national, earth-shaking decisions on which the people at home should have known how [their members] voted" (*Congressional Record*, 91st Congress, July 27, 1970, 25797).[17] While members recognized the folly in taking a public stance against transparency, not all believed the reform would make members more responsive to their constituents.[18] Political scientist Nelson Polsby argued that "only the lobbyists, for good causes or bad, [would] really keep tabs. [Recorded voting] will make their job easier" (Broder 1970). Other members presciently expressed concerns it would lead to more restrictive rules and omnibus lawmaking.[19]

Changes to legislative rules regarding amendment voting coincided with an increasing perception that roll calls on amendments were valuable for electoral purposes. This perceived increase in value is partially due to television advertising and increased electoral competitiveness between the two parties (Lee 2016). Amendments provide members with ample position-taking opportunities (Mayhew 1974). As a retiring Sen. Barry Goldwater (R-AZ) remarked in regards to one electorally motivated amendment, "[D]o we have to have this? The election is two years away. We do not have to start kissing this and rubbing that to get elected next time. And, thank God, I do not have to do it ever again" (96th Congress, *Congressional Record Daily*, December 11, 1980, S16227).

Additionally, as the Polsby comment suggests, there is a potential financial benefit to voting in line with the desires of outside groups. Aware that these groups are more likely to monitor their activity than general election voters, party leaders will acquiesce to, and occasionally press for, roll call votes in an effort to appeal to these groups for donations and to fend off potential primary challenges. This practice has increased sharply in the late 1970s and 1980s. Outside groups spent $3.47 billion on lobbying expenses in 2009, seven times more than they did in 1981 after controlling for inflation (Drutman 2015b).[20]

A Boon for Extremists

Diminishing practical barriers, combined with internal changes to legislative rules and increased electoral competitiveness, have served to both lower the costs and increase the value of roll call votes.[21] We believe this has benefited more partisan and ideologically extreme members like Flake, who first-dimension DW-NOMINATE score was more conservative than all but two other members of the 111th Congress, and Coburn, whose DW-NOMINATE score was the most conservative among senators in the 111th Congress. Ideologically extreme members are less likely to be vulnerable to a competitive primary election challenge than their more moderate counterparts. They frequently work closely with interest groups that represent more extreme constituencies.

Similarly, aggressive partisans and party leaders are motivated to build and maintain their party's national "brand name" in an effort to provide voters with a simplifying cue during elections (Cox and McCubbins 2007). This leads them to seek votes that both unify their membership and distinguish it from the opposition (Roberts and Smith 2003). This was evident in the House of Representatives during the 113th House, when the Republican-led chamber cast over 50 roll call votes on the floor to repeal President Obama's signature healthcare act (O'Keefe 2014). In previous work, we have demonstrated that during periods where House leaders enjoyed high levels of agenda control, proposals are screened in a way that reduces votes that split the majority party, making congressional policymaking appear more unidimensional than it would otherwise (Dougherty et al. 2014).

In contrast, centrists are more likely to offer amendments that would succeed and appeal to broader, cross-party coalitions. Often these members would prefer to go back to their district and emphasize their local legislative accomplishments, even if a recorded vote is not taken. A nice example of this behavior occurred during consideration of H.R. 3288, the Transportation-HUD Appropriations Act in the 111th Congress. Considered under a structured rule, majority-party Democrats allowed 22 amendments to be offered to H.R. 3288. Conservatives like Rep. Randy Neugebauer (R-TX) and Republican Study Conference Chair Jim Jordan (R-OH) were allowed to offer amendments slashing the total amount of spending in the bill.[22] Rep. Flake and Rep. Jeb Hensarling (R-TX) were allowed to select several amendments from a list of their proposed amendments, all of which cut specific earmarks from the bill. More moderate Republicans, like Rep. Joseph Cao (R-LA) and Rep. Aaron Schock (R-IL), offered modest proposals geared to specific constituencies.[23]

Of the 22 amendments offered, the House adopted six. Of those six, no roll call votes were requested. Four Republican amendments were approved by voice, including the Cao and Schock proposals. In contrast, all of the 16 rejected amendments were sponsored by conservative Republicans, and they insisted on recorded votes for each of these failed amendments. While those 16 amendment votes exposed splits within the Republican Party, they produced splits that largely followed traditional ideological differences between more moderate and more conservative members of the party.[24]

Failed amendment votes also allow some members, like Flake and Coburn, to craft fiscally conservative records that could be touted in upcoming political campaigns.[25] Flake featured his earmark amendments in a number of ads in his later election to the Senate. Amendment votes have also become fodder for conservative groups targeting moderate Republicans in primary elections. For example, Rep. Mike Simpson (R-ID) was criticized in primary challenger Bryan Smith's television ads for not supporting several Flake amendments, including one to cut $150,000 of funding for a South Carolina aquarium.[26]

Data and Methods

Determining whether an amendment is a "messaging" amendment is fairly arbitrary. As we have argued, many legislative proposals are enacted only after repeated defeats on the floor. For example, on July 18, 2001, Rep. Maurice Hinchey (D-NY) introduced an amendment that sought to bar the Department of Justice from enforcing federal marijuana laws in any of the eight states that had legalized the drug for medical purposes. While Hinchey withdrew the amendment after a brief debate, proposing it as an amendment allowed him to bypass the conservative Judiciary Committee (Higdon 2018).[27] Two years later the amendment was defeated on the floor overwhelmingly, failing 273–152. It would fail seven more times before being adopted in 2015 (Eddy 2010; Higdon 2018).

While it is difficult to tell the difference between a "sincere" and a "messaging" amendment, it is possible to assess how the pattern of recorded voting on amendments has changed across the history of Congress. If the roll call record is to be both interpretable to voters and a valuable tool of historical comparison for congressional observers, the roll call generating process for amendments should be consistent over time and sponsor ideology. Changing patterns would suggest otherwise.

Amendments to Important Legislation

Accordingly, to examine how the roll call generating process has changed over time, we needed a dataset that examines both amendments that did and did *not* receive roll calls. Existing roll call datasets already contain all amendments that received recorded votes, but no dataset was able to provide all amendments that could have received a roll call vote. Starting in 2010, we began construction of such a dataset by establishing the University of Georgia Congress Project. Our first step involved constructing a dataset of "important" legislation from 1905 to 2014. The decision to focus on important legislation was motivated by several factors, which are discussed in greater detail in Appendix B.[28] Altogether, this left us with a list of 2,036 enactments across 55 congresses.

Second, we tasked teams of coders to read through the *Congressional Record* and collect data on all amendments to those bills. Discussed in Appendix D, our primary dependent variable is whether or not the amendment received a recorded vote.[29] In total, 131 undergraduates, two faculty members, 17 graduate students, and three high school students collected data on 117,269 amendments. Figure 5.1 plots the amendments filed per congress by chamber from the 59th Congress (1905–1906) to the 113th Congress (2013–2014) in a stacked bar graph.

As Figure 5.1 demonstrates, the bulk of the amendments filed occur in the Senate. This is not surprising. While House leaders and bill managers have historically restricted members from offering amendments on the floor using special rules (Roberts 2010), the Senate lacks a comparable institutional mechanism. Of the 117,269 amendments filed from the 59th to 113th Congresses, 89,611 (or 76.41%) are Senate amendments.

However, this Senate bias is slightly mitigated if we look at amendments that are considered or offered on the floor. Of those 89,611 Senate amendments filed, 52,766 (or 58.89%) received consideration on the floor.[30] An amendment may be filed on the floor but not offered for a wide array of reasons. An amendment's sponsor may decide not to press the amendment. An amendment may be blocked by a later unanimous consent agreement or special rule. The measure the amendment sought to alter may be dispensed with, prior to consideration of the amendment. In recent Senates, the majority leader may "fill the amendment tree" to block amending opportunities. Figure 5.2 plots the number of filed and offered amendments per congress.

Figure 5.2 also demonstrates a sharp decline in the percentage of filed amendments formally offered on the floor. The bulk of this appears to be driven by the restriction on amending activity that has become more prevalent in recent congresses. For example, in the 112th Senate and 113th Senate, of the 4,479 amendments filed to important legislation in our dataset, just under 20% were formally offered and dispensed with on the Senate floor. This is consistent with anecdotal arguments that Reid employed filled amendment trees at a higher rate than his predecessors.

However, even before filling the tree became routine, many amendments were filed on the Senate floor, but not formally offered. This was often done by members in an effort to negotiate for leverage (Sinclair 1989). Amendments would get written and a negotiation would take place between their sponsors, leaders, bill managers, and committee chairmen over what would be offered on the floor or included in the bill. As Sen. Mary Landrieu (D-LA) remarked, "There was never a time as long I've been here where there's been a completely open, completely unlimited, completely freewheeling amendment process. That has never existed" (Everett and Raju 2014). Much of the amending behavior observed on the Senate floor is filtered through this selection mechanism.

The likelihood an amendment will be formally offered on the floor has fluctuated over time. This makes sense given the increasing likelihood a roll call will be taken on any amendment that is formally offered. From the 59th

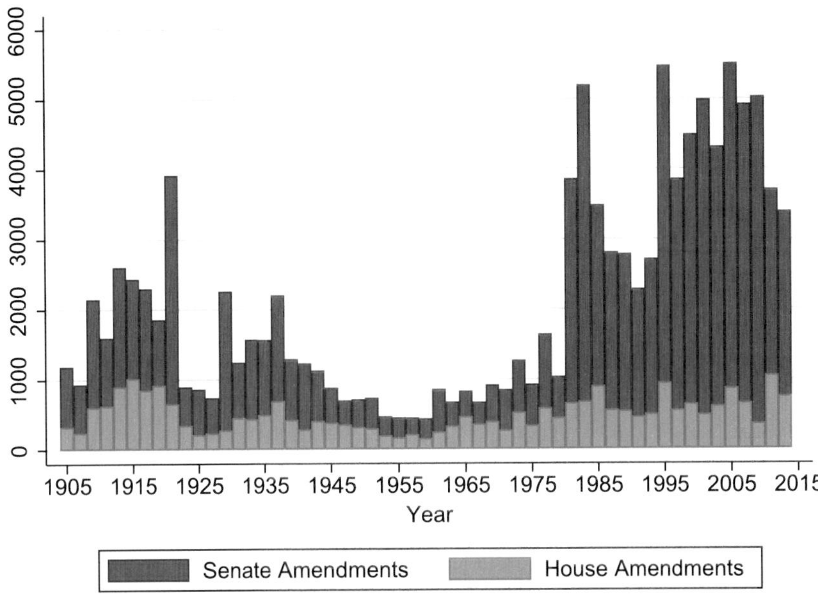

Figure 5.1. Amendments Filed per Congress by Chamber, 1905–2014

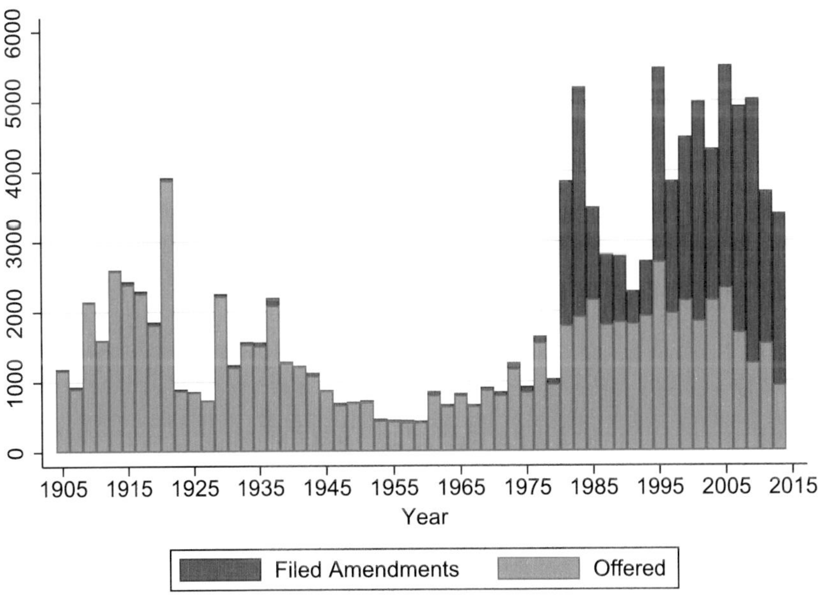

Figure 5.2. Filed and Offered Amendments per Congress, 1905–2014

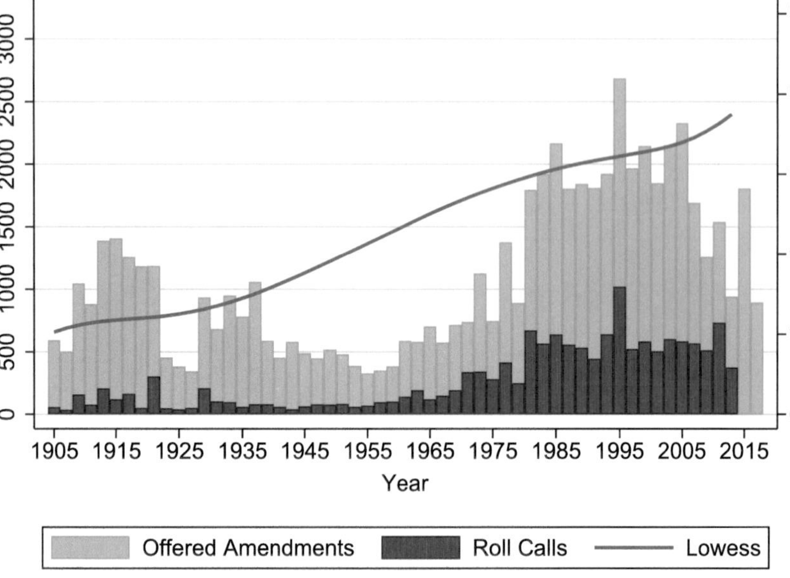

Figure 5.3. Roll Calls per Offered Amendments by Congress, 1905–2014

Congress to the 79th Congress, 7.35% of the 34,180 amendments received roll call votes. From the 80th to 113th Congress, 29.25% of the 44,717 amendments received roll call votes.[31] Figure 5.3 plots the number of amendments considered on the floor with the percentage that received roll call votes. The figure also includes a simple lowess smoothing line that reports the percentage of amendments that received recorded votes per congress (percentage reported on the right axis).

Modeling the Likelihood of a Roll Call Vote

In this chapter, our primary hypothesis is that the removal of practical barriers to roll calls, including improved travel, better staffing resources, and improved partisan coordination, combined with increased electoral competitiveness, have advantaged extremists. This, we have argued, has led some political observers to attribute increased polarization on roll call votes purely to shifts in member ideology. Consistent with some recent scholarship, we believe a substantial increase in this observed polarization is due to changes in legislative procedures and electoral incentives (Egar 2016; Dougherty et al. 2014; Lee 2009; Lynch and Madonna 2013b).

As we discuss further in Chapter 6, we argue that increased roll call voting on measures sponsored by more ideologically extreme members leads to

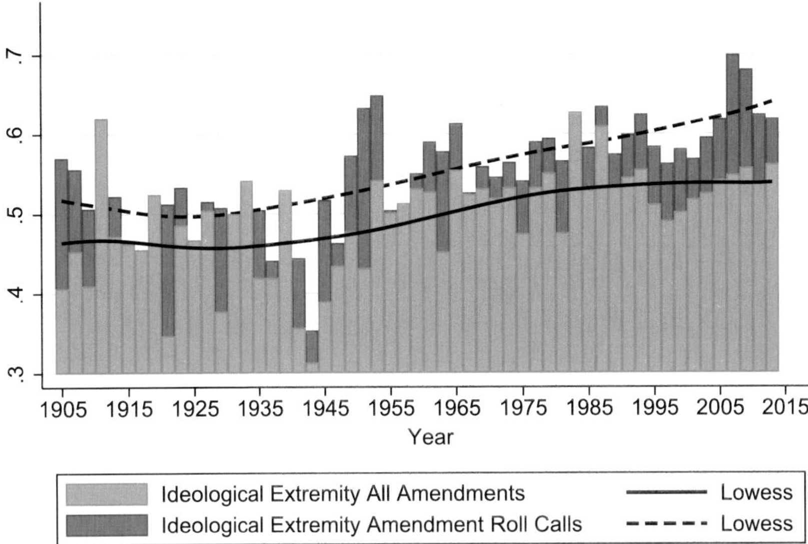

Figure 5.4. Average Ideological Extremity Rank by Amendment Sponsor per Congress, 1905–2014

more votes that divide the parties. These party votes accentuate the observed ideological distance observed between members of the two parties, creating artificially high measures of polarization. While roll-call-based measures of ideology, like DW-NOMINATE, may be susceptible to inflated measures of polarization, we do not think the changing patterns of roll call voting should affect how measures of ideology estimate the rank ordering of legislators. Accordingly, to examine the link between recorded voting and ideology, we created a measure accounting for each amendment sponsor's rank order distance from the chamber median in a given Congress or chamber, rather than use a more traditional NOMINATE scores as our measure of ideology.[32] Figure 5.1 plots all amendments' sponsors' average ideological extremity per congress versus the sponsors' average ideological extremity on amendments that received roll calls.[33] Lowess smoothing lines are included to indicate the general trends in the data.

Figure 5.4 suggests, consistent with our argument, that there has been a general increase in the ideological extremity of all amendment sponsors. Further, this trend has been much sharper for amendments that received roll call votes in recent congresses. In an effort to examine this more systematically, we fit separate probit models of recorded voting for three separate eras in our data. As we discuss in Chapter 4, we separate the data into three eras for the sake of comparison. Era 1 examines the 59th Congress (1905–1907) through the end of the 78th Congress (1943–1944), when attendance levels stabilized. Era 2 extends from the 79th Congress (1945–1946) through the 91st Congress (1969–1970), marking the period typically thought of as the "textbook" Congress era. Finally, Era 3 looks at the post-reform Congress period to the present—from the 92nd Congress (1972–1973) to the 113th Congress (2013–2014).

Our hypothesis suggests ideological rank should be positive and significantly related to recorded voting in recent eras. We also include a number of control variables. The majority party has a substantial advantage in drafting legislation, and majority-party members find it less necessary to seek policy changes via the amending process. Additionally, majority-party members have the ability to run on their record of legislative achievement and, accordingly, have less need for roll call votes for position-taking and electoral purposes. Hence, we include a dummy variable for whether an amendment's sponsor is in the majority party.

Because roll call voting was not permitted on amendments offered in the House Committee of the Whole for two of our three eras, we include a dummy variable for chamber (Senate amendments are coded 1, House amendments are coded 0).[34] In addition to majority-party status and ideological rank, we include several other member-specific variables. Gender is a dummy variable coded 1 if the member is female.

Committee chairs have significant influence on the content of the legislation prior to the bill coming to the floor. Given that, and the increased likelihood of their offering technical amendments, we anticipate amendments offered by chairs to be less likely to receive roll call votes. Ranking members, however, may have been shut out at the committee stage and thus more likely to receive roll calls.[35] Finally, we include controls for members of the majority and minority-party leadership.[36]

We also include controls for various amendment types. For much of congressional history, large numbers of committee amendments were adopted separately on the floor, as opposed to in committee or as a large committee substitute amendment on the floor. Committees were generally deferred to on these amendments and therefore generated higher success rates, minimal controversy, and fewer roll calls. In contrast, substitute amendments seek to replace entire texts of the pending proposal. These tend to be more controversial, and, thus, we anticipate more recorded voting on them. Finally, for enactments considered prior to the 97th Congress (1981–1982), we include motions to recommit. A motion to recommit with instructions in the House is often viewed as the final opportunity for the minority to amend the bill.

TABLE 5.1. Probit Models of Recorded Voting on Amendments, 1905–2014

Variable	Model 1 (1905–1944)	Model 2 (1945–1971)	Model 3 (1972–2014)
Ideological Rank	−0.1474	0.248*	0.533*
	(0.093)	(0.114)	(0.061)
Majority Party	−0.155*	−0.007	−0.080
	(0.060)	(0.059)	(0.067)
Chamber	1.264*	1.595*	−0.404*
	(0.083)	(0.162)	(0.114)
Gender	0.389	−.016	−0.093*
	(0.422)	(0.277)	(0.047)
Chair	−0.213*	−0.205*	−0.140*
	0.062	(0.074)	(0.032)
Ranking Member	0.070	0.168	−0.017
	(.081)	(0.105)	(0.043)
Majority Leadership	−0.326	−0.137	−0.031
	(0.172)	(0.142)	(.067)
Minority Leadership	−0.169	−0.227	−0.068
	(0.125)	(0.225)	(0.070)
Substitute Amendment	0. 625*	0.515*	0.528*
	(0.122)	(0.066)	(0.052)
Committee Amendment	−0.926*	−1.112*	−0.570*
	(0.030)	(0.155)	(0.258)
Recommit	2.185*	2.208*	0.630*
	(0.096)	(0.194)	(0.289)
Majority Seat Share	−0.873	0.545	−0.001
	(0.460)	(0.691)	(0.002)
Appropriation Bill	−0.155	0.054	−0.042
	(0.087)	(0.174)	(0.051)
Revenue	0.112	0.082	0.378*
	(0.102)	(0.098)	(0.086)
Tariff	0.380*	0.648*	−0.878*
	(0.129)	(0.129)	(0.041)
Civil Rights	-	0.635*	0.470*
	( )	(0.231)	(0.223)
Immigration	−0.059	0.497*	0.364
	(0.196)	(0.103)	(0.192)
Constant	−1.415*	−2.461*	−0.443*
	(0.282)	(0.476)	(0.094)
Observations	33,194	8,414	37,104
Pseudo R^2	0.221	0.274	0.052

These motions are generally controversial, and we anticipate more roll call votes on them.

The link between electoral competitiveness and roll calls suggests more recorded voting may occur when the majority party's seat share is smaller. Hence, we include a control for the share of seat held by the majority party. Finally, we include controls for the content of the underlying legislation. We anticipate more controversial issues like civil and voting rights, immigration, tariff legislation, and measures raising revenue through altering the tax code would lead to more electoral grandstanding. In contrast, appropriation bills and omnibus measures should suppress roll calls on amendments. Our results are presented in Table 5.1.

Results

The results show strong evidence of more roll call votes on proposals sponsored by more extreme members of Congress. In the earliest time period examined, ideological rank is negative and insignificant, suggesting that the ideology of an amendment sponsor did not help explain recorded voting. In the final two time periods, the coefficient is significant and positive, with the coefficient increasing from Era 2 to Era 3. This indicates that ideological extremists' amendments are more likely to receive roll call votes and that this likelihood increased from 1947 to 2013.

The negative coefficient on the majority-party variable indicates that minority-party members are more likely to receive roll call votes on their amendments than are majority-party members, although the effect is only significant in Era 1. In the first two time periods, Senate amendments are more likely to receive recorded votes than House amendments, although House amendments are more likely to receive roll call votes in the most recent time period.

Controls for different types of amendments perform as expected. Substitute amendments are more likely to receive roll call votes, while committee amendments are less likely to receive recorded votes. Motions to recommit are more likely to receive roll call votes across all time periods for which data are available. Issue type shows mixed results. Revenue bills are significantly more likely to see recorded amendment votes in the most recent era. Tariff issues are more significantly more likely to see recorded amendment votes in the first two time periods, but significantly less likely to see recorded amendment votes in the most recent period. Civil rights issues are more likely to see recorded amendment votes.

Conclusion

The roll call voting record is an invaluable tool for students of American politics. Candidates use recorded votes to attack electoral opponents. Interest groups employ the record in an effort to drum up financial or electoral support for their preferred candidates and positions. Students of political science use the record as a way to test theories of legislative behavior. However, we believe the literature has been hampered by undocumented changes in the roll call generating process.

We have argued that the removal of practical barriers to roll calls, internal changes to legislative procedures, and increased electoral competitiveness have led to more roll call votes on messaging amendments. Members frequently voice concerns over casting "tough" votes on messaging amendments like Flake's earmark restrictions and Coburn's Viagra amendment. It seems like that this has led those same members to allow leadership more control over the floor through procedural tactics like restrictive rules in the House and filled amendment trees in the Senate.

Moreover, we have argued that messaging amendments are more likely to be sponsored by extreme members. Using a new dataset of nearly 120,000 amendments to important legislation from 1904 to 2014, we document how the construction of the roll call record has changed over time. Consistent with our hypotheses, we find that in recent eras, proposals sponsored by more ideologically extreme members are more likely to receive recorded votes than measures sponsored by members ranked closer to the chamber median. This has led some to attribute increased polarization via roll call votes purely to shifts in member ideology. We examine this in greater detail in Chapter 6.

While changes in the roll call generating process do not alter the primary products of polarization, namely crippling gridlock on salient issues and anemic legislative productivity, it does suggest alternative means of reform. Specifically, if polarization is partially driven by electoral and institutions factors, then solving the problem requires a more nuanced set of solutions then simply replacing legislators. In the absence of specific procedural reforms and increased public education about how Congress operates, "voting the bums out" will only led to the creation of new bums.

Changes to the roll call generating process pose problems not only for scholars of political polarization. They also represent challenges for scholars seeking to examine the effects of institutional change across congresses (see, e.g., Madonna 2001; Wawro and Schickler 2004, 2006) and those characterizing the dimensionality of voting in Congress (see, e.g., Crespin and Rohde 2010; Dougherty et al. 2014; Noel 2013). Perhaps most importantly, though, it weakens the ability of the public to monitor legislative behavior.

SIX

Letting the Students Write the Exam

Coauthored with Alice Kisaalita

> Roll-call votes are only as useful as the underlying process by which they are generated.
>
> —Royce Carroll and Keith Poole (2014, 116)

The "Do-Nothing" 112th and 113th Congresses

When the 112th Congress finally adjourned in January 2013, it had racked up a great deal of criticism from political commentators. The *Washington Post* exclaimed "good riddance!" and noted that it "was the least popular since pollsters began keeping score" (Klein 2013). The *New York Times* argued it had made routine legislating "laborious and at times downright tedious" (Steinhauer 2012). A subsequent editorial pointed to its "reputation for monumental procrastination and toxic paralysis," and a number of outlets dubbed it "the worst [Congress] ever."[1] These arguments were bolstered by data demonstrating that it passed 100 fewer public laws (283 in total) than its predecessor, the 111th Congress. The 113th Congress did not fare much better, finishing with only 296 public laws and generating comparable criticism in the press (Bump 2014).[2] Their ineffectiveness was linked to their status as being two of the most ideologically polarized congresses in history, as measured by recorded votes (Matthews 2013).

While the 112th and 113th Congresses passed few laws, they did not shirk their duties when it came to taking recorded votes. Excluding lopsided votes, the 112th House and Senate cast a total 1,795 recorded votes, roughly 15% more than its predecessor.[3] The 113th Congress performed comparably, enacting nearly as few public laws despite recording 1,537 non-lopsided roll call votes. Much of this voting occurred on issues that did not become law. Only 23.56% of roll calls cast in the 112th and 11.78% roll calls cast in the 113th Congress occurred on measures enacted into law.[4] There were a lot of party votes to repeal or replace the ACA, as well as many party votes on cloture, nominations, and procedure.[5] While all this voting did not lead to a lot of lawmaking, it did present to the public an image of two highly unified and polarized political parties.

Both the House and Senate use the agenda-setting process to choose what measures receive consideration (Stage 1 from Chapter 1). They also choose which measures, on both procedural and substantive issues, receive recorded votes (Stage 2 from Chapter 1). Why is Congress choosing to hold so many time-consuming recorded votes in the course of passing so few public laws? Previous chapters indicate that parties have increasing incentives to hold party votes as a way to highlight party differences. In this chapter, we consider what impact these frequent party votes have on our ability to analyze the roll call record. We argue that the changing roll call generating process has made it increasingly difficult to understand Congress by just looking at roll call votes.

In this chapter, we first discuss how Congress has the ability to strategically construct the roll call record, avoiding votes they do not want the public to see and repeating votes that they do want the public to see. Then, using simulations, we show that measures of congressional behavior, like polarization rates, are highly sensitive to changes in the roll call generating process. We conclude by arguing that changes in how Congress builds the roll call record are inhibiting the public's and researchers' ability to accurately access Congress.

Strategic Construction of the Record

The roll call record can be thought of as closely resembling an exam, with each vote by a member of Congress being equivalent to answering a question on an exam. Political scientists and other Congress watchers have used this exam analogy for years to think about roll calls and congressional members' voting behavior. As early as the 1940s, interest groups, such as the Americans for Democratic Action, began developing interest group scores. These scores identified a limited number of key votes, important to the interest group, and noted the position the interest group preferred. Groups then tallied up the proportion of time each member voted the "correct" way and issued annual scores. Political scientists use similar techniques, typically aggregating all roll call votes, and using them to estimate members' relative ideologies via the "revealed preferences" derived from a member's votes.

There is one major difference between traditional exams and the roll call record that make this exam analogy problematic: the students get to write their own exam questions. As such, Congress picks what questions they answer and how often they answer them. Votes that reveal intraparty divisions can be avoided, allowing parties to appear highly unified, and votes that highlight interparty differences can be repeated, inflating the appearance of polarization. Through strategic construction of the roll call record, Congress has a role in determining how it is perceived.

Hidden Divisions

In the spring of 2021, President Joe Biden introduced two major infrastructure plans. The first plan proposed spending $2.3 trillion on physical infrastructure projects, while the second proposed $1.8 trillion of so-called human infrastructure. This second proposal, eventually dubbed the Build Back Better Act, focused new spending on education and support for families and children. It included new programs such as free universal preschool, increased spending on higher education, extension of child and earned income tax credits, expanded ACA subsidies, and money for childcare and family leave (Parlapiano 2021).

While Democrats and some Republicans generally supported Biden's physical infrastructure proposals, there was much less agreement on how much should be spent for the Build Back Better Act.[6] Progressives, like Sen. Bernie Sanders (I-VT), argued for even more spending than outlined in Biden's plan. Sanders circulated an almost $6 trillion proposal that included $500 billion to add hearing, dental, and eyecare coverage to Medicare and expanded Medicare coverage by changing the eligibility age from 65 to 60, among other proposed additions (McPherson 2022). In July, the White House and Senate Majority Leader Chuck Schumer (D-NY) developed a $3.4 trillion compromise plan that combined Biden's plan with some programs supported by progressives. Sens. Joe Manchin (D-WV) and Krysten Sinema (D-AZ) soon objected to the total cost of this compromise plan. After months of negotiations among Democrats, Manchin eventually countered that he would only be willing to support, at most, a $1.5 trillion package.

In November 2021, the House passed a version of Build Back Better that contained $2.2 trillion of new spending to confront climate change and improve healthcare and other social programs (Cochrane and Weisman 2021).[7] It was now up to Democrats to craft a version of the bill that could pass in the Senate.

The makeup of the 117th Senate required every Democrat to support the proposal. Democrats held 50 seats in the 100-seat chamber, and frequently had to rely on Vice President Kamala Harris to provide the tie-breaking vote to give Democrats a 51-vote majority. Democratic leaders planned to pass Build Back Better via reconciliation. The reconciliation process would allow Democrats to avoid a Senate filibuster by Republicans, lower the number of votes needed for success from the normal 60 down to 51. With no Republican senators willing to support the measure, Democrats needed every single Democratic senator to vote for the measure for it to be successful.

Negotiations between the White House, Senate Democrats, and Manchin extended through the end of 2021 and into 2022, with seemingly little progress. On October 27, 2022, Manchin and Schumer announced they had reached a deal on the reconciliation bill, to the surprise of even some of those involved in the negotiations (Friedman and Plumer 2022). The new plan, now called the Inflation Reduction Act, spends more than $450 billion to combat climate change and lower healthcare costs, was much smaller than any previous version of the Build Back Better Act.[8] But with Manchin's support, the bill was able to pass the Senate on 50 to 50 vote, with Vice President Harris casting the tie-breaking yea vote. Sen. Brian Schatz (D-HI) noted, "This is pretty nearly a political miracle to negotiate with a caucus that is as diverse as we have, from Bernie to Manchin. This thing got killed and got revived and got killed and got revived—all the way to the end" (Cochrane 2022).

While the Washington press corps dutifully reported the extended back-and-forth of Senate Democrats' intraparty negotiations on the Inflation Reduction Act, the roll call record tells a different story. The policy differences that divided Senate Democrats and made it so hard for Democrats to build a winning coalition are not apparent in the roll call record. From the initial 51–50 party-line vote that allowed the bill to be considered, to the 51–50 party-line final passage vote, Democrats looked highly unified during recorded voting. There were 39 total votes on the Inflation Reduction Act in the Senate.[9] In 29 of those votes, all Democrats voted as a unified bloc. In the other 10 votes, a small number of Democrats defected from the rest of the party. Of the 1,950 individual votes that Democrats could have cast on the Inflation Reduction Act, Democratic senators only bucked their party 29 times.[10] Only once did a Republican-authored amendment gain enough Democratic support to pass and alter the bill, despite the majority of the Democratic caucus voting against the amendment.[11]

The Senate's consideration of the Inflation Reduction Act is a nice example of how Congress strategically constructs the roll call record. Despite there being deep policy divisions within the Democratic Party, those policy difference were debated and negotiated off the floor of the Senate. Voting on the floor featured repeated party-line votes that showed a largely unified Democratic Party working together to pass a bill, opposed by an equally unified Republican Party.

What tools do members of Congress and congressional leaders use to strategically construct the roll call record? Majority party leadership controls which bills are allowed to come to the floor in both the House and Senate. In the House, the Speaker's agenda-setting powers allow her to keep votes off the floor that risk showing splits within a party. In the Senate, the majority leader's right of first recognition gives him the ability to schedule what legislation comes to the floor and to prevent bills from coming to the floor that may reveal party divisions.

Leaders can also prevent amendments from being offered that risk revealing policy divisions in the majority party. The House Rules Committee, through the use of restrictive rules, can prevent amendments from being considered that may split the majority party. As documented earlier in this book, the use of restrictive rules has dramatically increased in congressional history. Recent congresses have seen most major bills considered under either closed or structured rules. In the Senate, leaders can fill the amendment tree as a tactic to prevent minority amendments from being offered that could divide the majority party.

Repeated Agreement

On February 24, 2021, House Speaker Pro Tem Jim Costa (D-CA) announced he would entertain up to 15 one-minute speeches. These one-minute speeches typically are allowed at the start of a legislative day and may cover any topic of a member's choosing, as long as they only last one minute. On this particular day, members gave speeches covering a variety of parochial interests, including Rep. Tim Burchett's (R-TN) speech recognizing WJBE as a cornerstone of Knoxville, Tennessee's media, and Rep. Claudia Tenney's (R-NY) speech celebrating Utica, New York, resident Jessie Clemente's 103rd birthday. When Rep. Majorie Taylor Greene (R-GA) rose to speak, rather than give a speech about a topic of interest to her district, she moved that the House adjourn for the day. Greene's attempt to adjourn was a protest against the Equality Act, a bill that sought to prohibit discrimination based on sex, sexual orientation, and gender identity.

Greene tweeted that she sought adjournment "in order to give every Member of Congress time to rethink destroying #WomensRights and #WomensSports and #ReligiousFreedom before voting the #Equality Act." When Costa announced that the motion failed, Greene demanded "the yeas and nays." All 202 Republicans that made it to the floor for the surprise vote supported adjournment, while all 214 Democrats voted against adjournment.[12] The Equality Act passed the next day, with all 221 Democrats voting for the measure and all 206 Republicans voting against. Greene's failed adjournment vote, while having no impact on policy, did allow Republicans the chance to twice show their opposition to the Equality Act.

Marjorie Taylor Greene and her fellow House Republicans are not the only ones that might want to add a party-splitting vote to the roll call record. All members of the House and Senate have strong incentives to build a roll call record that highlights party differences. As we have argued, there are strong theoretical reasons why lobbyists, activists, and their supporters in the electorate want to see stark differences between the parties. Deep divisions between the two parties—or at least the perception of deep divisions between the two parties—gets those actors to put skin in the game. Outside groups and more extreme voters are more likely to financially support legislators whose roll call voting records appear more extreme (Barber 2016; Barber et al. 2017; Stratmann 2002). While general election voters may prefer bipartisan approaches, they lack the resources to monitor member behavior in most policy areas (Dancey and Sheagley 2013; Miller and Stokes 1962; Sulkin 2009). Moreover, increased procedural and issue complexity renders it difficult for voters to determine which party is at fault for conflict.

Members provide voters, activists, and interest groups with the conflict they desire by repeatedly showing them party-line votes (Harbridge 2015). These votes can take many different forms. Frequent votes on procedural matters, substantive issues that have no chance of becoming law, nominations, or carefully screened amendments, while failing to provide much information about how Congress makes new laws, successfully fill the record with durable documentation of ideological division.

As an example, during the first session of the 117th Congress, the Senate held recorded confirmation votes for 147 nominees to fill a variety of positions in the new Biden administration. Most of these votes showed high levels of polarization, with most or all Democrats voting in support of Biden's nominees and most or all Republicans voting against. For 128 or these 147 nominees, there was also a recorded cloture vote that preceded the confirmation vote. For 12 of the 147, a motion to discharge from the Judiciary Committee preceded the cloture vote, meaning three nearly identical votes occur for each of these 12 nominees. Vanita Gupta, Biden's nominee for associate attorney general, received four total confirmation-related votes: a motion to discharge, a motion to proceed, a cloture motion, and final confirmation vote. All Democrats voted in support of Gupta across all four votes. All Republicans, with the exception of Lisa Murkowski (R-AK), voted against Gupta in all four votes.[13] These extra confirmation-related votes typically show the exact same or very similar patterns of voting as the final confirmation vote. While these effectively duplicate votes provide no real additional information about senators' ideological preferences, these 141 nomination-related procedural votes made up 26.7% of the 528 roll call votes the Senate held in 2021.

In aggregate, Congress's recent voting patterns raise concerns about the roll call record and its use by both the public and scholars. If members of Congress feel pressure to increase the number of party-line votes, while simultaneously repressing votes that reveal intraparty ideological divisions, the roll call record could be overreporting party differences and polarization rates. In the next section we will examine how these voting patterns have changed over time and will consider what effects these have on roll-call-based measures, like polarization rates.

Risks of Changing Voting Patterns

The preceding discussion suggests some reasons for scholars to be cautious of employing roll-call-based measures, like NOMINATE, as a proxy for ideology. Skepticism due to changes in the roll call generating process is not new. Scholars of comparative politics, recognizing the variation in rules for generating roll calls across legislatures, have been particular sensitive to the limitations of roll call analyses (see, e.g., Carruba et al. 2006; Finke 2015; Hug 2010; Thierse 2016). Carroll and Poole (2014, 116) put this succinctly, noting that "roll-call votes are only as useful as the underlying process by which they are generated."

In the US context, scholars have acknowledged the substantial advances made by the NOMINATE technique (Poole and Rosenthal 2007). However, scholars have questioned specific applications of NOMINATE. One of the earliest arguments on this front was offered by Wilcox and Clausen (1991). While conceding its many benefits (including ease of interpretation), they argue that it should not be used exclusively, as an overreliance would cause scholars of legislative politics to miss issue dimensions converging and diverging. Others have questioned the unidimensionality assumption (Aldrich et al. 2014; Crespin and Rohde 2010; Dougherty et al. 2014; Noel 2013), whether it actually measures ideology (Bateman et al. 2017; Lee 2009), and whether it adequately accounts for selection effects that generate record votes (see, e.g., Vandoren 1990).

In this section, we explore the implications of these changes to the roll call generating process. There is no doubt that members of Congress have been incentivized to hide intraparty differences and highlight interparty differences across the years we analyze in this book. The question is whether this pressure has been constant across the time series, or whether recent congresses are both more likely to strategically restrict votes that divide a party and more likely to add votes that divide the parties.[14] Historical measures of congressional behavior, like polarization rates, rely on a consistent data-generating process (Morton 1999). If members are systematically changing the way they build the roll call record across the history of Congress, aggregate measures like polarization rates can only be reliably interpreted if systematic changes to the data-generating process are accounted for.

Several factors are combining to increase the number of roll call votes where most members of one party are voting against most members of the other party. Increased procedural votes, more roll call votes that are unrelated to lawmaking, more voting on failing amendments, and more omnibus legislation all combine to increase the raw number of party votes. As we have discussed throughout this book, the roll call record provides both the public and scholars with a powerful tool to both monitor the work of Congress and understand how Congress has changed across its history. As party-line votes become more common, we must assess how the changing practices that cause increased party voting are changing the public's and scholars' ability to understand Congress.

We focus our assessment on polarization rates. Polarization rates are calculated using the roll call record and are interpreted by comparing how rates change across the history of Congress.[15] Polarization rates have been steadily increasing since the 1970s, with recent congresses displaying record levels of polarization. Political scientists' default measure of polarization rates in Congress through time comes from DW-NOMINATE scores. These scores are computed by analyzing the full roll call record for all congresses and all legislators simultaneously, allowing legislators' ideal points to vary through time. Although Poole and Rosenthal recognize the limits that changing agendas place on their model, they argue that any concerns that changes in the creation of the roll call record introduce are largely mitigated by the success their model has in reproducing a consistent liberal-conservative first dimension. As Poole (2005, 185) argues:

> [T]he selection of what roll calls to scale can definitely affect the structure of a spatial map. This is particularly true if a single legislative session is analyzed, but will be less true if legislative sessions are analyzed over longer periods of time. The reason is simple. Over time, short-run agenda effects will be smoothed out because the primary issues dividing the political parties . . . represented in the parliament will tend to be voted on in every legislative session.

But it remains true that to accurately compare measures of congressional behavior—such as polarization rates—across history, the process that generates the roll call record must remain consistent across that same historical period. If the process changes in a substantive way, or at least something beyond the "short-run agenda effects" that Poole considers, then it is impossible to assess the cause of changes in polarization rates. Are changes in polarization solely due to changes in parties and their members' ideologies, or is change also influenced by major changes in the roll call generation process. As we document throughout this book, the process has been anything but consistent across the history of Congress. Parties and their leaders are incentivized to add more and more party votes to the roll call record. This has the potential to both alter measures of congressional behavior and scholars' ability to accurately compare them across time.

We use simulation techniques to examine how susceptible measures like polarization rates are to changes in congressional process and procedure. We use simulations to demonstrate that changes to the roll call generation process have the theoretical potential to drastically alter measures of polarization. We first examine these theoretical impacts in a single congress, and then think about the potential impact of changing voting patterns across the history of Congress.

The Problem of Artificial Polarization

In this section, we use simulations to demonstrate that increased party voting has the potential to inflate polarization scores. As we show in the preceding chapters of the book, party voting is on the rise in Congress. Party votes are increasing on both procedural votes (Figure 3.4) and on amendment votes (Figure 3.5). The number of straight party-line votes, where one party votes entirely against the other party, are also on the rise, with the more recent congresses producing between three and 24 more party-line votes than the historical average.

To illustrate the theoretical effect of increasing the number of party votes, we conduct simulations that consider the effect of additional partisan votes on the measurement of polarization. To highlight how increased party voting can change how individual members' ideology is estimated and how that, in turn, affects polarization rates, we first select a prior House with a low level of relative polarization. The 79th House (1945–1947) fits the bill. Speaker Sam Rayburn (D-TX) led the Democratic majority party, during an era where liberal Republicans frequently received more liberal NOMINATE scores than their conservative Southern Democratic colleagues. We then estimated W-NOMINATE scores using the entire roll call record from the 79th House.[16] These estimated ideal points are plotted as x-coordinates on all four panels of Figure 6.1. We also plot these same ideal points as y-coordinates, creating the top left panel, where all points are located on a 45-degree line.

We then add 100 straight party-line votes, votes where all Democrats vote one way and all Republicans vote the other, to the original roll call record and re-estimate W-NOMINATE scores using this augmented roll call data. We plot the new ideal points as y-coordinates in the top right panel. The effect of new party-line votes can be seen by comparing the top left and top right panels. If the new votes do not change the NOMINATE scores, then all points should remain at the 45-degree line, as they are in the top left panel. The top right panel shows that the addition of 100 party-lines votes had a substantial impact on the members' estimated-NOMINATE scores. The overlap between liberal Republicans and Southern Democrats disappears completely, as moderates are pulled to more extreme positions. The most liberal Republican in the 79th House (1945–1947), Rep. Richard Welch (R-CA), moved over .6 units on the −1 to +1 scale. While Republicans show the most movement, Democrats x-axis scores fall, indicating more extreme ideological scores after the addition of the party-line votes. Overall, adding 100 party-line votes moves the 79th House's polarization rate from 0.688 to 1.251.[17]

Reassessing the 112th and 113th Congresses

The previous section shows that ideological scores, like NOMINATE scores, are theoretically susceptible to members adding party-splitting votes to the roll call record. Early chapters have highlighted how voting on issues that frequently lead to party-splitting, such as procedural votes and votes on measures that do not end up becoming law, have increased in recent congresses. Taken together, this calls into question how much of the high levels of polarization seen in recent congresses is the result of true ideological polarization and how much is a result of changing voting patterns.

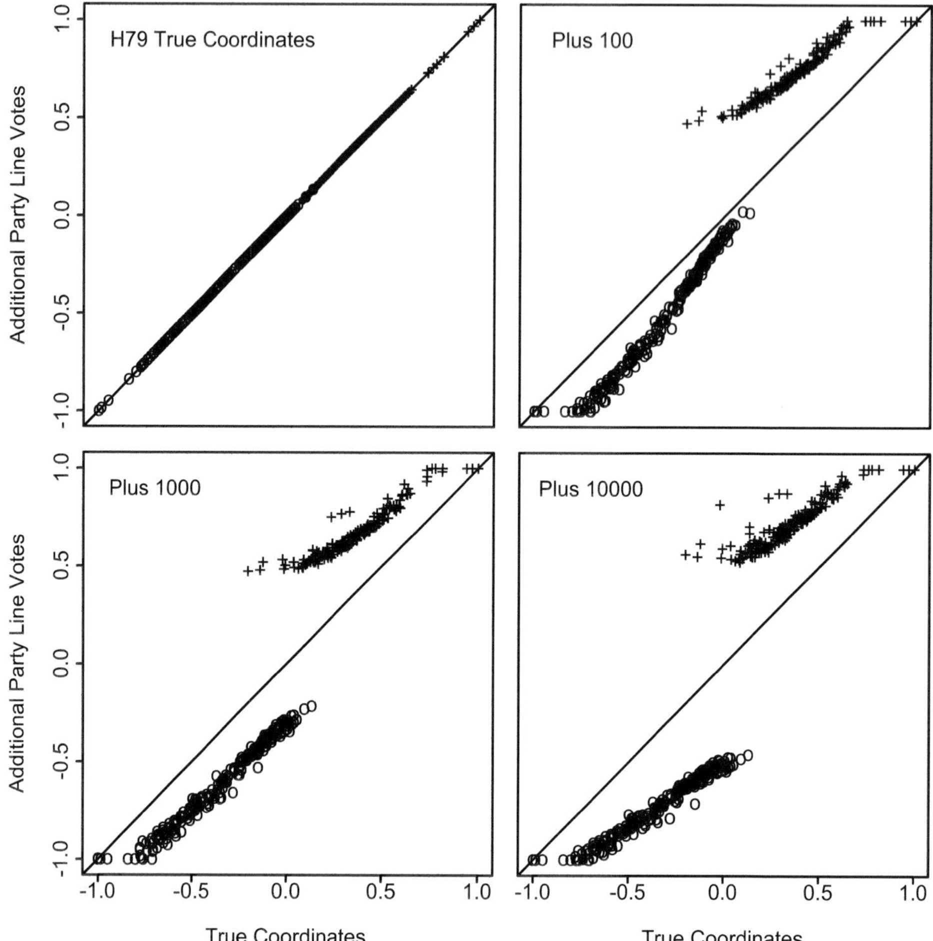

Figure 6.1. Effect of Additional Party-Line Votes on Ideal Point Estimation

We do not believe that all recent increases in polarization are the result of changes in voting patterns—certainly the parties have experienced increased levels of polarization in recent decades. We instead seek to argue that *some* of recent polarization is the result of changing patterns in the type of votes that Congress chooses to record. To that end, we analyze roll call votes from the 112th and 113th Congresses that began this chapter. We look specifically at increased voting in procedural votes and votes on matters that do not become law and ask the following question: What would ideological scores and polarization rates look like if we account for increased voting on these two vote types?

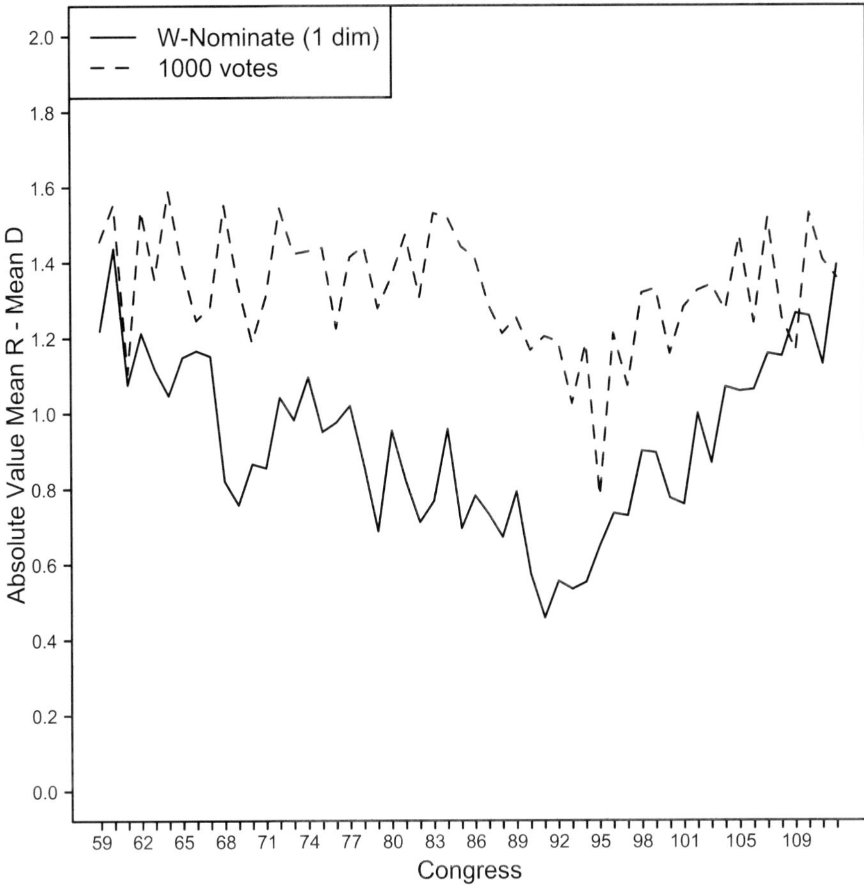

Figure 6.2. Polarization Rates with Additional Party-Line Votes Added

Procedural Votes

Procedural votes represent an obvious starting place to examine increases in party-line votes. As we discuss in Chapter 3, party unity on procedural votes tends to be substantially higher than on substantive votes (Cox and Poole 2002; Crespin 2010; Jessee and Theriault 2014). Minority-party members, in an effort to make the parties appear more polarized, frequently request roll call votes on procedural issues (Egar 2016).

Procedural votes, which show high levels of party voting even in times of relatively low polarization, have greatly increased in recent congresses. Figure 3.4 reports this increase. From 1905 to the 1950s, Congress typically had around 200 recorded procedural votes per congress. From the mid-1950s to the mid-1990s, this number tripled, to around 600 votes per congress. It has remained around an average of 600 per congress since. These votes tend to have high level of party voting, even in time periods with low polarization rates, but the percentage of party voting is over 80% in recent congresses.

To assess the impact these procedural votes have on measures of ideology and polarization, we compare NOMINATE scores from the 112th and 113th House and Senate with scores estimated using a roll call record with all procedural votes removed. When Democrats appear above the 45-degree line and Republicans appear below the 45-degree line, this indicates reduced polarization. When Democrats appear below the 45-degree line and Republicans appear above the 45-degree line, this indicates increased polarization. These results are reported in Figure 6.3.

The scores calculated with procedural votes removed show a less polarized House in both the 112th and 113th Congresses. Both House Democrats' and House Republicans' ideologies appear more moderate than when all votes are included. Results from the Senate are less consistent. In both the 112th and 113th Senates, removing procedural votes makes Senate Democrats appear less polarized. These results do not hold for Republicans. They appear slightly more polarized in the 112th Senate and effectively unchanged in the 113th Senate.

Votes on Failing Measures

Chapter 3 documented the rise of votes on issues that do not become law. From 1905 to the mid-1940s, Congress held, on average, around 200 votes per congress on bills that did not become public laws. From the 1940s till now, that number steadily increased, reaching an average of over 1,500 votes per congress. In the 113th Congress only 15.4% of all roll calls were on measures that became law. In this section we assess the difference between ideological scores and polarization measures when we compare votes on measures that become laws to votes on measures that fail to become law. We do this by estimating NOMINATE scores only for votes that occurred on passing measures and comparing these scores to scores estimated with the full roll call record for the House and Senate for both the 112th and 113th Congresses. The results are reported in Figure 6.5.

For the 112th House, both Democrats and Republicans appear less polarized when votes that become law are analyzed. Republicans appear more moderate in the 113th House, while Democrats are not systematically more or less moderate. The 112th Senate appears less moderate across both parties,

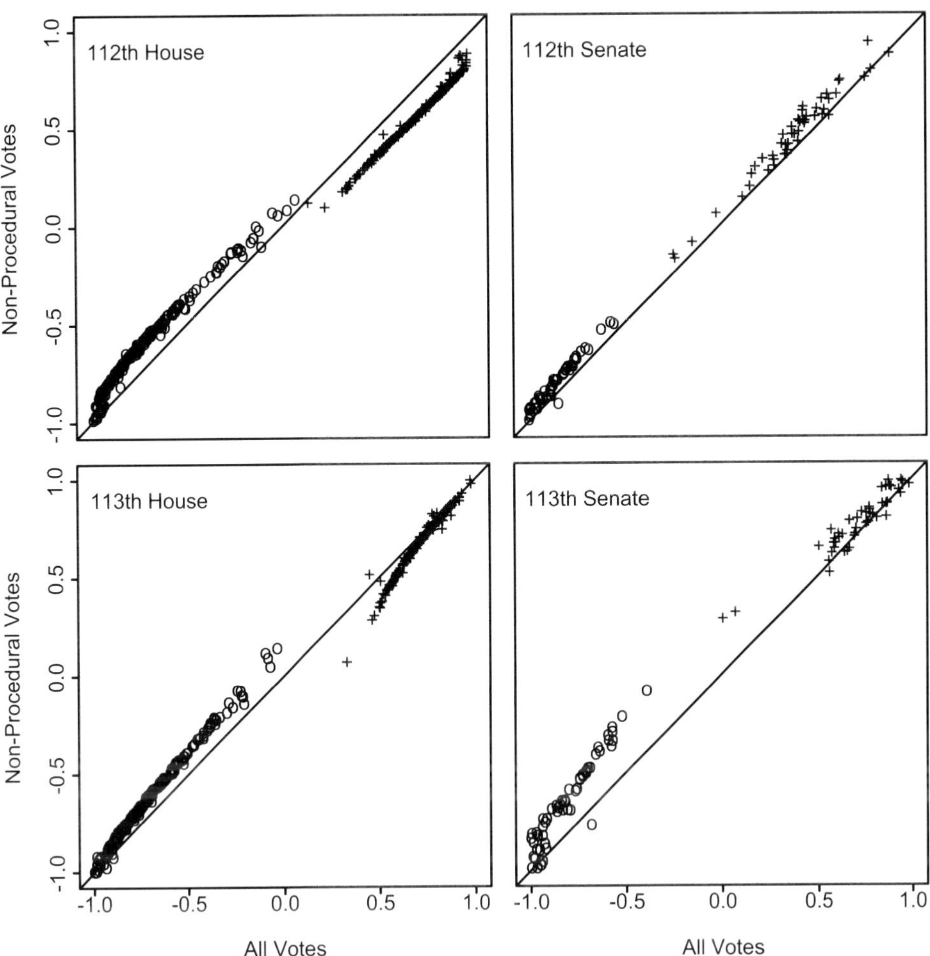

Figure 6.3. NOMINATE and Non-Procedural Votes

while the 113th Senate shows moderation among Democrats but little change among Republicans.

Compare this to score measures using only votes on failing measures. These are reported in Figure 6.6. Voting on failing measures and voting on the full record appear virtually indistinguishable in the 112th and 113th House. This is at least in part because the vast majority of the full roll call record was on failing measures in these two Houses. Senate voting also appears similar between voting on the full record and voting only on failing measures. The exception to this is that Republicans appear more polarized on failing measures than on the full record in the 112th Senate.

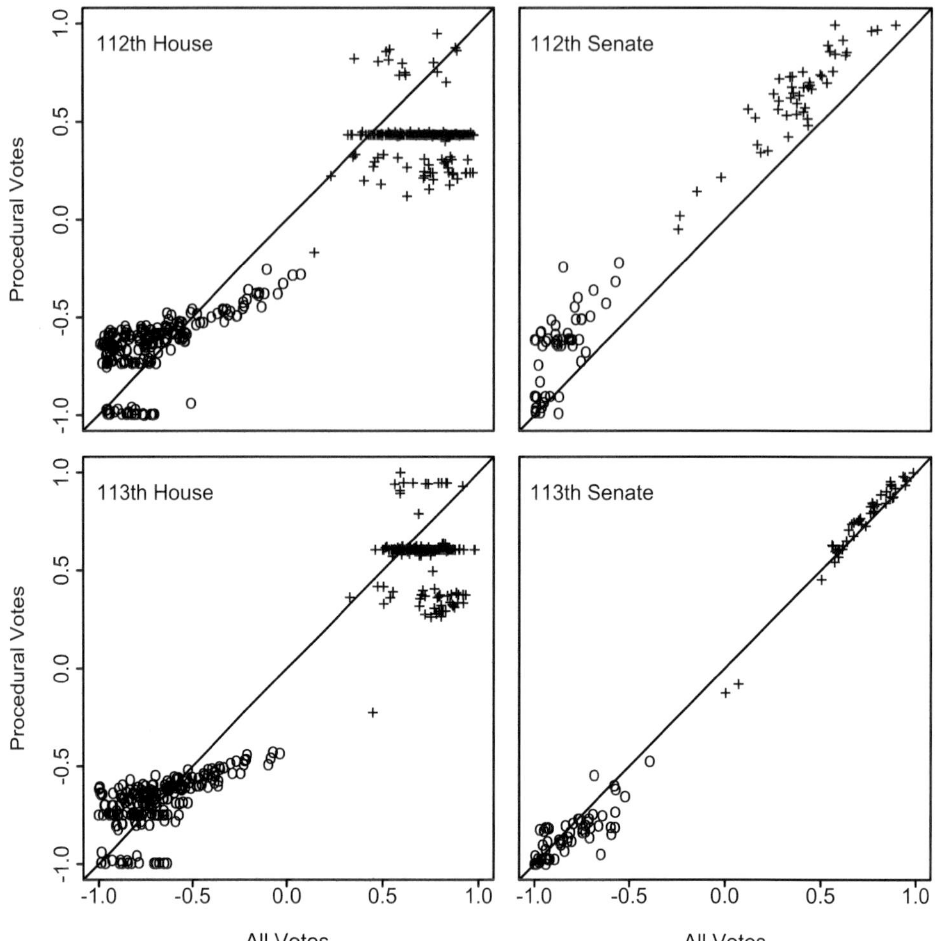

Figure 6.4. NOMINATE and Procedural Votes

Conclusion

It seems that the voting patterns found in the 112th and 113th Congresses are the new normal. The roll call record is filled with party voting, much of it on procedural votes and failing amendment votes that have little to do with policymaking. If parties have splits in their caucuses, they can pull bills to avoid revealing those in the record. If there are issues that must pass, they can be packaged in omnibus legislation that makes it difficult for voters to track or understand.

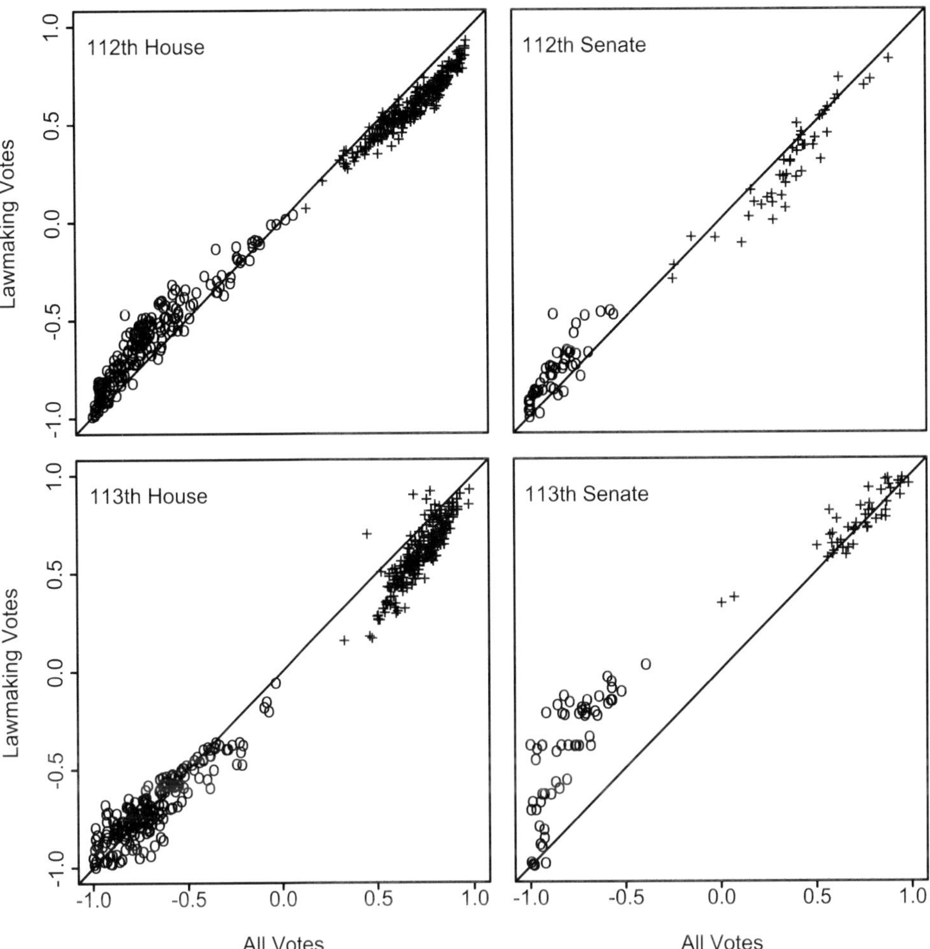

Figure 6.5. NOMINATE and Passing Measures

The simulations presented in this chapter make it clear that changing patterns of roll call vote generation make it difficult for congressional scholars to measure legislative behavior. Since the process that generates roll call votes has changed drastically in the last several decades, it is hard to evaluate changes in legislative behavior. Simulations indicate that increased party voting can greatly inflate the observed level of polarization in Congress. Measures of legislative behavior, like polarization rates, are susceptible to fairly limited increases in the number of party-line votes.

So how polarized is today's Congress? It is hard to know how much higher levels of polarization are driving Congress to hold more party votes and how

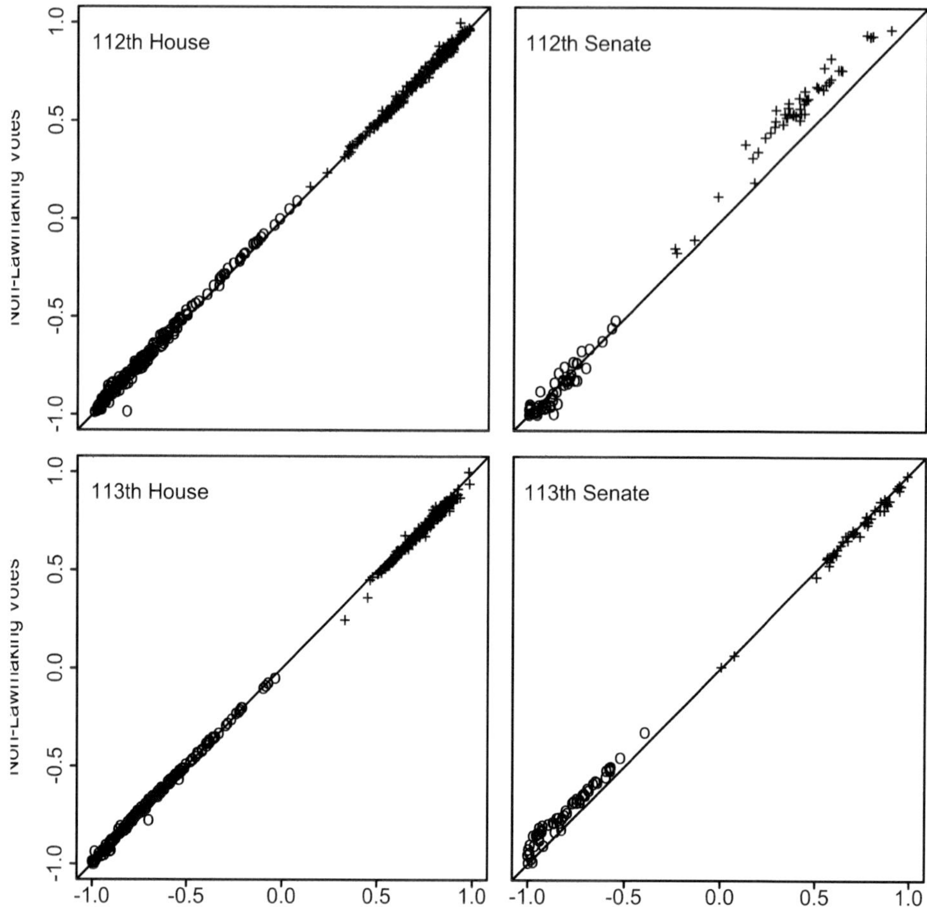

Figure 6.6. NOMINATE and Failing Measures

much higher levels of party votes are driving increases in measures of polarization. Congress is clearly more polarized than it has been in the past, but it is also clear that Congress is writing its own test. Party leaders are in full control of the agenda that scholars use to assess polarization. They can add party votes at will, and party leaders, from both the majority and minority, can work together to alter the roll call record such that Congress can effectively choose how polarized it would like to appear.

SEVEN

The Roll Call Record

Endless Loops, Skipped Tracks, and a Distorted Sound

> Mr. Gorham was opposed to the motion for allowing a single member to call the yeas and nays, and recited the abuses of it in Massachusetts; first, in stuffing the Journals with them on frivolous occasions; secondly, in misleading the people, who never know the reasons determining the votes.
>
> —Max Farrand, 1966

> When things are driving me insane; / Let me hear that same rhythm ring; / Over and over and over; / And over and over and over and over again.
>
> —Van Morrison

Institutional Design and Recorded Voting Revisited

It is nearly impossible to overstate the importance of the roll call voting record in Congress to both scholars of American politics and the general public. For scholars, roll call votes are attractive because they represent "hard data" that can be both "simple and precise" (Truman 1951, 12; Rice 1925, 60). Given this, it is not surprising that searching for "roll call" and "Congress" in J-STOR generates nearly 13,000 results. For the public, the casting of recorded votes is, as John Jay argued in 1779, "almost the only way in which our constituents can be informed of the conduct of their respective delegates."[1] Echoing that sentiment nearly 200 years later, Rep. John Emerson Moss (D-CA) argued that an expanded roll call voting record was necessary because "There is a need to know how we vote in order that an honest evaluation of our effectiveness as a Representative may be made by the voters in the election" (*Congressional Record*, 91st Congress, July 27, 1970, 25804).

Does the roll call voting record provide scholars and the general public with the ability to honestly evaluate congressional behavior, as Jay and Moss suggest? Has it ever? This study has attempted to gain leverage on these questions by providing a broad examination of the creation and evolution of roll call voting in Congress. After discussing the institutional design chosen by the Founders to set the rules for recorded voting, we sought to determine how the record evolved through the history of Congress. We also attempted to assess the degree to which the record is representative of the lawmaking undertaken by Congress. To examine the makeup of the roll call record, we need data not just on recorded votes, but on measures that passed via unrecorded voting. Accordingly, we expanded existing roll call vote databases but also collected new data on major federal legislation, floor amendments to major federal laws, and House special rules that passed by both recorded and unrecorded votes.

We began this book by laying out several questions related to the roll call voting record in Congress. First, we set out to document the origins of recorded voting. Where did the practice of recording votes for public consumption originate? How widely accepted was it? What motivated the Framers to design such a formal rule providing for roll call votes in the Constitution? Finally, we asked if their design worked as it was intended. We argue in this chapter that the rules provided by the Framers did not prevent frivolous and misleading votes.

Second, we sought to document how the roll call record has changed. How often have roll call vote requests been denied? What factors led to the massive increase in recorded voting? How have party leaders and bill managers responded? Are certain types of motions, votes, and proposals more represented in the modern roll call record than in previous eras of Congress? Overall, the data show the biggest change in the roll call record is a sharp rise in redundancy. The contemporary roll call record has become an endless loop, with parties documenting their differences with repeated party-line votes, frequently on measures that never become law. While Congress still occasionally skips tracks by strategically avoiding uncomfortable recorded votes, the key change revealed in our analyses is that Congress is effectively playing the same song, over and over again.

Finally, we endeavored to examine what implications the changing roll call record has for voters, scholars, and members themselves. Is the record "broken," as some have suggested? We find the answer is yes. The sheer volume of recorded voting, combined with the fact that so little of this voting is on measures that become law, means that the roll call record has become less useful for the public, scholars, and Congress. The current record distorts as much as it informs. Without reform, the public will struggle to effectively monitor Congress and understand lawmaking.

Transparency and the Origins of the Roll Call Record

Few concepts are more positively ingrained in American democracy than transparency. And rightfully so. Voters need information in order to make informed decisions and to hold their elected representatives accountable for the policy positions they take. Referring to transparency as "sunlight," former Supreme Court Justice Louis Brandeis (1913) is frequently quoted as saying it is the "best of disinfectants" for combating social and industrial diseases. In congressional politics, roll call votes represent a vital component of transparency. In contrast to speeches or debates, they are said to provide "hard data" for voters seeking information on their members' policy positions (Truman 1951).

As we have argued throughout this manuscript, the relationship between transparency and democratic governance is rarely this straightforward. The Founders grappled with this during the Constitutional Convention. Ultimately, they decided secrecy—not transparency—was essential to forming and ratifying a new Constitution (Beeman 2010; Berkin 2002; Hoffman 1981). They adopted a rule barring the publication or communication of anything "spoken in the House" during debate (Berkin 2002, 64). James Madison would later declare, "No Constitution would ever have been adopted by the convention if the debates had been public" (Hoffman 1981, 21).[2]

While we often take recorded voting in Congress for granted, the decision to provide for a yeas and nays clause in the Constitution was not something the Founders settled on lightly. As we detail in Chapter 2, a formal yeas and nays clause was an American phenomenon and not a mechanism with a long, successful track record in democratic legislatures. Moreover, most members were aware of the limitations of roll call voting from their experiences under the Articles of Confederation, as well as some problems in early state legislative assemblies. In arguing against roll call voting, Nathaniel Gorham pointed to abuses of it in his home state of Massachusetts, noting that it led to members "stuffing the Journals with [votes] on frivolous occasions" and "misleading the people, who never know the reasons determining the votes" (Farrand 1966, 255). On one hand, Gorham's concerns could be viewed as his being skeptical of providing the public with information. An alternative interpretation is Gorham was concerned about how recorded voting could be constructed such that votes confused and misled the public, rather than providing them with a representative record of the legislative work of Congress.

Specifically, his motivation was not to hide the records of members on important policy questions. Rather, he was concerned the recorded voting provision would incentivize members to produce more roll calls in order to distort the policymaking process in Congress. In this respect, Gorham and others were not challenging the notion that Congress should be transparent to voters; rather they were suggesting "more information" did not necessarily result in "more transparency." In more contemporary terms, they were concerned roll call voting would result in "information overload" (Gross 1964; Toffler 1970). The prevalence of large amounts of information, often disorganized and presented without context, allows activists ample material that they can use to spin multiple narratives to confuse voters (Andrejevic 2013).

Gorham and others' skepticism was mollified at the convention by the inclusion of a sufficient second provision with a comparatively higher threshold. As we detail with both assorted cases and data in Chapter 2, the sufficient second clause did provide some relief for members looking to bypass "journal stuffing" votes—at least initially. But was it successful overall at preventing members from filling the record with the type of frivolous and misleading votes that Gorham feared? The evidence is this book indicates the answer is no.

The sufficient second clause was effective at deterring roll call requests early in congressional history. When congressional attendance was low, members were hesitant to record votes that documented their fellow members' absences, making denials of roll call requests common. But as attendance has improved, aided by members' ability to travel more easily to and from Washington, recorded vote requests became more and more likely to receive a sufficient second.

While the sufficient second clause is technically in effect in the House and Senate, roll call requests have effectively become pro forma in the modern Congress. Rather than use the sufficient second clause to limit recorded votes, modern congressional leaders have instead controlled the creation of the roll call record via agenda-setting mechanisms like omnibus lawmaking, restrictive rules, and the scheduling of votes on measures that are redundant and/or unlikely to ever become law. When a measure is allowed a vote on the floor, contemporary agenda setters understand they can do little to prevent a recorded vote.

In fact, the rare denial of a sufficient second is newsworthy because of its novelty.[3] In 2020, in the face of an emerging covid outbreak, Congress crafted the bipartisan $2.2 trillion CARES Act to combat the pandemic.[4] Due to the potential risks of infection for members packed in the House chamber, leaders sought to pass the measure via voice vote (Stolberg 2020). However, in the days leading up to floor consideration, Rep. Thomas Massie (R-KY) announced his intentions to request a recorded vote. This request drew a wide range of criticism from Republicans and Democrats alike. Rep. Peter King (R-NY) complained that large numbers of members "had to be in House Chamber and risk infection to themselves & others because of 1 arrogant Member." Rep. Dan Kildee (D-MI) dubbed it an "an act of vanity and selfishness that goes beyond comprehension" (DeBonis 2020a). And President Donald Trump called Massie a "third-rate grandstander" (Forgey 2020).[5]

Massie argued that by pressing for a voice vote on the "biggest spending bill in the history of mankind," Speaker Nancy Pelosi (D-CA) and House Minority Leader Kevin McCarthy (R-CA) were trying "to insulate members of Congress from accountability." The CARES Act was brought to the House floor on March 27, 2020. Members then filled the chamber, including seats in the gallery, to maintain appropriate social distancing. Following debate on the bill, Massie said, "I came here to make sure our republic doesn't die by unanimous consent in an empty chamber and request a recorded vote" (Forgey 2020). The request was denied and the bill was adopted via voice vote.[6]

Despite Massey's rebuke, it is much more typical for recorded votes to be granted to all requests, even the most egregious attempts to fill the record with meaningless votes. As discussed in Chapter 6, Rep. Marjorie Taylor Greene (R-GA) repeatedly attempted to adjourn the House during morning speeches during the 117th Congress. She requested and was granted recorded votes after each of these attempts. Even though these unplanned roll call votes angered and disrupted members of both parties, no attempt was made to deny Greene the sufficient second technically needed to receive a recorded vote. The Founders' hopes that the sufficient second clause would protect the record from frivolous votes have not come to pass.

The Changing Content of the Record

During consideration of H.R. 5161, the Commerce, Justice, State, and Judiciary Appropriations Act for 1987, Rep. Bob Walker (R-PA) offered an amendment that sought to strike $50 million in funds from the bill and allocate them to the "war on drugs." The amendment fell 256–150. A gleeful Walker would later tell a reporter, "Any congressional candidate worth his salt can figure out how to use a no vote on my amendment to say that either the guy doesn't understand the issue or he chose pork over a war on drugs." The amendment was just one of 38 offered by Walker in the 99th Congress, the most by a House member. His behavior drew the ire of not just majority-party Democrats, but the media as well, leading to a *Washington Post* article that asked whether "Bob Walker [was] the most obnoxious man in Congress" (Carlson 1986). What constituted obnoxious behavior in 1986 is routine in the contemporary US Congress.

Since the sufficient second clause has not restricted recorded voting in the ways intended by the Founders, what impact has this had on the content of the roll call record? The data presented in this book show that the record is filled with the type of frivolous votes the Founders feared. There is an endless loop of votes that highlight the differences between the parties but do little to inform the public about lawmaking. The sharp increase in messaging votes, like Walker's failing amendment, is an example of the type of frivolous votes increasingly occurring within the record (see, e.g., Lee 2009; Lee 2016). Other changes, like the increase of procedural roll calls and the increased likelihood proposals by more ideologically extreme members will get recorded votes represent notable departures from previous congressional eras. Parties and members are increasingly using recorded votes to document their political differences rather than their policy accomplishments.

The Founders also feared that Congress might try to avoid recorded votes to prevent the public from having a transparent view of Congress's work. While it is much rarer than Congress's habit of filling the record with frivolous votes, Congress still occasionally prevents measures from receiving a recorded vote. These attempts to prevent recorded votes, or "skipped tracks" as we call them here, inhibit the transparency hoped for by the Founders.

The result is a roll call record that does not inform the public of Congress's lawmaking activities, but instead distorts the meaning of votes and misleads the public. There has been a significant increase in roll calls on measures with limited policy impact. As noted in Chapter 3, the percentage of recorded votes on measures eventually enacted into law during the last 10 congresses in our dataset is nearly half that of the first 10 congresses. As documented in Chapter 4, the rise in recorded votes on process motions that theoretically lack any "traceability" to voters has mirrored increased procedural warfare in both the House and the Senate. Minorities transform these votes into messaging opportunities, claiming majority-party members' votes on things like motions to recommit and previous question motions are not boring procedural votes, but rather evidence of their political opponent's unpopular, and possibly dangerous, views on the key political issues of the day. When votes on actual lawmaking do take place, omnibus legislation obscures members' positions on the multiple issues contained within these bills. This all combines to make the modern roll call record simply too confusing for the public to follow and understand; sometimes the record even confounds the authors of a book about the roll call record.

Endless Loops

Perhaps the most substantial shift in the record is the sharp rise in redundancy. The contemporary roll call record tends to play the same song over and over again. Through control over the agenda-setting process, the majority party is bringing measures to the floor it knows will present a united front. Moreover, improved coordination allows it the ability to make post hoc adjustments and pull measures before potential embarrassment may occur. Such behavior may overstate the degree of unity a party may have on a given policy.

The 50-plus roll call votes taken by Republicans on repealing the Affordable Care Act are instructive on this point. Republicans appeared unified against the ACA throughout the Obama presidency, knowing Obama's veto power meant none of these 50-plus repeal attempts risked becoming law. Things changed in 2017, when Republican control of the House, the Senate, and the presidency meant Republicans could repeal ACA without any Democratic support. Now that the Republicans' repeal-and-replace bill, the American Health Care Act, had the possibility of becoming law and radically altering the American healthcare system, Republican unity on healthcare suddenly faded. There were 20 Republicans who voted against the American Health Care Act in the House. Of those 20, all but a freshman member had voted for at least one measure that would have repealed the ACA without a replacement during the 112th, 113th, and 114th Congresses. One of those members, Rep. Dave Reichert (R-WA), voted in favor of the American Health Care Act in committee, but ultimately changed his position, justifying his no vote on the grounds that "the GOP plan fell short in protecting poor kids and those with pre-existing conditions" (Person 2017). Notably, none of the previous repeal measures Reichert voted for contained any such protections. Despite the endless loop of votes recording Republican opposition to the ACA, Republican efforts to repeal and replace the ACA ultimately failed due to a lack of Republican unity on the issue, leaving the ACA to remain the law of the land.

As we have demonstrated, this is further muddled by a significant increase in roll calls on measures with limited policy impact. As noted in Chapter 3, the percentage of recorded votes on measures eventually enacted into law during the last 10 congresses in our dataset is nearly half that of the first 10 congresses. This increase in recorded voting on substantive "messaging" bills is accompanied by a rapid rise in roll call votes on procedural issues.

Skipped Tracks

Problems stemming from the roll call record repeating the same types of votes are compounded by the number of important policy choices made by Congress that do not receive recorded votes. This has been fairly well documented by earlier scholarship (Clinton and Lapinski 2008; Lynch and Madonna 2013a) and ample anecdotal evidence. Additional data from our amendment dataset further illustrates this point. Simply because a proposal did not receive a recorded vote, does not mean it lacked conflict or disagreement. As we have documented in Chapter 2 (see Figure 2.3), requests for the yeas and nays were frequently rejected, even in the latter half of the 20th century.

Additionally, measures that have been passed via voice vote, may still mask some disagreement. For example, final passage of the Legislative Reorganization Act of 1945 was adopted in the Senate via voice vote.[7] However, immediately afterward, a number of senators announced their opposition to the motion in the *Congressional Record*. Sen. Walter George (D-GA) held the floor and yielded to these members to make their announcements. Eventually, George announced that he had "better decline to yield further, or else a majority of the Senate may go on record as being opposed to the reorganization bill" (*Congressional Record*, 79th Congress, July 26, 1946, 10152).

In more recent congresses, major pieces of legislation will still occasionally pass without recorded votes. From the 104th to the 113th Congresses, the last 10 congresses in our data, 33 out of 360 (9.2%) pieces of important legislation did not receive a final passage vote in the House. And 67 out of 360 (18.6%) did not receive one in the Senate. The vast majority of these were due to broad support and a lack of interest on the part of individuals in pursuing a roll call. However, there are notable cases even in the contemporary period where roll calls were blocked on important measures.

Several high-profile cases further illustrate this point. The 2015 episode involving Cruz discussed in Chapter 2 is one. Other cases had even greater policy implications. In 2014, Speaker John Boehner (R-OH) angered many conservatives in his caucus when he worked with minority Democratic leadership to pass a short-term "doc fix" bill via a voice vote.[8] The maneuver was done while most members were out of the chamber and, thus, unable to request a roll call vote. Members were highly critical of the maneuver. Rep. Steve King (R-IA) said "[the vote] erodes our confidence in our own system" and expressed skepticism that the extension would have passed if there had been a recorded vote (Newhauser and Fuller 2014). Despite these public complaints, a number of "opponents" of the bill still supported the policy but feared the electoral consequences of voting for it.[9] In perhaps the most unusual example of unrecorded voting, in 2018 the US Senate adopted a treaty making it easier for the disabled to gain access to music and literature by division vote despite only one senator, Majority Leader Mitch McConnell (R-KY), being present (Ota 2018).

Distorted Sounds from a Broken Record

Skipped tracks may deprive political campaigns from the "smoking gun" roll call vote they can use to "persuade citizens how poorly their current representatives have served their interests" (Arnold 1990, 49). However, modern majorities recognize the difficulty in preventing a recorded vote once a measure reaches the floor. As detailed in Chapter 3, they combat this primarily through agenda-setting techniques. This includes both blocking potentially divisive proposals from floor consideration and crafting large, omnibus pieces of legislation. While this tactic doesn't allow them to "skip" a track or a vote, it does let them pack so much into the vote that they can spin it a number of ways in a campaign or election. As a result, the sound the public hears is highly distorted.

For example, in 2016, the Zika virus had become a pressing issue in Florida. In February, President Obama had called for $1.9 billion in funds to combat the disease, and Sen. Marco Rubio (R-FL), who was up for reelection against House Rep. Patrick Murphy (D-FL), immediately cosponsored a bill with Sen. Bill Nelson (D-FL) that provided the requested funding. After the bill was passed, House Republicans balked at the price and instead passed a bill providing for only $622 million in funds, and also including an amendment barring any of those funds from going to Planned Parenthood in Puerto Rico (Herszenhorn 2016; Shutt 2016). Murphy had announced his support for the Rubio-Nelson Senate bill but joined nearly all Democrats in voting against the House bill. While a compromise amount of $1.1 billion eventually passed both chambers, both the Rubio and Murphy camps were able to pull votes out of episode they could use to justify attacking each other for not properly supporting Zika funding. Specifically, Rubio's camp claimed that "Patrick Murphy is the only candidate to have voted against every measure to fund Zika." And NARAL Pro-Choice America sponsored a television ad on behalf of Murphy that asserted "Marco Rubio voted against funding health clinics that provide critical care during this public health emergency." *PolitiFact* rated both claims as false (Gillin 2016; Sherman 2016).

Much like the 2016 Zika vote, attack ads are "dueling" in nature, meaning both candidates attack each other for the exact same vote. For example, during one of their gubernatorial debates in 2015, Sen. David Vitter (R-LA) accused former state house Rep. John Bel Edwards (D-LA) of voting to raise his own pay as a state house member. In response, Edwards asserted that Vitter had "been lying sideways in the public crawl since 1992. You make $40,000 a year more now in the Senate than when you got elected to the Senate." Another example occurred in the 2012 Montana Senate general election, where Rep. Denny Rehberg (R-MT) ran ads asserting Sen. John Tester (D-MT) voted to "raise his own pay." Tester ran a similar ad asserting Rehberg voted to "raise his own pay five times." This also occurred in the 2016 Arizona Senate race, where Sen. John McCain (R-AZ) attacked Rep. Ann Kirkpatrick (D-AZ) for voting to increase her own salary.[10]

Misleading advertisements like these are quite common. Indeed, the website *PolitiFact* checked the accuracy of the 243 statements and advertisements referencing a politician's voting record from 2010 to 2018 and reported that just over half of them could be classified as "mostly false," "false," or "pants on fire."[11] False campaign advertising is nearly impossible to regulate. The courts will not enforce statutes barring false campaign advertising unless a plaintiff can demonstrate "actual malice" (Goldman 2008).[12]

Most of the few attempts to regulate false campaign advertising through statute have been done at the state level. These attempts have either been ineffective or, in several instances, successfully challenged on First Amendment grounds (Lieffring 2012). This was reinforced at the federal level by *United States v. Alvarez*, which struck down the Stolen Valor Act of 2005. The act made making a fraudulent claim about receiving a decoration or medal awarded by the president or armed forces a federal crime. Xavier Alvarez, a member of a district water board in Claremont, California, violated the act and was indicted. Alvarez's indictment was originally upheld but overturned by the Ninth Circuit Court of Appeals. The Supreme Court then upheld the Ninth Circuit decision and struck down the Stolen Valor Act on First Amendment grounds (Lieffring 2012). The courts' rulings on these cases has led legal scholars to conclude "because of the *New York Times Co. v. Sullivan* line of cases, requiring proof of actual malice in the form of knowledge of falsity or reckless disregard for the truth," there is virtually no remedy for [false advertising]" (Ashdown 2011, 1087).

The public's ability to figure out what is true and false about the activities of Congress is further hampered as the volume of voting activity has increased. As an example, consider the rise in recorded voting on previous question motions. Demanding recorded votes on previous question motions has become a popular tool of electoral messaging among minority-party members. For example, in 2009, the House considered H.R. 1388, the Serve America Act. This measure, which expanded service programs like AmeriCorps, SeniorCorps, and Learn and Serve America, had broad bipartisan support. The structured rule, under which the bill was considered, made in order all proposed amendments by minority-party Republicans, giving Republicans little reason to demand a recorded previous question vote as a form of protest about the rule. While Republicans praised the rule, they still urged a no vote on the previous question motion. Explaining his position, Rep. Steven LaTourette (R-OH) stated that his no vote was a function of Republicans wanting to offer an amendment to the rule calling up an unrelated bill. He argued, "I intend to vote 'no' on the previous question on this particular rule. I don't have any big problem with the rule, but it is my understanding that Mr. Diaz-Balart will, if it is defeated, offer an amendment to the rule that will address a topic that isn't the subject of the GIVE Act, but the AIG bonuses" (*Congressional Record*, 111th Congress, March 18, 2009, H3540).[13]

From the 59th Congress to the 115th Congress, minority-party members have requested and received 1,089 recorded votes on previous question motions.[14] Holding a recorded vote on whether the chamber should precede to a vote tells the public very little about lawmaking. Indeed, who votes yea or nay for a previous question motion typically looks very similar to who votes yea or nay for the underlying measure. These 1,089 votes provide minority-party members with an opportunity to talk about issues, like bonuses for AIG executives, that have nothing to do with the legislation under consideration. Unfortunately, this messaging opportunity comes at the cost of a roll call record filled with repetitive votes that confuse, rather than inform, voters about lawmaking.

The other side of this story is the dramatic drop in the percentage of recorded votes on measures eventually enacted into public law. From 1905 to 1994, the average percentage of roll calls on measures enacted into law was around 55%. In the most recent 12 congresses in our dataset, it has averaged 29.5%. Our data suggest the increase in recorded voting documented in Chapter 1 is heavily driven by messaging votes on substantive policies, many of which have little chance of becoming law, and procedural votes that produce a glut of party-line votes. The roll call votes provide campaign consultants with fodder come election season but do little for the media and general public. As Congress fills the record with electorally motivated votes, less and less of the roll call record represents actually lawmaking. When the public looks to the record to monitor their representatives or understand lawmaking, the record plays a distorted sound, masking both the true positions of members and the legislative output of Congress.

Implications of a "Broken Record"

The utility provided by the modern roll call record is likely overstated, especially as a source of information for the public. While information about Congress is easy to find, it is difficult to understand. The sheer volume of votes, combined with a complicated legislative process, can leave visitors to websites like Congress.gov quickly overwhelmed. Procedural votes can be difficult to understand, as can concepts that are unique to Congress, such as cloture, reconciliation, or structured rules. Members of the public are unlikely to have the specialized knowledge to track a bill and understand how it is moving through the legislative process.

A nice example of this is the 118th Congress's H.R. 2872. This bill began as a House effort to amend the Permanent Electronic Duck Stamp Act of 2013 to allow states to issue electronic stamps that lasted the entire hunting season, removing the 45-day limit currently placed on duck stamps. The seemingly uncontroversial bill passed the House on September 20, 2023, via a voice vote under suspension of the rules. On January 11, 2024, the Senate brought the duck stamp bill up for consideration. On January 16, a successful cloture vote on the motion to precede opened the path for the Senate to consider the bill, but why did a duck stamp bill need a cloture vote? Was someone filibustering the bill? The apparent opposition to the bill makes more sense when Sen. Patty Murray (D-WA) proposed a substitute amendment on January 17 that struck all language about hunting stamps and replaced it with language turning the bill into the Further Additional Continuing Appropriations Act of 2024. This humble duck-related bill was transformed into a continuing resolution negotiated by Majority Leader Chuck Schumer (D-NY) and Speaker Mike Johnson (R-LA) that provided the government funding through March 1, 2024, preventing a shutdown of part of the government, when funding was scheduled to run out on January 19.[15]

Implications for the Public

The difficult paths often taken by legislation, coupled with the sheer volume of information about Congress, leave the public with simply too much information. In addition to official congressional records, public statements and speeches by members of Congress are readily available, as are news stories and commentary from a plethora of social media posts and news outlets. The result is information overload.

Curtin and Meijer (2006) discuss the concept of "information overload" in regards to an online collection of European Union policy documents. They argue that information overload

> refers to the fact that it is impossible for a normal citizen to understand all information on policymaking processes both because of the quantity of the information available or received as well as the specific terms and explanations used. . . . Even experts have a hard time in dealing with the incredible amount of information. In this situation one can question whether more information indeed leads to more legitimacy. (Curtin and Meijer 2006, 116)[16]

The large amounts of information created by Congress creates a similar information overload for voters interacting with the roll call record and the multitude of other sources of information about Congress.

When the public can't make heads or tails of information on Congress, there are plenty of actors willing to help. Politicians, interest groups, and media sources with a defined ideological bias are more than happy to help the public understand the work of Congress. Unfortunately for the public, these actors are not incentivized to provide an objective look at Congress. Misleading and incorrect explanations of its work abound.

The media plays a role in providing the objective examination of Congress that would help the public better understand Congress. And many in the media do an excellent job of documenting and explaining how Congress works. We are personally indebted to the many congressional reporters whom we have relied on to help us understand Congress. Unfortunately, the number of media outlets that actively report on Congress has been in decline in recent history. In 1975 there were 858 daily press media outlets and 160 periodical press outlets that were officially credentialed by Congress (Eckman 2017). By 2015, these numbers had fallen to 192 print media outlets and 143 periodical press outlets. While traditional media sources continue to work to explain the work of Congress, fewer outlets support this work, and nontraditional media sources, like social media, explain the work of Congress without the benefit of the training nor code of ethics shared by traditional journalists.

Implications for Scholars

The changing roll call record presents a series of challenges for scholars of Congress. First, scholars must recognize that the data-generating process that creates roll call votes is very inconsistent across the history of Congress. Comparing roll-call-derived data from recent congresses and historical congresses should be done with caution. When measures like polarization rates change across the history of Congress, it is difficult to assess how much of the reported increases in polarization are the result of true increases in polarization, as opposed to changes that are an artifact of a changing roll call record. As Chapter 6 demonstrated, small increases in party-line votes lead to large increases in polarization rates.

Scholars should also reconsider which votes to include in their analyses. While the "all votes" approach used by NOMINATE and most other scaling techniques has afforded a great deal of utility, less may be more in many contexts. Some types of votes should never be included in analysis. Indeed, NOMINATE excludes votes on quorum calls from its datasets. Votes to approve the journal do not provide any information about ideology and should be added to the list of votes to exclude from analysis.

Knowing which votes to drop is challenging. For example, measures like previous question motions rarely appear in the record in early congresses and are very common now. Would removing recorded votes on the previous question motions improve historical comparison, without the loss of much important information? It seems the answer is yes. But what other measures to exclude and when to stop? It might be more fruitful to think about what data to retain. Clinton (2007) makes a compelling case that using only successful final passage votes is a good choice for his study examining competing lawmaking theories. Limiting analysis to final passages votes provides the votes most emblematic of lawmaking while excluding those most susceptible to a changing roll call record. There is no right answer here, other than that the inconsistent roll call generating process must be recognized and accounted for.

Implications for Congress

Despite the lack of consensus among scholars about whether the electorate is influenced by recorded voting in Congress, members have clearly demonstrated they believe recorded voting could be determinative to the outcomes of both primary and general elections. Discussions of recorded voting dominate Congress. As we documented through case studies and quotes, the increased use of omnibus lawmaking, the rise in messaging votes on bills and amendments unlikely to become law, the increase in roll calls on procedural matters, the use of restrictive floor rules in the House, and filled amendment trees in the Senate all partially stem from a desire to avoid or mitigate the impact of "tough votes." Consistent with this, scholars have observed that greater transparency in Congress, while providing many normative benefits, has made dealmaking more difficult and the lawmaking process less efficient (Binder and Lee 2016).

To curb electorally motivated usage of the roll call record, Congress could alter its rules. While any specific rules reforms would need to account for the differing procedural environments in the House and Senate, we do believe a broader alteration of standing rules could benefit Congress, provided this was done with an eye toward simplification and a reduction of redundancy. There are some precedents for this approach. Speaker Thomas Reed (R-ME) and his Reed's Rules provide an example of a Speaker taking actions to limit dilatory motions and thus reduce votes on these now disallowed motions. Speakers in this era used their powers as Speaker in combination with formal rules changes to limit voting in a variety of ways. For example, changing the rules to limit or eliminate roll calls on the previous question motion seems to be an obvious area for potential reform. Their documented usage against incumbents during primary campaigns (e.g., see the "pay raise" examples discussed earlier in this chapter) might provide members with the electoral incentives needed to support such reform efforts.

While reforming standing rules to minimize the potential for redundant roll calls may provide normative benefits for both Congress and the public, we do not think efforts to restrict voting are likely to be successful. As we have documented, congressional reforms regarding recorded voting have largely been geared toward making recorded votes easier to obtain. As an example, the House changed its rules in 1970 to allow for recorded amendment voting. This change increased transparency but was quickly met with some regret, as recorded votes on floor amendments skyrocketed (Smith 1989). Attempts to roll back this new transparency, by making it more difficult to achieve a sufficient second for amendment votes, were not successful. Convincing voters that reducing transparency is in their best interest is a challenging argument to make. While members express sincere concerns about how increased recorded voting harms chamber efficiency, they still tend to oppose reforms that would improve efficiency. In short, systematic efforts to restrict recorded voting once a proposal is on the floor appear to be unlikely.

Apart from institutional reforms, a second approach would involve disincentivizing members from using the record for electoral posturing. Perhaps the most obvious way to do so would be through a substantive reform of our campaign finance system. But this approach also seems to be politically impracticable. As has been well documented, legal challenges have substantially complicated campaign finance restrictions. Even if there were no constitutional issues, it is unclear whether the quality of the information voters receive would improve.

Another approach to disincentivizing electorally motivated votes could involve convincing members that these votes don't influence voters or elections, or at least not in the way the members intend. Members think these types of votes matter, but there are plenty of reasons to be skeptical of such a conclusion. As we have argued, monitoring legislative behavior through recorded voting is difficult. Voters lack the time and capacity to observe and process all roll calls. This is especially true in recent congresses, as votes and issues have covered increasingly complex topics. The public is generally not getting the message that messaging votes are intended to send. On the rare occasions when voters are informed about roll call behavior, it is often via negative advertising, and campaigns have virtually no incentives to portray roll call votes truthfully. False or misleading campaign advertising is nearly impossible to regulate. In this political environment, there should be minimal incentives for members to vote strategically for electoral purposes. Why hold messaging votes when the message either goes unheard or is distorted by political opponents?

Final Thoughts

In our view, the project presented in this book highlights the need for more research within the intersection between American political institutions and voting behavior. While scholars have made great strides in this area in recent years, there are still a number of questions regarding the ability of the public to monitor their elected officials that we don't know the answer to. Does the public hold strong, consistent opinions on certain legislative rules or features? Do these opinions ever trump ideological or partisan views? Are they impacted by issues like legislative complexity and salience? Are advertisements highlighting a member's vote or voting record effective compared to advertisements drawing attention to a member's position or statement on an issue? More work on questions like these is necessary in order draw a consensus on the utility of messaging votes and potential internal reforms.

Additionally, our examination of the construction of the roll call voting record suggests the record might be beneficial to scholars in new applications. Congressional scholars have traditionally used the record as a tool to evaluate the ideology of individual members. As we have argued, that may be problematic. However, we believe the study of the construction of the roll call record reveals useful information about the priorities of parties and individual members. Utilizing data on what does and does not receive a roll call may help scholars better determine what policies are more likely to change in a given congress. This is a rich and underutilized resource for scholars of congressional politics.

Finally, the story of the roll call record demonstrates the importance of having a consistent data-generating process while conducting any longitudinal analysis. Changes to the roll call generating process not only pose problems for scholars of political polarization but represent challenges to all scholars looking at historical change in Congress. To understand how Congress changes over time, we must first understand how the data we use to study Congress have changed.

Appendixes

Appendix A

Roll Call Vote Type Data

Extending the PIPC Data

Coding roll call vote types began in the fall of 2016. We started with the PIPC Roll Call dataset, which codes each roll call vote by vote type starting with 83rd House (1953–1954) and 91st Senate (1969–1970) (Crespin and Rohde 2016). We then extended it back to the 59th Congress (1905–1906) for both chambers in order to match our unrecorded amendment time series (discussed in Appendix D). In this appendix, we detail our coding process and provide, for robustness purposes, several graphs that utilize the data.

In extending the PIPC dataset, our graduate student coder relied first on original Inter-university Consortium for Political and Social Research (ICPSR) vote descriptions. When questions or ambiguities arose, she then consulted the *Congressional Record* directly. She then matched the procedure used to one of PIPC's 110 different categories of vote type. We then placed those different vote types into one of four categories: (1) passage/final passage; (2) amendment votes; (3) procedural/miscellaneous; and (4) nominations. These categories, as well as a breakdown of the raw number and percentage of the 61,525 roll call votes in our dataset that correspond to each vote type, are presented in Tables A.1 through A.5. An aggregate breakdown across our four categories is presented in Table A.6.

TABLE A1. Passage/Final Passage Vote Types

Code	PIPC Description	count	%
1	Amendments to the Constitution (usually titled a Joint Resolution)	76	0.12
11	Final Passage/Adoption of a Bill	7,312	11.89
12	Final Passage/Adoption of Conference Report	2,245	3.65
13	Final Passage/Adoption of Resolution	1,226	1.99
14	Final Passage/Adoption of Joint Resolution	693	1.13
15	Passage/Adoption of a Bill under Suspension of the Rules	3,336	5.42
16	Passage/Adoption of a Joint Resolution under Suspension of the Rules	162	0.26
17	Final Passage/Adoption of Concurrent Resolution	369	0.6
18	Passage/Adoption of a Concurrent Resolution under Suspension of the Rules	438	0.71
19	Passage/Adoption of a Resolution under Suspension of the Rules	1,008	1.64
30	Passage over Presidential Veto	294	0.48
31	Adoption of First Part of Resolution	26	0.04
32	Adoption of Second Part of Resolution	18	0.03
33	Suspension of Rules for Conference Report	42	0.07
34	Treaty Ratification	421	0.68
68	Motion to Suspend the Rules and Concur	109	0.18
130	Election of Pro Tempore	43	0.07
144	To Terminate Debate	1	0
150	Final Passage of a Private Bill	0	0
155	Final Passage (ratification) of Resolution—Treaties Convention and Associated Protocols	0	0
180	Agree to Committee Report	0	0
181	Agree to a Reservation to a Resolution	101	0.16
184	Adopt Majority Report	1	0
185	Contempt of Congress	0	0
192	Rules of Trial Impeachment	14	0.02

Coding Decisions

Perhaps the most consequential coding decision we made was to place motions to table amendments in the procedural category as opposed to the amendments category. There are 3,678 tabling motions to amendments in our dataset. We placed it in the procedural category as it is not a direct vote on the amendment. Most members tend to complain about use of the motion to table on these grounds. For example, during debate over the Keystone Pipeline, Senate Majority Leader Mitch McConnell (R-KY) tabled a number of Democratic amendments, prompting Democrats like Sen. Edward Markey (D-MA) to complain their amendments were "blocked" (Barron-Lopez 2015).

Our graduate student coder was also tasked with identifying bill numbers for measures subjected to roll call votes. Again, she relied first on the

TABLE A2. Amendment Vote Types

Code	PIPC Description	count	%
21	Straight Amendments (includes en bloc & amendments in the nature of a substitute)	19,982	32.48
22	Amendments to Amendments	1,584	2.57
23	Substitute (to an amendment)	363	0.59
25	Amendment to Amendment to Substitute	29	0.05
26	Perfecting Amendment	64	0.1
27	Amendment to Substitute	536	0.87
28	Perfecting Amendment to Substitute	4	0.01
29	Suspension of Rules to Amend Bill	75	0.12
73	Motion to Agree	187	0.3
75	Motion to Delete	25	0.04
79	Motion to Disagree	100	0.16
82	Motion to Recede	117	0.19
90	Motion to Strike	131	0.21
97	Motion to Recede and Concur (also includes motion to concur)	795	1.29
143	Remove Injunction of Secrecy	3	0
191	Rules of Evidence Impeachment	7	0.01
195	Amendment to Order Impeachment	0	0

original ICPSR vote descriptions generously provided by Keith Poole. When questions or ambiguities arose, she then consulted the *Congressional Record* directly. As we have noted, not all votes can be paired with bills. For examples, votes on nominations, treaties, and pure procedural motions like adopting the House journal could not be matched. Ultimately, we were able to match an underlying bill number to 56,731 of our 61,525 roll calls (92.2%). This was then used in our enactment-level data described in Appendix B.

Additional Graphs

Additional figures are included here for robustness purposes. Figures A.1 and A.2 provide the roll call vote series in the House and Senate from the first Congress (1789–1791) through the 113th Congress (2013–2014). The figures demonstrate relatively low levels of roll call voting in the early congresses, though a spike in the Civil War and Reconstruction eras. Notably, this increase is still markedly lower than the contemporary period.

TABLE A3. Procedural and Miscellaneous Vote Types, Part 1

Code	PIPC Description	count	%
9	Quorum Call	18	0.03
24	Motion to Table Amendment	3,678	5.98
52	Judgment of the Senate	119	0.19
53	Motion to Instruct Sergeant at Arms	20	0.03
54	Motion to Suspend Senate Rules	47	0.08
55	Motion to Extend Debate	1	0
56	Motion to Discharge	53	0.09
57	Point of Order	83	0.13
58	Motion to Go into Executive Committee	23	0.04
59	Unanimous Consent Motion to Table	3	0
60	Motion to Waive Gramm-Rudman Requirements	18	0.03
61	Budget Waivers	673	1.09
62	Motion to Invoke Cloture	1,198	1.95
63	Motion to Reconsider	271	0.44
64	Motion to Waive	2	0
66	Motion to Proceed	314	0.51
67	Appeal of the Chair's Ruling	155	0.25
69	Miscellaneous	302	0.49
72	Motion to Recommit to Conference	218	0.35
74	Motion to Postpone	59	0.1
76	Motion to End Debate	52	0.08
77	Motion to Rise from the Committee of the Whole	152	0.25
80	Amendment to Special Rule	30	0.05
81	Passage of Rules (Special Rule)	2,335	3.8
83	Motion to Commit	70	0.11
84	Motion to Consider	275	0.45
85	Demand for a Second	46	0.07
86	Motion to Permit to Read from Record	13	0.02
87	Motion to Refer	122	0.2
88	Motion to Order Previous Question	372	0.6
89	Election of Speaker	65	0.11
91	Motion to Approve House Journal	961	1.56

TABLE A4. Procedural and Miscellaneous Vote Types, Part 2

92	Motion to Adjourn	690	1.12
93	Motion to Recommit	2,131	3.46
94	Motion to Resolve into the Committee of the Whole	421	0.68
95	Motion to Instruct Conferees	457	0.74
96	Motion to Table	1,340	2.18
98	Dispense with Further Proceedings under the Quorum Call	74	0.12
99	Previous Question on Special Rules	924	1.5
107	Motion to Discharge and Refer to Different Committee	8	0.01
108	Election of Committee Chairman	33	0.05
111	Adjourn to a Day Certain	6	0.01
112	Recess	169	0.27
113	Executive Session	32	0.05
116	Postpone to a Day Certain	1	0
118	Insist and Ask	0	0
120	Ask for Further Conference with the House	2	0
124	Compel Attendance by Absentees	328	0.53
128	Proceed to Consideration of Conference Report	20	0.03
133	Second Reading	0	0
134	Engrossment and Third Reading	16	0.03
135	Dispense (Suspend) with the Rules (and pass) Various Respects	0	0
138	Determine Germaneness	54	0.09
139	Insist	30	0.05
141	Return from the House	3	0
142	To Make Special Order	7	0.01
145	Discharge Committee	0	0
159	Final Passage of Senate Rules	2	0
162	Executive Amendments	1	0
163	Conference Report Amendments	0	0
167	Adopt Part of Joint Resolution	1	0
168	Amend Journal / Write into the Record	10	0.02
171	To Adopt a Preamble or Section of a Bill	2	0
172	Final Passage of a Preamble to a Resolution	0	0
183	Adopt Minority Report	1	0
193	Guilt or Innocence Impeachment	35	0.06
194	Pass Order Impeachment	3	0

TABLE A5. Confirmation Vote Types

Code	pipc_description	count	%
65	Confirmation	1,035	1.68

TABLE A.6. Aggregate Vote Types

Vote Category	Total Roll Calls	Percentage
Passage/Final Passage	17,666	28.72
Amendment	22,638	36.80
Procedural	20,182	32.81
Confirmation	1,035	1.68

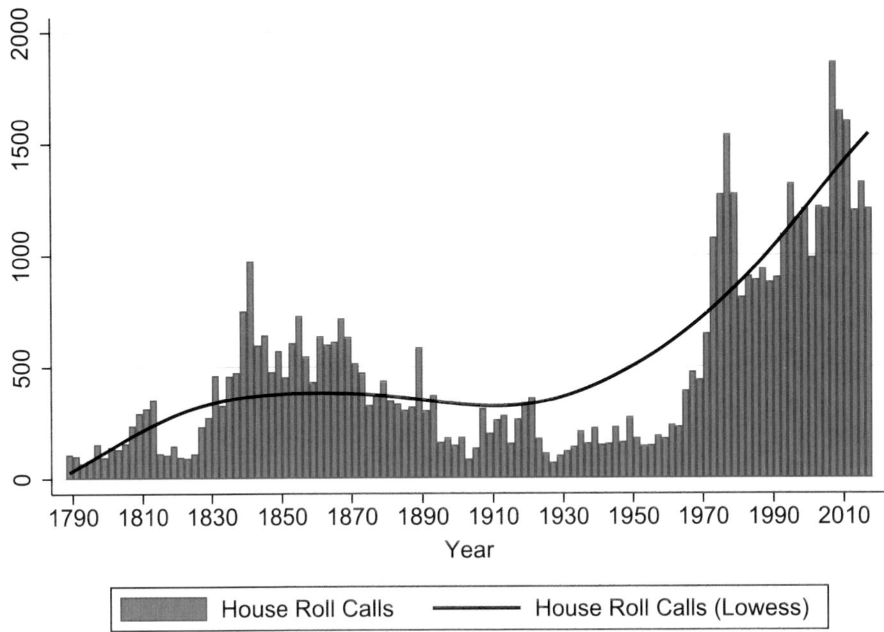

Figure A1. House Roll Call Votes, 1789–2014

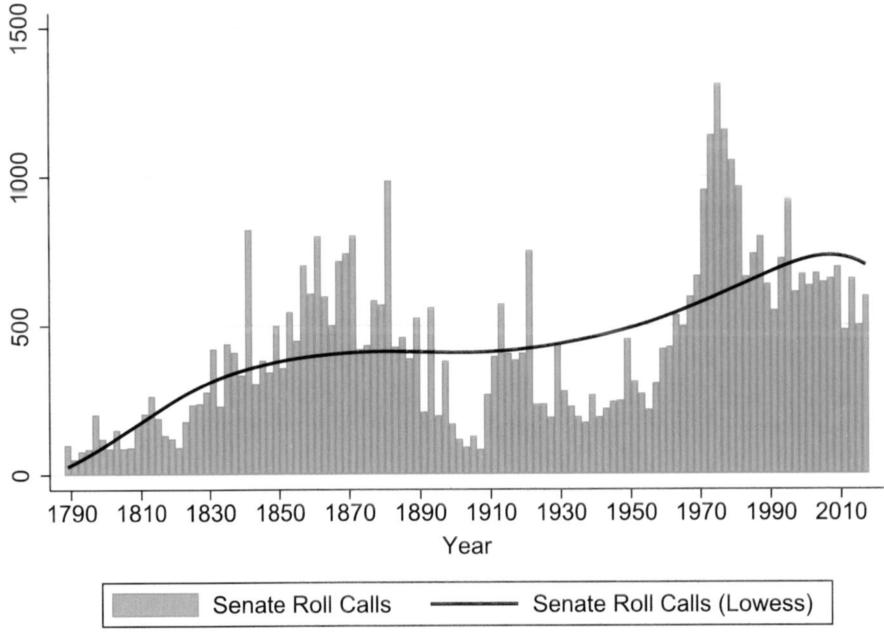

Figure A2. Senate Roll Call Votes, 1789–2014

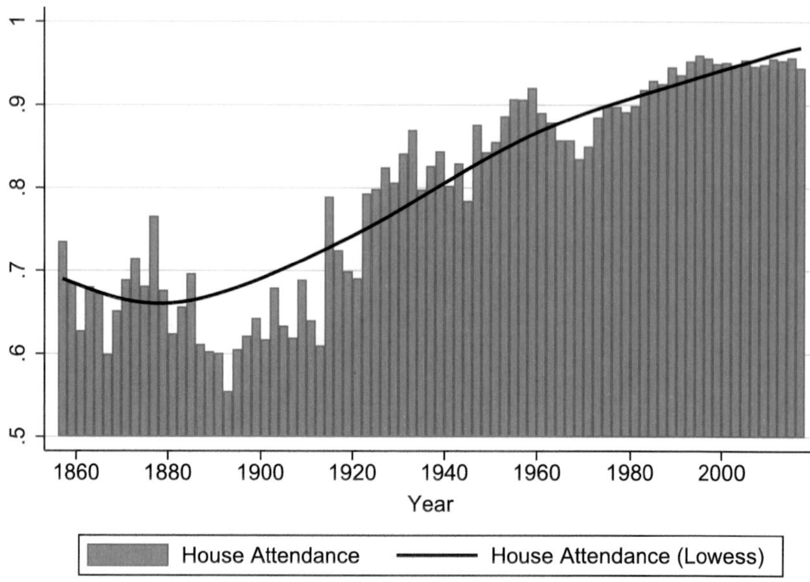

Figure A3. House Attendance, 1859–2014

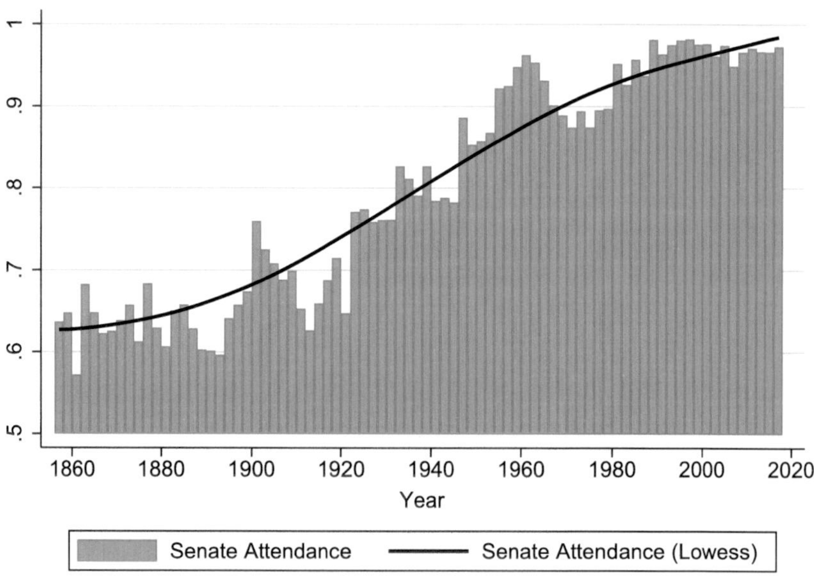

Figure A4. Senate Attendance, 1859–2014

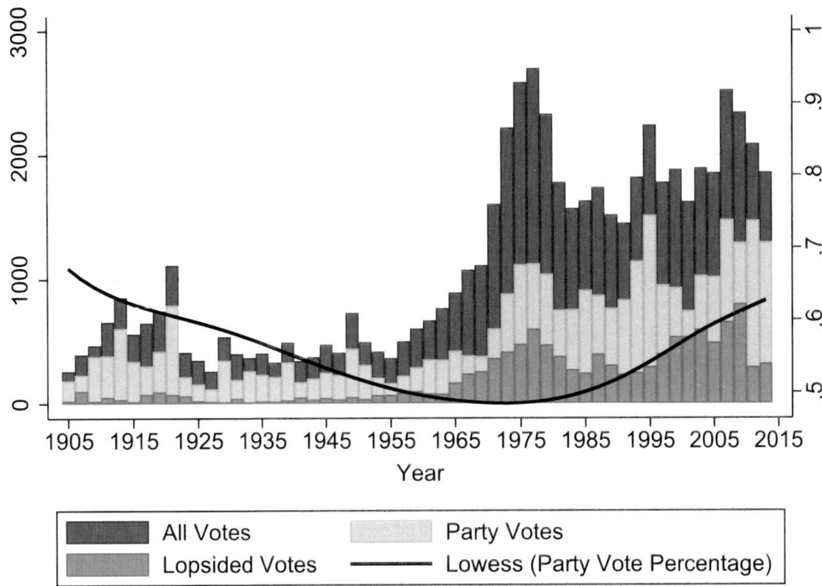

Figure A5. Lopsided and Party Votes per Congress, 1905–2014

Appendix B

Generating a List of Important Legislation

Coding on this project began in the spring of 2010. Our initial intention was to code all special rules, orders, and amendments to legislation considered on the floor of the House and Senate from the 45th Congress (1877–1878) to present. While we completed coding on all amendments offered during the 45th Congress, it was apparent that attempting to do so for every Congress would be too labor intensive.[1] Accordingly, we sought to narrow the data collection effort by compiling a list of "important" legislation. To do so, we combined several lists of landmark enactments with at least two routine appropriation bills per congress. In this appendix, we describe those efforts below.

"Landmark" Legislation and Political Science

Focusing on landmark bills allows scholars to minimize biases stemming from the large amount of trivial legislation the US Congress produces (Clinton and Lapinski 2006). For example, approximately 20%–30% of all bills passed in a typical Congress rename public buildings. Accordingly, landmark legislation allows researchers to ensure a certain level of salience.

Perhaps the most notable list of landmark legislation was created by David Mayhew for his book *Divided We Govern* (1991, 2005). In it Mayhew sought to evaluate whether the presence of divided government depressed the numbers of laws produced in a Congress. To do so, he generated a list of important enactments from contemporaneous accounts from journalists. This list—dubbed "Sweep One"—provided a contemporaneous measure of legislative significance. It differed from his "Sweep Two" list, which was generated retrospectively based on laws identified by policy experts.[2] Using these lists, Mayhew reported that, contrary to the conventional wisdom, divided government did *not* suppress productivity.

This measure was challenged by a number of scholars. Howell et al. (2000) and Kelly (1993a, 1993b) focused on Mayhew's decision to pool legislation judged as "landmark" by contemporaneous and retrospective raters. Howell et al. (2000) argue that retrospective ratings are likely to be vulnerable to selection bias. They broadened Mayhew's Sweep One list to create a four-category measure using all laws enacted and report that divided government systematically depressed legislative productivity using this measure. Arguing that legislation should be both "timely and enduring," Kelly (1993a, 478) reported a similar finding by examining only legislation that appeared on both the Sweep One and Sweep Two lists.[3]

Mayhew's book was followed by a number of attempts to either extend his list—which began in 1947—to earlier congresses or to produce a more systematic measure of legislative productivity. For example, Petersen (2001) extended Mayhew's Sweep One list from 1881 to 1946. Stathis (2003, 2014) generated a list that extended to the 1st Congress.[4]

Perhaps the most systematic effort was by Clinton and Lapinski (2006). They employed an item-response model and information gleaned from 19 scholarly works rating congressional legislation (including Howell et al. 2000; Mayhew 1991, 2005; Petersen 2001; and others) to generate a significance score for each statute passed by Congress from 1887 to 1994. These statutes can then be rank-ordered by their significance both within and between congresses. This allows researchers to employ their own theoretical assumptions to generate their own list of landmark legislation.

From Landmark to "Important" Legislation

This is not to say that landmark enactments are a panacea. Determining what constitutes a landmark enactment introduces an arbitrary element. Given this, scholars will often differ on certain methodologies and measures (Clinton and Lapinski 2006). These choices can bias empirical results and lead to differing normative conclusions.[5] These lists also vary substantially in the time series they employ.

Fortunately, the purpose of our study is not to determine which measures are the most important (or most "landmark"). Instead, we wanted to ensure we had a large enough sample to track changes in the roll call generating process over time. To both ensure a large enough sample and provide us with opportunities to test the robustness of our findings, we take a broad view of landmark legislation. To do so, we combined multiple "landmark" enactment lists generated by Stathis (2003, 2014), Petersen (2001), Mayhew (1991, 2005) and *CQ Almanac* with the 10 most important bills per congress as coded by Clinton and Lapinksi (2006) and at least two "routine" appropriation bills per congress. Given the length of our time series, the list of enactments employed varies across congresses. Specifically, our broadly defined set of landmark legislation, which we will refer to as a list of "important legislation," comes from the following sources:

1905–1944: The 59th Congress (1905–1906) to the 78th Congress (1943–1944) use data from Stathis (2003); Petersen (2001); and Clinton and Lapinski's (2006) top 10 enactments per congress and top 400 landmark enactments from 1877 to 1946.

1944–1945: The 79th Congress (1945–1946) use data from Stathis (2003, 2014); Petersen (2001); and Clinton and Lapinski's (2006) top 10 enactments per congress and top 400 landmark enactments from 1877 to 1946.

1947–1978: The 79th Congress (1947–1948) to the 96th Congress (1977–1978) use data from Stathis (2003, 2014); Clinton and Lapinski's (2006) top 10 enactments per congress; and Mayhew's (1991) Sweep One list of landmark enactments.

1979–1996: The 97th Congress (1979–1980) to the 104th Congress (1995–1996) use data from Stathis (2003, 2014); Clinton and Lapinski's (2006) top 10 enactments per congress; Mayhew's (1991) Sweep One list of landmark enactments; and bills subject to *CQ Almanac*'s key votes.[6]

1997–2000 The 105th Congress (1997–1998) and the 106th Congress (1999–2000) use data from Stathis (2003, 2014); Mayhew's (1991, 2005) Sweep One list of landmark enactments; and bills subject to *CQ Almanac*'s key votes.

2001–2012: The 107th Congress (2001–2002) through 112th Congress (2011–2012) use data from Stathis (2014); Mayhew's (1991, 2005) Sweep One list of landmark enactments; and bills subject to *CQ Almanac*'s key votes.

2013–2014: The 113th Congress (2013–2014) use data Mayhew's (1991, 2005) Sweep One list of landmark enactments and bills subject to *CQ Almanac*'s key votes.

Appropriation Bills

As a robustness check, we later included a dataset of appropriation bills to our list of important legislation. Even when they do not constitute "landmark" measures, routine appropriation bills are exceptionally important measures for Congress and often highly controversial. Accordingly, our dataset includes at least two routine appropriation bills per congress from the 59th Congress (1905–1906) to the 96th Congress (1977–1978). To be consistent, whenever possible, we selected an agriculture appropriations act and a legislative branch appropriation act. In cases where those acts were already listed as landmark bills or they failed to pass, another appropriations act was selected.

The data also includes all appropriation bills from the 97th Congress (1979–1980) to the 113th Congress (2013–2014). As we discuss in Appendix D, amendment data for this period was not manually entered. Rather it was downloaded from Congress.gov using govtrack and then coded for vote type. There are 641 appropriation bills in our dataset. Of these, 64 were also considered landmark measures.

Additionally, primarily due to the addition of legislation related to CQ "key votes," we have 250 measures that were not enacted into law. We fit our models in Chapter 5 with and without the failed measures and find doing so does not alter the conclusions drawn from our results.

In total, we have coded important legislation data for 2,036 measures across 55 congresses. This ranged from a high of 82 proposals in the 106th Congress (1999–2000) to a low of 13 proposals in the 72nd Congress (1931–1932). The mean and median number per congress was 37.02 and 27 proposals. Figure B.1 plots total important legislation per congress, broken up by appropriation bills, failing measures and all other passing proposals.

Pairing Bills with Important Legislation

We then paired our list of important legislation, with a bill or set of bills. Identifying the bills that correspond to important enactments proved to be a difficult endeavor for several reasons. First, on rare occasions, there are multiple landmark policies listed in a given public law. Mayhew (1991, 40), for example, had a rule against counting multiple landmark policies in one law. However, he notes that he "fudged [his] rules" in a few select cases.

Second, on rare occasions, a landmark policy may be passed across several pieces of legislation. Perhaps the most notable instance of this was the passage of the Affordable Care Act (ACA). For procedural purposes, the ACA was

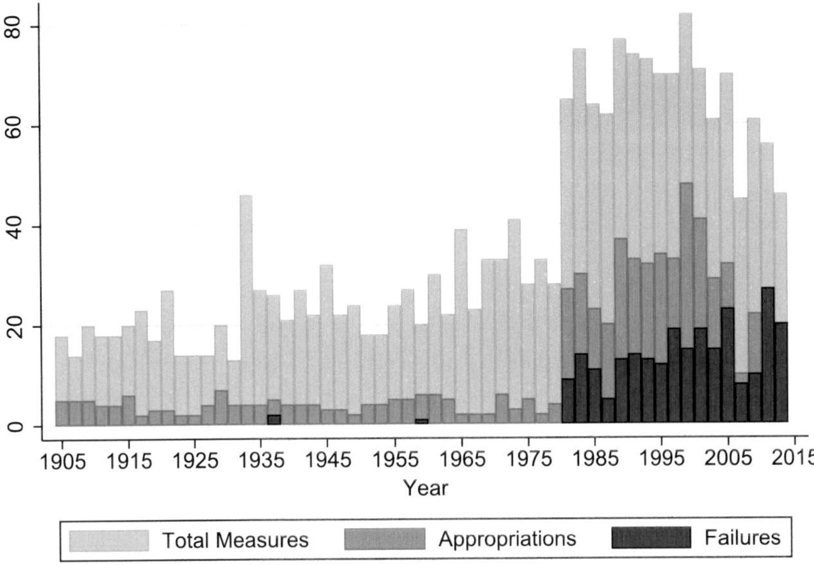

Figure B1. Important Legislation per Congress by Type, 1905–2014

passed as part of two separate public laws (111 P.L. 148; 111 P.L. 152) (see, e.g., Oleszek and Oleszek 2012). Hurricane Sandy Relief was also parceled out in two separate legislative installments (113 P.L. 1; 113 P.L. 2). In these cases, the policy was treated as two enactments.

Finally, it is common for there to be a substantial number of bills included in a given landmark enactment. Often times, these bills are debated and amended separately on the floor before being folded into one landmark act. For example, Mayhew's (1991) list of "landmark bills" includes the Higher Education Act of 1972. The measure was passed in the 92nd Congress (1971–1972) and Mayhew listed it as a landmark measure that provided $20 billion for Pell grants to low-income college students. The public law also included $2 billion for emergency school aid and desegregation and several highly controversial antibusing provisions. It is perhaps most well known for Title IX, which barred education programs from discriminating on the basis of sex. The Higher Education Act of 1972 was covered by not only the enacted bill, S. 659, but a House companion, H.R. 7248, and another Senate bill, S. 1557, which passed the Senate separately but was folded into S. 649 in the House.

Given the increasing usage of vehicles and omnibus lawmaking in contemporary congresses, we felt coding only the enacted bill for a given landmark measure would introduce bias by masking conflict.[7] It is common in the modern Congress for enacted laws to pass easily after substantial conflict occurred on earlier companion or related measures. This occurred on occasion in older congresses as well.

For example, the Agriculture Appropriations Act of 1919 (66 P.L. 22) is in our important enactment dataset. The enacted bill is H.R. 7413. It featured one recorded vote in the House, none in the Senate. It passed both chambers by voice vote and was subject to only three amendments. On its face, this presents a fairly simple picture for the legislative process on that bill. However, H.R. 7413 passed with minimal conflict only after a related bill, H.R. 3157, failed earlier. H.R. 3157 featured six recorded votes and 183 amendments across the two chambers. It was eventually vetoed by President Woodrow Wilson because it contained language repealing daylight saving time. A House attempt to override the veto was defeated by eight votes, 253–138.

Accordingly, we opted to code all companion and related bills that received floor consideration. This was done using a combination of the *Congressional Record* index, *CQ Almanac*, and Congress.gov when available.

Congress.gov defines a companion measure as an "identical or substantially similar measures introduced in the other chamber." We attempt to distinguish between companion and related bills by identifying companion bills as being those formally linked up to the enacted measure (i.e., the Senate struck all after the enacting clause on H.R. 1 and replaced it with S. 2, or if the index specifically lists the Senate as passing H.R. 1 in lieu of S. 2).

Congress.gov defines a related measure as either a "companion measure, an identical bill, a procedurally-related measure, or one with substantive similarities. Bill relationships are identified by the House, the Senate, or CRS, and refer only to same-Congress measures." Related bills represent a much broader category than companions. Congress.gov will list related bills if informed by staffers that a given measure is "related," so the listings can be arbitrary.

For our purposes, related measures generally include three types of bills.

Bills Considered Related

1. Bills that dealt with the same content, albeit usually unsuccessfully (e.g., if a landmark act raising the minimum wage, H.R. 2452, passes later in a Congress after an earlier measure, H.R. 15, failed in that same Congress, H.R. 15 is considered related). This often happens with vetoed bills.
2. Bills that were eventually packaged into the final enactment (e.g., if H.R. 5214 is the final bill and it included S. 12, which passed the Senate separately, then S. 12 is a related bill). This often occurs with omnibus continuing appropriation bills.

3. Measures where the substantive debate and amending activity related to the underlying substance, even if they were eventually enacted as something else. These are generally vehicles (e.g., if a landmark act on busing, H.R. 567, passes the House and the Senate opts to use a minor House-passed bill, H.R. 67, as a vehicle for busing amendments, H.R. 67 will be considered related even if the amendments are stripped from it and it is enacted as a minor bill).

Bills Not Considered Related

Bills that originally contained the final enactment. For example, H.R. 638 is a bill that contained a provision cutting funds to the EPA; that provision was removed before final passage but included in the landmark bill, H.R. 2319. In this case H.R. 638 would not be a related bill.

The 2,036 pieces of important legislation left us with a total of 3,199 bills over the 55 congresses. The median number of bills per important legislation was 1 in 47 out of the 55 congresses.[8] However, the large number of bills associated with omnibus appropriation bills in recent congresses has generally led to an increase in average bills per important legislation over time. Figure B.2 plots the number of bills per enactment for each congress.

A complete important legislation list is available online at thecongressproject.com/data-and-links/

Coding Supplementary Variables

Our list of important legislation was then paired with the bill numbers in our expanded roll call vote dataset (see Appendix A). Bills in our list accounted for just over 43% of all roll call votes from the 59th Congress (1905–1907) to the 113th Congress (2013–2014). Moreover, roll calls on just amendments to our important enactments accounted for over 10% of all roll calls in all but two congresses in our dataset. In our view, this gives adequate leverage in evaluating the roll call generating process.

Students and faculty members were then tasked with coding additional variables to our important legislation dataset. When feasible, these variables were supplemented by data on bills and public laws made public by Adler and Wilkerson (2019). Given our extended time series, we then extended back these variables through the 59th Congress. This includes variables like

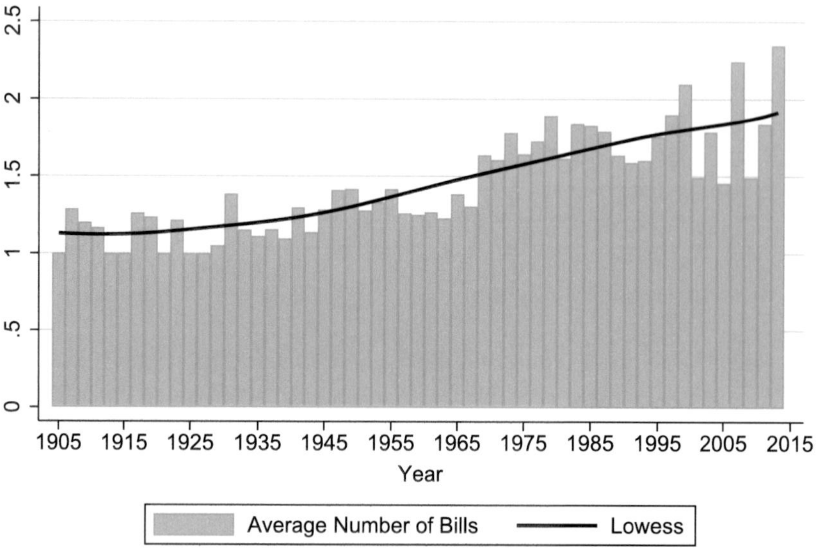

Figure B2. Average Number of Bills per Enactment by Congress, 1905–2014

introduction date, whether a bill was vetoed, and if it went to a conference committee.

We also coded how the enacted bill was brought to the floor in the House. This includes whether it was passed through suspension of the rules or brought forward under a special rule or some other procedure (including Calendar Wednesday, unanimous consent, or a similar process). If a special rule was employed, it was coded for rule type. That process is described in Appendix C.

Finally, student coders were tasked with going through pdfs of the enacted bill (or last bill considered in the event it failed) and coded the number of pages per bill. Figure B.3 plots the average number of pages per important enactment. We observe a substantial increase in these measures over time, consistent with all public laws.

Additional Graphs

Additional figures are included here for robustness purposes. Figures B.4 and B.5 track the likelihood an important enactment receives a recorded vote on final passage in the House and the Senate. The numbers exclude failed measures and House and Senate simple resolutions. A lowess smoothing line was

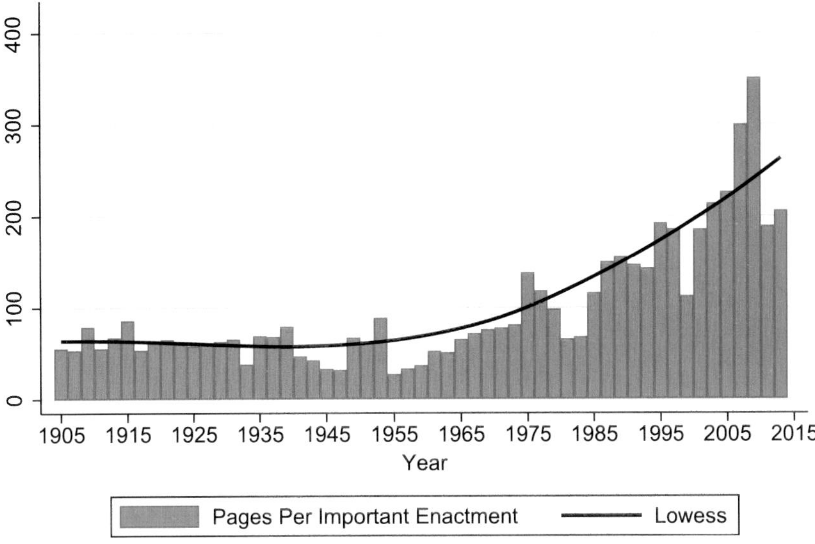

Figure B3. Average Page Length of Important Legislation per Congress, 1905–2014

added to illustrate the percentage of all enactments that received a recorded final passage vote. Unsurprisingly, there is a sharp increase in both chambers over time.

Figure 4.2 plots non-lopsided roll calls per congress by vote type, pooling both chambers. Figures B.6 and B.7 break the data up between the House and the Senate. Consistent with our expectations given the institutional reforms of the 1970s, we observe a substantial increase in House recorded amendment votes per enactment. The Senate's roll call distribution per enactment has remained roughly stable with fewer amendment votes per enactment and more procedural votes. However, interpreting this is complicated by the categorization of tabling motions.

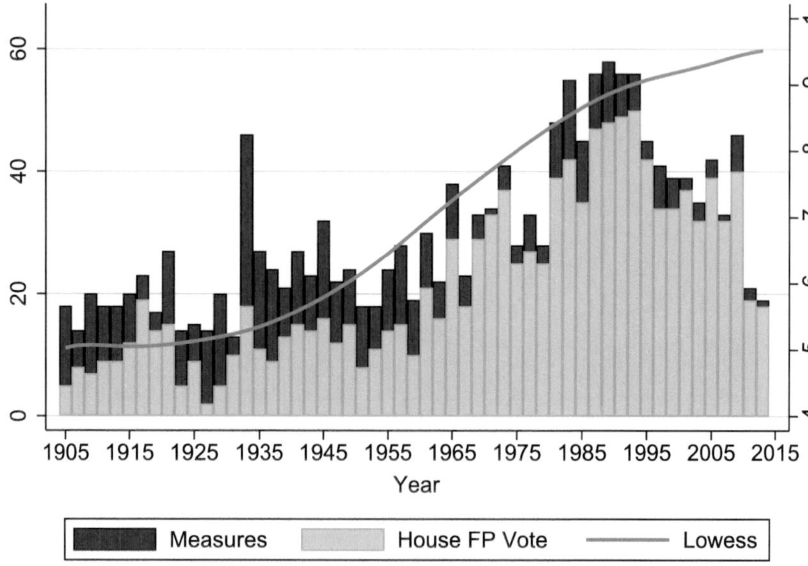

Figure B4. Important Enactments and House Final Passage Votes, 1905–2014

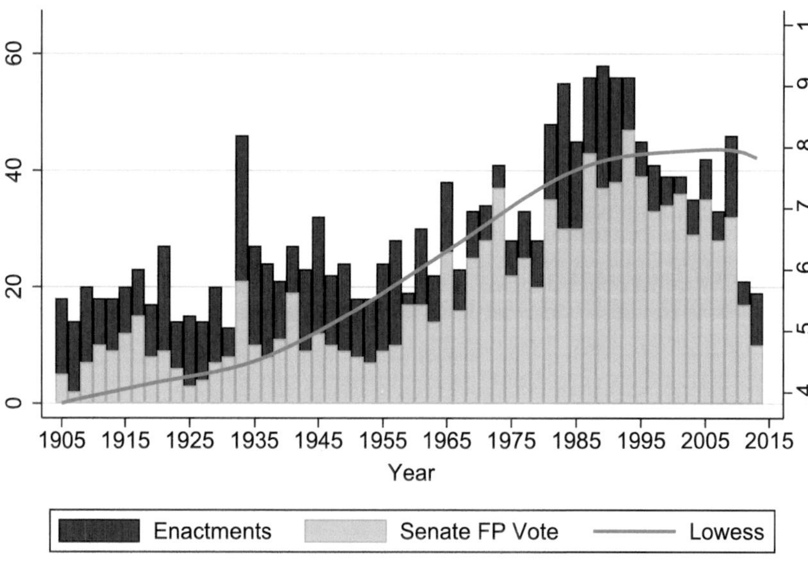

Figure B5. Important Enactments and Senate Final Passage Votes, 1905–2014

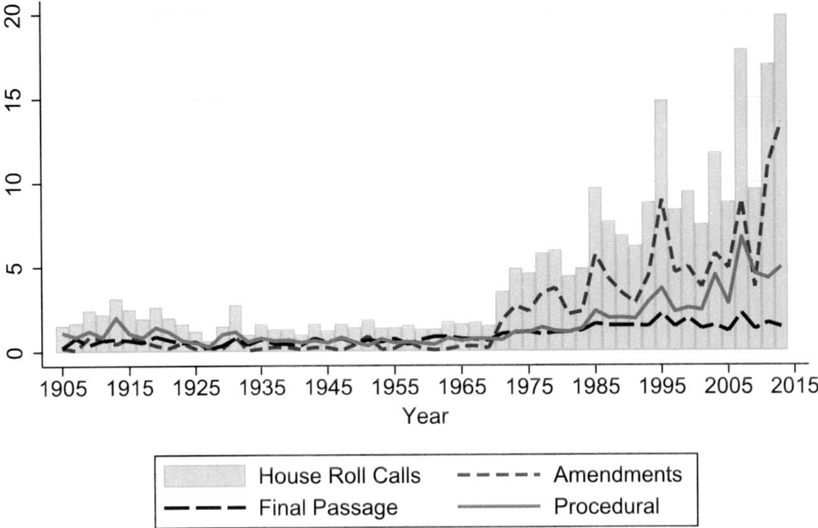

Figure B6. Average House Votes per Enactment by Type, 1905–2014

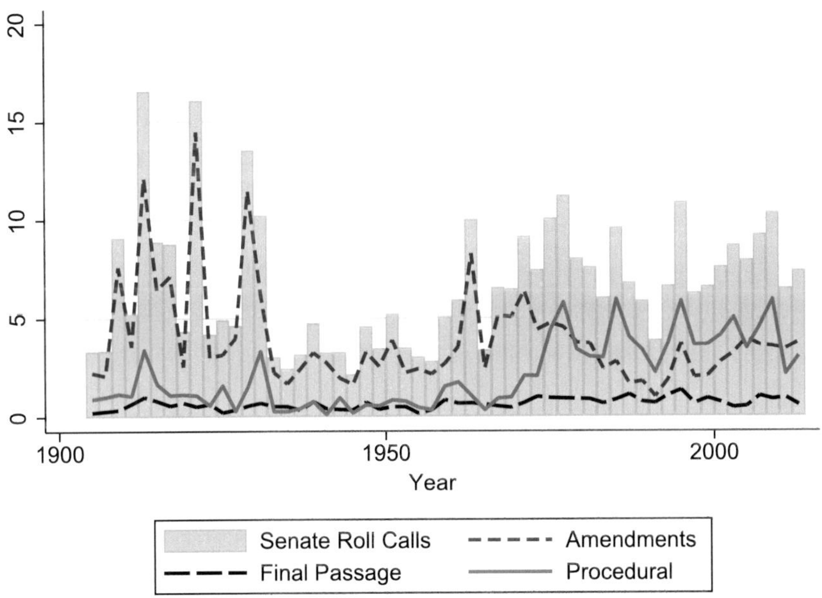

Figure B7. Average Senate Votes per Enactment by Type, 1905–2014

Appendix C

Coding Special Rules

Coding these data began in the spring of 2018. The dataset was put together using a variety of sources. First, an initial list of special rules from 1905 to 1937 was provided by Roberts (2010).[1] Using the *Congressional Record* index, we then expanded this list through the 92nd Congress (1971–1972). Specifically, a faculty member and a graduate student coder went through the "House Resolutions" subsection of the History of Bills and Resolutions and checked each resolution that received floor consideration.[2] The dataset includes 3,120 resolutions that included special rules from the 59th Congress (1905–1907) to the 92nd Congress (1971–1972).[3]

Special rule information for the 93rd Congress (1973–1974) through the 115th Congresses (2017–2018) were downloaded from Congress.gov. Initially, we downloaded all 9,313 House resolutions that received floor consideration during this time frame. Through keyword searches of the rule descriptions, we were able to distinguish between special rules and simple House resolutions. This resulted in 4,209 resolutions that included special rules from the 93rd Congress (1973–1974) through the 115th Congresses (2017–2018).

We employed four additional sources to ensure we did not miss any special rules that received floor consideration. First, we compared our final dataset with our dataset of important legislation.[4] For all bills in our important legislation data, we went through the index and separately coded any special rules related to the bill. All of these rules were present in the Congress.gov data. Second, we compared our data to a dataset from voteview.com for all special rules subjected to roll call votes. Third, when the time series matched, we compared our data to data collected by Stiglitz (2008).[5] Finally, for the

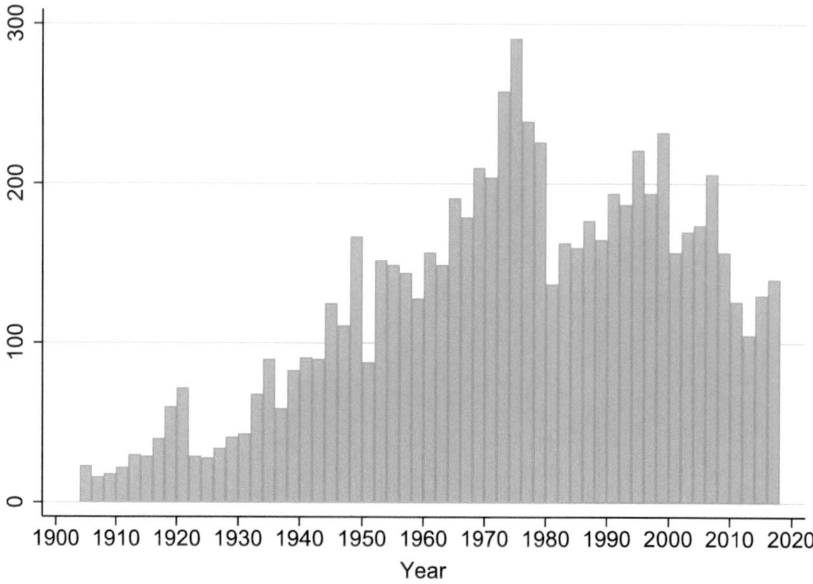

Figure C1. House Rules by Congress, 1905–2018

98th Congress through the 115th Congress, we checked to ensure the rule was listed in the Rules Committee's *Annual Survey of Activities Reports*.

The final dataset includes information on 7,329 House resolutions considered on the floor that provide special rules for legislation. Of these resolutions, 494 provided special rules for multiple bills, resulting in 8,027 rule-bill level observations. Figure A.1 plots the 8,027 rules per congress. The full dataset ("House Rules, 59th (1905–1907)—115th (2017–2018) Congresses") is available here: https://www.thecongressproject.com/data-and-links/

Once our list of rules was established, we had faculty, two graduate students, and 25 undergraduates code rule and vote types. While our primary interest was in coding whether the rule received a recorded vote or not, we had the student coders collect supplemental variables that are discussed below.

Coding Rule Types

Student coders were initially tasked with coding the bill or bills the rule corresponded to. Rules that cover multiple bills, often either bifurcated or multi-measure (also referred to as "grab-bag" rules) are common in recent congresses.[6] For rules that cover multiple bills, students would code the bill numbers and code a dummy variable denoting a multi-measure rule as a "1." As discussed above, 494 resolutions in our dataset provided special rules for multiple bills, resulting in 8,027 rule-bill level observations. Using our team of undergraduate researchers, we collected the text of these rules and coded them into 12 rule types (categorizing each as either "restrictive," "open," or "other"). These are listed in Table C.1 and discussed below.

Unfortunately, there is no set definition for special rule types, and terminology used by the Rules Committee has shifted over time even for the most commonly used rule types (i.e., open, modified-open, closed, modified-closed, and structured rules). Broadly, we coded any rule that bars all amendments as "closed," rules that allow a vote on only a select set of amendments stated in the rule as "modified-closed," and rules that allow a vote on amendments specified in the accompanying report as "structured." Rules allowing for any germane amendments were classified as "open." Open rules with some nondiscriminatory limitation, generally through a time limit on amending or a requirement that amendments be preprinted, were categorized as modified-open. These rule types are discussed in greater detail below.

Open Rule

The most common rule type for many congresses is the open rule. An open rule will include language to the effect of "amendments will be considered under the 'five-minute' rule." This means any germane amendment can be offered and five minutes will be permitted for debate and/or discussion. An example of an open rule from the 97th Congress (1981–1982) is the following:

TABLE C1. House Special Rules by Rule Type, 1905–2018

Rule Type	Count	Category
Closed	782	Restrictive
Modified-Closed	580	Restrictive
Structured	782	Restrictive
Open	3,976	Open
Modified-Open	168	Open
Waiver Only	301	Other
Conference Report	519	Other
Senate Amendment	283	Restrictive
Go to Conference	52	Other
Special Order/Miscellaneous	175	Other
Martial Law	169	Other
Suspension of the Rules	240	Other
Total	*8,027*	

> Resolved, that upon the adoption of this resolution it shall be in order to move that the House resolve itself into the Committee of the Whole House on the State of the Union for the consideration of the bill (H.R. 3462) to authorize appropriations to carry out the activities of the Department of Justice for fiscal year 1982, and for other purposes, and the first reading of the bill shall be dispensed with. After general debate, which shall be confined to the bill and shall continue not to exceed one hour, to be equally divided and controlled by the chairman and ranking minority member of the Committee on the Judiciary, ***the bill shall be read for amendment under the five-minute rule***. It shall be in order to consider the amendment in the nature of a substitute recommended by the Committee on the Judiciary now printed in the bill as an original bill for the purpose of amendment under the five-minute rule, and all points of order against said substitute for failure to comply with the provisions of clause 5, rule XXI are hereby waived. At the conclusion of the consideration of the bill for amendment, the Committee shall rise and report the bill to the House with such amendments as may have been adopted, and any Member may demand a separate vote in the House on any amendment adopted in the Committee of the Whole to the bill or to the committee amendment in the nature of a substitute. The previous question shall be considered as ordered on the bill and amendments thereto to final passage without intervening motion except one motion to recommit with or without instructions. (*Congressional Record*, 97th Congress, June 9, 1981, 11854)

Modified-Open Rule

A modified-open rule is generally considered an open rule with some nondiscriminatory limitation. Generally, this takes the form of a time limit or a preprinting requirement. In the case of a preprinting requirement, the rule specifies that amendments will only be considered if they are printed in the *Congressional Record* by a certain time period. Practically, what this means is that the majority wants to know what amendments are coming ahead of time. Modified-open rule language will look like this rule from the 104th Congress: "No amendment to the committee amendment in the nature of a substitute shall be in order unless printed in the portion of the *Congressional Record* designated for that purpose in clause 6 of rule XXIII before the beginning of consideration of the bill for amendment." Time limits will simply state that any amendments can be offered, but they will state that consideration of the bill and amendments will end at a specified time (e.g., at 5:00 p.m.) or after an allotted time period (e.g., two hours).

Closed Rule

A closed rule is the most restrictive type of rule. It bars any amendments from being offered. The rule text will generally not reference amendments of any kind. Instead, it will specify control over debate and then include language like the following: "The previous question shall be considered as ordered on the joint resolution to final passage without intervening motion except the motion to recommit with or without instructions."

Structured Rule

A structured rule is a restrictive rule that provides for only certain amendments to be in order (Lynch et al. 2016). These are usually listed in a report of the Committee on Rules. An announcement for a structured rule is typically made several days in advance. Amendments are then proposed and screened by the Rules Committee. Those found to be acceptable are printed in the report. The language will often look like this: "No amendment to the committee amendment in the nature of a substitute shall be in order except those printed in part B of the report of the Committee on Rules accompanying this resolution."

Notably, the term "structured rule" first appears in the Rules Committee year end reports at the conclusion of the 103rd Congress. It is not used to characterize a specific type of rule; rather it is used as a "catchall" term to describe rules that are not purely closed or open. Democrats claimed the rising use of these "structured rules" reflected "the desire of the membership for more structured debate, more certainty in the schedule, and advance notice of the amendments to be debated" ("Survey of Activities of the House Committee on Rules, 103rd Congress," House Rules Committee, Report 103-891, January 2, 1995, 23).

The following year, the new Republican majorities characterized rules as "structured/modified closed." This category was defined to include rules that "limit[ed] the amendments that may be offered only to those amendments designated in the special rule or the Rules Committee report to accompany it, or which precludes amendments to a particular portion of a bill, even though the rest of the bill may be completely open to amendment" ("Survey of Activities of the House Committee on Rules, 104th Congress," House Rules Committee, Report 104-868, November 26, 1996, 30). This change, according to Democrats, was so Republicans could put a more positive spin on their record of employing restrictive rules in that Congress: "Essentially the Republicans decided to change the rules of the game in order to make their manipulation of the rules process look more open than that of the Democrats" ("Survey of

Activities of the House Committee on Rules, 103rd Congress," House Rules Committee, Report 103-891, January 2, 1995, 144).

Modified-Closed Rule

A modified-closed rule is also highly restrictive. It will bar nearly all amendments but may specify that an amendment will be offered by the committee chair or his or her designee (or a set of amendments may be offered that have been approved of by the committee). Under our criteria, a modified-closed rule may also be open in parts but bar all amendments to one section. Our primary way of distinguishing between modified-open and structured rules was to identify language providing for amendments printed in the resolution, which led to the rule being classified as modified-closed, from language providing for amendments printed "in the resolution," which was coded as structured.

Additional Rule Types

Rules that provide for consideration of a bill and waiving certain or all points of order, but do not mention amending otherwise, were classified as "waiver only" rules. These were especially common on appropriation bills and were occasionally controversial. In the House, amendments have to be germane to the bill. Accordingly, legislation could be written in such a narrow way that only a handful of amendments could be proposed even under an open rule. The majority could then provide waivers for only amendments they viewed as important but still claim credit for issuing an open rule. After one such instance in 2003, Rep. Dave Obey (D-WI) complained that "[we] have just been told that this rule is an open rule. That is an absolutely meaningless statement."[7]

Approximately 11% of the rules in our dataset cover secondary consideration. This includes rules providing for consideration of and/or waiving points of order against conference reports and those agreeing to or separately requesting a conference with the Senate on a bill. As conference reports are not amendable under House rules, these were classified as neither restrictive nor open. Rules providing for consideration of a Senate amendment with an amendment or simply concurring with a Senate amendment (and barring other amendments) were coded as restrictive.

In addition to rules covering secondary consideration, special rules waiving "availability requirements" are increasingly common in contemporary congresses. House rules specify that legislative text must be available to members for a certain period of time before floor consideration. For bills and conference reports, this is 72 hours. For special rules, it's one day (Rybicki 2017).[8] Special rules waiving these requirements are often referred to as either "same-day rules" by their supporters or "martial law rules" by their opponents.

House rules also provide for consideration of motions to suspend the rules only on certain days. These rules can also be waived through a special rule and are occasionally controversial. Bills passed via suspension necessitate two-thirds support and, accordingly, typically have a great deal of support. But it does preclude amending opportunities. For example, in 2009, news broke that insurance companies had paid executive lucrative bonus checks after receiving federal bailout funds. Democrats moved to suspend the rules and pass a bill that would recoup much of that money. Despite supporting the bill, minority-party Republicans complained that suspension barred them from offering an amendment ensuring more funds would be recouped.[9] Suspension and martial law rules were classified as neither restrictive nor open.

We included a final category titled "Special Order/Miscellaneous" to account for rules that provide for consideration of a bill but do not waive points of order. Measures providing for the rules of the House are included in this category, as are a handful of resolutions that could not be categorized.

Supplemental Variables

In addition to the rule type variables, our research term coded a number of supplemental variables. These include identifier variables like the resolution number, the bill or bills covered by the special rule, the date the rule was last voted on, and a unique, seven- to eight-digit identifying variable for each resolution.[10] Perhaps most useful of the supplemental variables coded is the full text of the rule. Student coders copied the text of the rule as reported in the *Congressional Record* into a variable denoted text. This was done to ensure it would be easier for future researchers to recode the rule type should they want to employ an alternative coding scheme.

As we would anticipate, rules have been increasing in their complexity throughout congressional history. This is evident when we consider the increase in the median number of words per rule. Figure C.2 plots the average number of words per rule by Congress. The figure also includes a simple lowess smoothing line to indicate the general trend in the data.

Coders were also asked to code how the resolution was finally dispensed

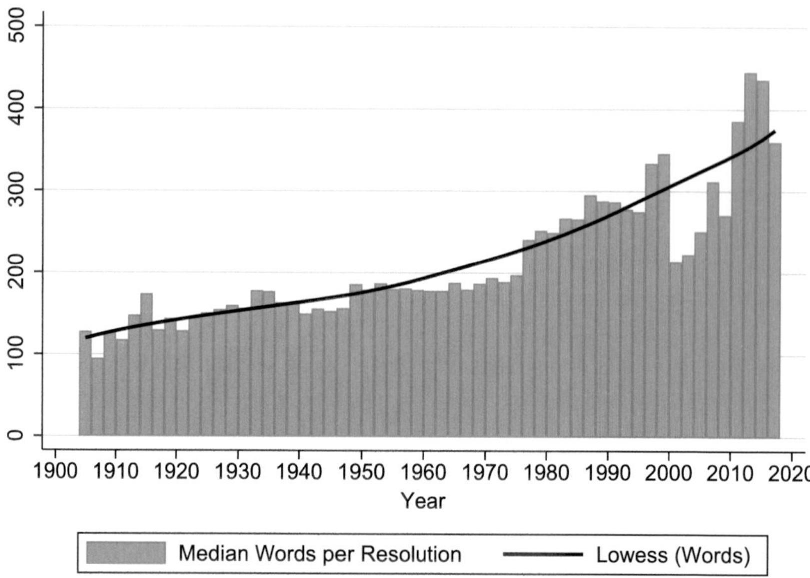

Figure C2. Median Words per House Rule by Congress, 1905–2018

with. Specifically, there should be at least two votes for special rules. The first of these is ordering the previous question motion. The previous question motion requires a simple majority to enact and serves to terminate debate. The motion is present in the House, but not the Senate, and is frequently described as an important procedural difference between the two chambers. Defeating the previous question motion allows the minority to amend a rule, and a defeat is devastating to majority-party agenda control (Finocchiaro and Rohde 2008). Once the previous question motion is ordered, a vote is taken on the rule itself. For each resolution, our research team coded whether the vote on the previous question motion and the rule itself was recorded (as opposed to a voice vote or unrecorded teller or division vote). Those data are presented in Figures C.3 and C.4.

Additional supplemental variables were also coded. These include notes, which often contain quotations from the majority and minority rule managers. For example, for H.Res. 108 in the 101st Congress, there is language in the rule that states "the bill shall be considered for amendment under the five-minute rule." Subsequent language adds that "consideration of all amendments to the committee amendment in the nature of a substitute shall not

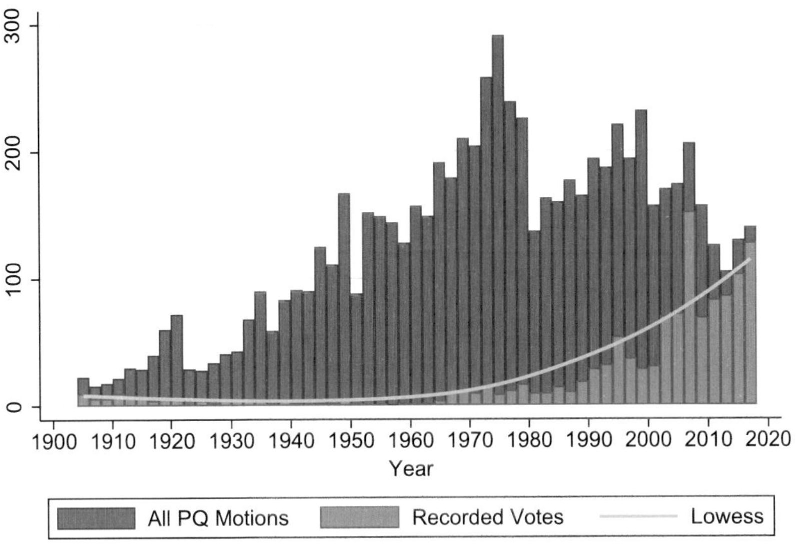

Figure C3. Previous Question Motions by Vote Type, 1905–2018

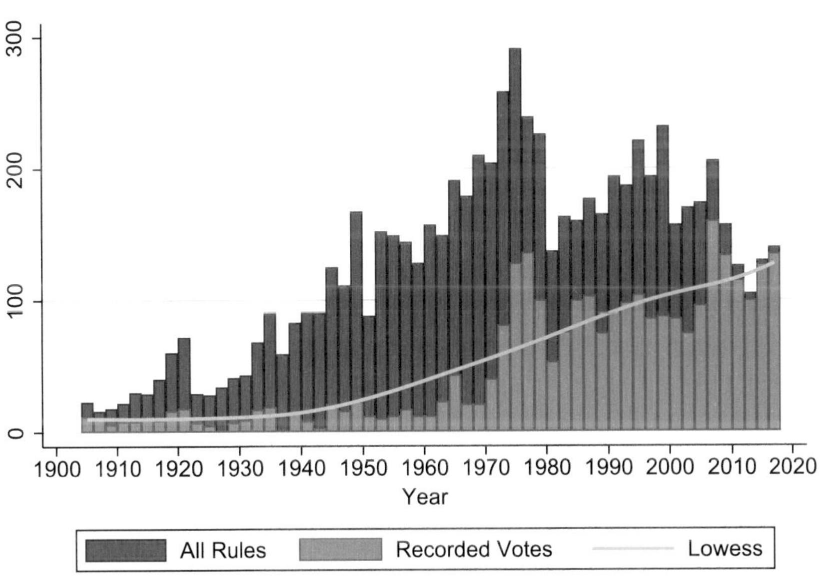

Figure C4. Special Rules by Vote Type, 1905–2018

exceed three hours." This suggests that we're looking at a modified-open rule. That suggestion is confirmed by the subsequent debate.

Specifically, right after the text of the rule is presented, the sponsor, Rep. Claude Pepper (D-FL), explicitly states, "House Resolution 109 is a modified open rule providing for the consideration of H.R. 1231" (*Congressional Record*, 101st Congress, March 15, 1989, 4158). The minority manager for the rule, Rep. Lynn Martin (R-IL), concedes the rule is "modified-open" but takes issue with its construction. She characterizes it accordingly:

> But lo and behold, when we returned in the afternoon we had a new wrinkle called a modified open rule. This is modified open about as much the Incredible Hulk is a modified ballerina. The modified rule says that no matter how worthwhile your amendments may be, when we reach the 3-hour mark, we must stop debating and offering amendments and come to a final vote. (*Congressional Record*, 101st Congress, March 15, 1989, 4158)

The exchange between Pepper and Martin is included in the notes variable. Other supplementary variables include dummy variables denoting whether or not the rule provided for a full-text substitute amendment, whether it provided for en bloc amendments, and information on related or companion bills that may have been mentioned in the rule, and dummy variables denoting self-executing and/or king or queen of the hill rules.

A self-executing rule is one that provides "that the House—upon adoption of the special rule—is considered or 'deemed' to have taken some other action as well" (Binder 2010). Usage of these rules has also increased throughout the history of the House, and they are commonly included in rules resolving differences between House and Senate bills. For example, in the 88th Congress, H.Res. 789 provided for House consideration of H.R. 7152, the Civil Rights Act of 1964, which had just been amended by the Senate. The bill manager, Rep. Emanuel Celler (D-NY), attempted to concur in the Senate amendments by unanimous consent, but this request was blocked. H.Res. 789 provided that the bill "with the Senate amendment thereto, be, and the same is hereby taken from the Speaker's table, to the end that the Senate amendment be, and the same is hereby agreed to."

Queen of the hill and king of the hill (or "mountain") rules are unorthodox rules that allow the floor to consider multiple competing proposals, but specify how a winner will be decided. They generally will say something to the effect of "the amendment with the greater number affirmative votes is to be considered adopted" or "the last amendment to receive a majority of affirmative votes shall be considered adopted." For example, H.Res. 198, during the 97th Congress, had a hill rule provision in it. Specifically, it provided that "if more than one amendment in the nature of a substitute has been adopted in the Committee of the Whole, only the last such amendment adopted shall be reported to the House."

A full listing of supplemental variables can be found in the codebook tab of the data and is available at thecongressproject.com/data-and-links/.

Appendix D

Coding Recorded and Unrecorded Amendments

This appendix details the data collection process used to code amendments to landmark legislation. Since 2010, the project has been serviced by 131 separate undergraduates, two faculty members, 17 graduate students, and three high school students. Undergraduate student coders participate in the project while taking an undergraduate research course. The students are trained in legislative politics while reading debates in the *Congressional Record* and coding data on amendments to landmark bills.

Why Amendments?

We choose to focus on the decision to record votes on amendments for several reasons. First, the amending process has historically provided members with greater opportunities to influence policy output than bill drafting. By offering an amendment on the chamber floor, members can guarantee their position will get considered, discussed, and voted upon. While institutions governing members' abilities to offer amendments on the floor have varied in their restrictiveness over time and by chamber, they are far more permissive than those that alter members' abilities to introduce and pass specific bills (Carson et al. 2012).

Second, amendment voting contains a level of depth and nuance that is simply missing from analyses of final passage votes. The decision to record roll call votes on final passage votes had been considered by several other papers (Clinton and Lapinski 2008; Lynch and Madonna 2013). While these works

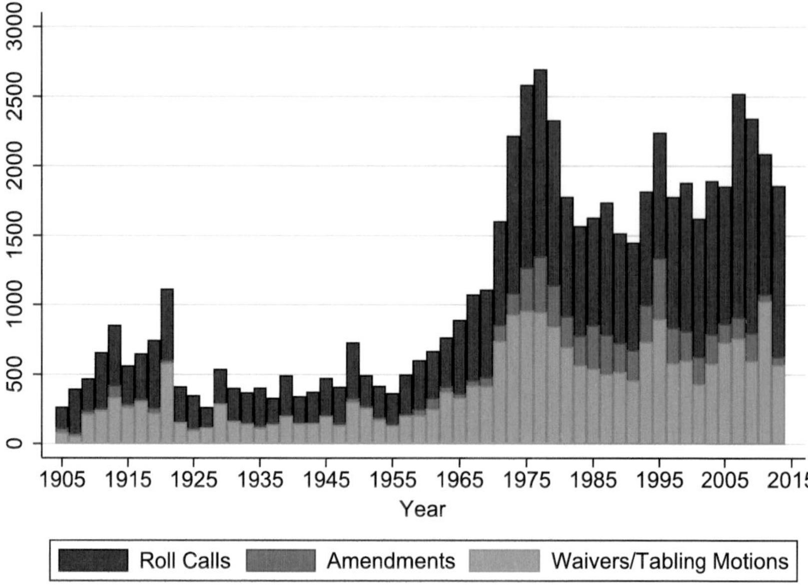

Figure D1. Amendment Votes as Part of the Roll Call Record

certainly represent substantial improvements in the effort to examine the roll call generating process, they are limited by the scope of the bill's content. A specific bill may contain a vast array of policy provisions reflecting the contributions of many specific members, staffers, and committees. Amendments, by contrast, are generally narrower and reflect a specific policy position. This makes them an ideal vehicle for forcing opponents into taking uncomfortable votes that may be used in election campaigns.

Third, amendments have been recognized by scholars as a tool for minority parties to put majority-party members on the record by requesting difficult votes (Smith 1989; Roberts and Smith 2003). Roberts and Smith (2003) found that the increase in political polarization in the House during the late 20th century was significantly influenced by the House's adoption of electronic voting in the Committee of the Whole. This led to a sharp increase in the number of amendments sponsored by minority-party members, who were simply trying to force majority-party legislators to cast embarrassing or unpopular votes.

Finally, amendments represent a substantive portion of the roll call record. From the 59th Congress (1905–1906) to the 113th Congress (2013–2014), amendments represented 58.89% of all votes cast in the Senate. In the House, amendment votes represented 29.11% of all votes cast during the same time period. Figure D.1 plots all roll calls (pooling the House and the Senate) with roll calls on amendments. The figure also stacks procedural roll calls (motions to waive and tabling motions) that dispense with amendments.

Coding Assignments

Research assistants working on congresses prior to the 96th Congress (1979–1980) were tasked with coding all amendments that were "disposed of" by some sort of vote, be it unrecorded voice vote, unrecorded teller votes, unrecorded division vote, or recorded roll call vote. Thus, amendments offered on the floor but withdrawn or adopted by unanimous consent were often omitted from the data collection process. This was done primarily to make the coding process easier. Amendments dispensed through other procedural means, including points of order or motions to table, are also included, as are amendments offered through motions to recommit.

After the 96th Congress, the Congress.gov website makes tracking amendments far easier. Until recent congresses, it was very unusual for an amendment to filed but not dispensed with by some form of vote. For example, in the 95th Congress only 22 of the 952 amendments filed did not receive consideration. Of the 22, 19 were withdrawn and three fell when the underlying measure was dispensed with. In recent congresses amendments are frequently filed that are never considered on the floor. These amendments are almost exclusively filed in Senate and are the result of the practice of filling the amendment tree. For example, in the 111th Congress, 3,900 amendments were filed but never considered on the floor.

After the 96th Congress, all amendments were downloaded from Congress.gov using govtrack and coded for vote type, including those never formally dispensed with. Research assistants than went through the downloaded datasets and added information related to the sponsor, the manner in which the amendment was dispensed with, and its final result. Notably, motions to recommit were not tracked after the 97th Congress.

Amendment Data

This left us with 117,269 filed amendments to important legislation from the 59th Congress (1905–1906) to the 113th Congress (2013–2014).[1] An amendment may be filed on the floor but not offered for a wide array of reasons. These include the member deciding not to press the amendment, its being

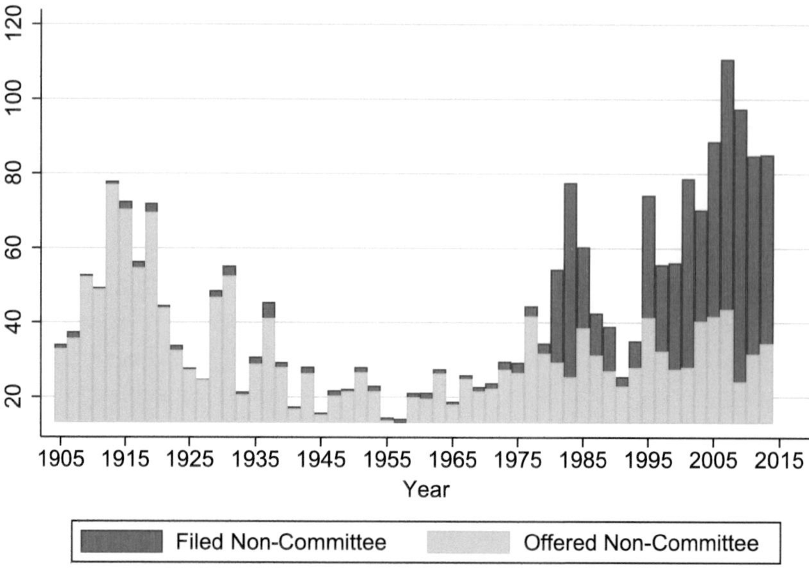

Figure D2. Amendments per Enactment, Filed and Offered, 1905–2014

blocked by a later unanimous consent agreement or special rule, the measure the amendment sought to alter being dispensed with, and, in recent Senates, the majority leader's "filling the amendment tree" to block amending opportunities.

Figure D.2 plots the average number of filed amendments per important enactment and the average number of offered amendments per important enactment. Figure D.2 is restricted to non-committee amendments. Committee amendments were often considered on the floor in the early 20th century and generally noncontroversial.

Coding Selected Variables

To accomplish their coding, research assistants scanned the online *Congressional Record*. Once an amendment was identified, a number of descriptive variables were entered. This primarily included information pertaining to the timing of the vote (the Congress number and chamber; month, date, and year the amendment was dispensed with; and the *Congressional Record* page number). Numerous additional variables were then coded. Those are discussed below; a full copy of our codebook is available online at thecongressproject.com/data-and-links/

Vote Type

Next all votes taken on the amendment were coded. This was accomplished by filling in a series of variables labeled vtype1, vtype2, vtype3, vtype4. For example, in the 43rd House (1873–1875), Rep. Frank Morey (R-LA) moved to

> Offer the following as a substitute for the resolution submitted by the gentleman from New York, [Mr. COX]:
>
> Resolved, That the name of George L. Smith be placed upon the roll, as the Representative from the fourth congressional district of Louisiana. (*Congressional Record*, 43rd Congress, December 3, 1873, 49)

Debate ensued before the speaker put the question:

> The first question was upon the amendment moved by Mr. MOREY, to substitute the name of George L. Smith for that of E. C. Davidson, as having the *prima-facie* right to a seat as the Representative from the fourth district of Louisiana.
>
> The question was taken, and upon a division there were—ayes 81, noes 78.
>
> Before the resolute of the vote was announced, Mr. SPEER called for the yeas and nays.
>
> The yeas and nays were ordered.
>
> The question was again taken, and there were—yeas 161, nays 94, not voting 261. (*Congressional Record*, 43rd Congress, December 3, 1873, 49)

In this example, vtype1 would be coded as a division vote and vtype2 would be listed as a recorded roll call vote. The remaining two categories—vtype3 and vtype4—would be coded as "Not applicable. No additional vote taken." In the event a recorded vote was taken, recorded vote data originally coded by Poole and Rosenthal (1997) was merged into the database. This includes the yeas, nays, missing votes, party, and sectional splits.

Information regarding the amendment was coded next. This included the amendment sponsor, the underlying measure, and additional information regarding the vote. Specifically, students would enter a description of the amendment. When feasible, this involved taking the description of the amendment directly from the record. For example, in the preceding example, the description would read "substitute the name of George L. Smith for that of E. C. Davidson, as having the prima-facie right to a seat as the Representative from the fourth district of Louisiana."

Other examples include "amendment to change expenses for Naval Department from 100k to 50k" or "Amendment to strike out clause instructing Secretary of Treasury to cover into the Treasury all undrawn monies from 1873 salary act." Coding descriptions of the amendments allows us the flexibility of going back and conducting a measure that assesses the importance of the amendment.

Amendment Sponsor

Determining the sponsor of each amendment offered some challenges. In the rare cases where a member introduced an amendment on behalf of himself or herself and other senators, only the member introducing the measure on the floor was coded as the sponsor. However, the name of the additional sponsors was coded in the notes section. For example, in the 88th Congress (1963–1965), the *Congressional Record* noted, "Mr. Williams of Delaware (for himself and Mr. Case) submitted a resolution (S.Res. 330) to inquire into the financial of business interests or activities including use of campaign funds, of any Member of former Members of the Senate, officer, employee, or former employee of the Senate, which was ordered to lie on the table and to be printed" (*Congressional Record*, 88th Congress, May 13, 1964, 10757). In this instance, Sen. John Williams (R-DE) was coded as the sponsor.

When an amendment was described as a "committee amendment," a more detailed reading of the record was undertaken to determine whether the member who sponsored the amendment in the committee was identified. This was frequently the case. In the 77th Congress (1941–1943), Sen. Walter George (D-GA) stated that an "amendment was presented to the committee by the Senator from Michigan [Mr. Vandenberg], and the committee voted favorably on the amendment offered" (*Congressional Record*, 77th Congress, October 9, 1942, 10757). In this instance, Sen. Arthur Vandenberg (R-MI) was listed as the sponsor.

In other cases, the member indicated that the amendment he or she was presenting was a committee amendment. In the 60th Congress (1907–1909), Rep. Reuben Moon (R-PA) stated, "Mr. Chairman, I send up to the desk a committee amendment, which I ask to have read" (*Congressional Record*, 60th Congress, February 18, 1909, 2649). In this instance, Rep. Moon would be coded as the amendment sponsor and the amendment would be coded as a committee amendment.

If the committee sponsor was not explicitly listed, students listed the sponsor as the member who consumed the most floor time advocating for the adoption of the amendment. For example, in the 85th Congress (1957–1959), Sen. Robert Kerr (D-OK) stated, "Speaking for that committee and for what I believe to be the rights of the people of a great State and of a great metropolitan area, and in the conviction that it can do no harm to any area, I urge the passage of the proposed legislation by the Senate" (*Congressional Record*, 85th Congress, August 22, 1958, 19125). In this case, Kerr was listed as the sponsor.

In a few instances, an amendment was reported as a committee amendment and there was no debate or advocacy for the bill on the floor. In the 64th Congress (1915–1917), the Senate began consideration of H.R. 15522, which established the National Park Service, with a committee amendment. Upon bringing the bill up for the consideration, the secretary stated, "The bill has been reported from the Committee on Public Lands with an amendment," and the amendment was agreed to after being read (*Congressional Record*, 64th Congress, August 5, 1916, 12150). In this case, the sponsor of the bill would be coded as the chairman of the Committee on Public Lands since the amendment had no identifiable sponsor. A dummy variable (1, 0) for committee amendments was also coded, granting us some flexibility in how we deal these moving forward.

In a limited number of cases, neither the identifying amendment sponsor nor committee could be accurately determined. When this occurred, the amendment sponsor information was coded as missing data.

Underlying Measure

Data was also collected regarding the underlying measure. This allows us to better assess the characteristics of bills and motions that receive large numbers of amendments. Thus, students were asked to list the underlying landmark enactment being amended (e.g., H.R. 478). Much like the amendment sponsor variable, research assistants would then code the primary sponsor of the root measure. Occasionally this information was not made clear in the *Congressional Record*. In these instances, students were encouraged to utilize the *Congressional Record*'s index. The student looked up the name of the member who sponsored the amendment and the page number where the amendment was introduced. The index then provided the underlying bill that was being amended and any companion bills that might be considered. In the event a companion or related bill was considered, amending activity on that bill was coded.

Occasionally, the underlying measure was another amendment. As successful secondary amendments can significantly alter the content of the underlying amendment, we coded a dummy variable denoting that the amendment was a secondary amendment that sought to amend another amendment. In these instances, the underlying bill, resolution, and motion, as well as information on the amendment being amended, were coded. Once sponsors were identified, the member's ICPSR numbers were entered.

Additionally, research assistants were asked to code an assortment of other institutional factors related to the amendment. For example, scholars of the Senate have argued that the motion to table plays an important role in restricting measures on the chamber floor. Students coded whether or not a tabling motion was offered and information regarding who offered it.[2] Students also coded whether the amendment was considered in the Committee of the Whole, whether it was considered under the suspension of the rules procedure, and whether a motion to reconsider was offered.

Finally, information pertaining to the specific votes was coded. This can provide scholars with some leverage in analyzing how different vote types can alter policy outcomes. For measures that passed without a recorded vote, students coded the announced result. For example, on September 15, 1944, the *Congressional Record* noted the following announcement by the presiding officer:

> The PRESIDING OFFICER (Mr. THOMAS of Oklahoma in the chair). The next amendment was, on page 13, line 14, after the word "Roads" to strike out "Administration; and the Commissioner of Public Roads is hereby directed to concur only in such installations as will promote the sage and efficient utilization of the highways."
>
> The amendment was agreed to.
>
> Mr. BRIDGES. Mr. President, I was absent in the cloakroom a moment ago when action was taken on the so-called McClellan amendment. I am told that it was agreed to before my return to the floor, and that there was no opportunity to request a yea-and-nay vote on the amendment, that action on it was taken very quickly. Therefore, I ask unanimous consent that the Senate reconsider the vote by which the amendment was agreed to. (*Congressional Record*, 78th Congress, September 15, 1944, 7802)

Later in the debate, the chair announced that no objection to Bridges's request was heard, and a recorded vote was taken. In this case, the announced result was that the amendment passed. For division and teller votes, students coded the results of those votes as well as the yeas and nays. For amendments that received more than one type of vote, scholars can compare the size of coalitions on each vote, as well as the final result.

Yeas and Nays Information

In an effort to assess how members use the record to publicize their positions on issues, we also had research assistants code who requested the yeas and nays when a recorded vote was taken. For example, during consideration of H.R. 15455, the Merchant Marine bill, in the 64th Congress, Sen. Albert Cummins (R-IA) stated, "I am not for any part of the bill—I want no misunderstanding about that. I think it is fundamentally wrong; but as to this section, there is nothing but mischief in it. It can accomplish no good, and there is in it the opportunity for a great deal of wrong and evil. Upon the motion I have made, Mr. President, I ask for the yeas and nays" (*Congressional Record*, 64th Congress, August 18, 1916, 12814). The *Congressional Record* went on to note that the yeas and nays were ordered, indicating that a sufficient second was present. In this episode, Cummins would be listed as the member ordering the yeas and nays.[3]

Amendment Information

Finally, information was coded pertaining to whether the amendment was a substitute, second-degree or motion to strike, whether cloture was filed on the amendment, whether voting took place only in the Committee of the Whole, whether a yeas and nays request was made but not supported by a sufficient second, whether a motion to reconsider was offered, information regarding who—if anyone—moved to table the amendment or raised a point of order against it, and whether the amendment was dispensed with en bloc.

Additional Figures and Tables

In Chapter 5, we argued there was a sizable increase in the number of "messaging amendments" in both the House and the Senate. Additional evidence suggesting the growth in amendments is primarily reflective of an increase in electoral position-taking is evident when we look at party status. Figures D.3 and D.4 plot the number of non-committee amendments by party status. The figures include amendments that were filed on the floor but not formally offered (which primarily affected only the Senate). Lowess smoothing lines were included to reflect the general trend toward minority-sponsored amendments.

As Figures D.3 and D.4 demonstrate, there is a general trend toward minority-party-sponsored amendments. This trend is magnified when we

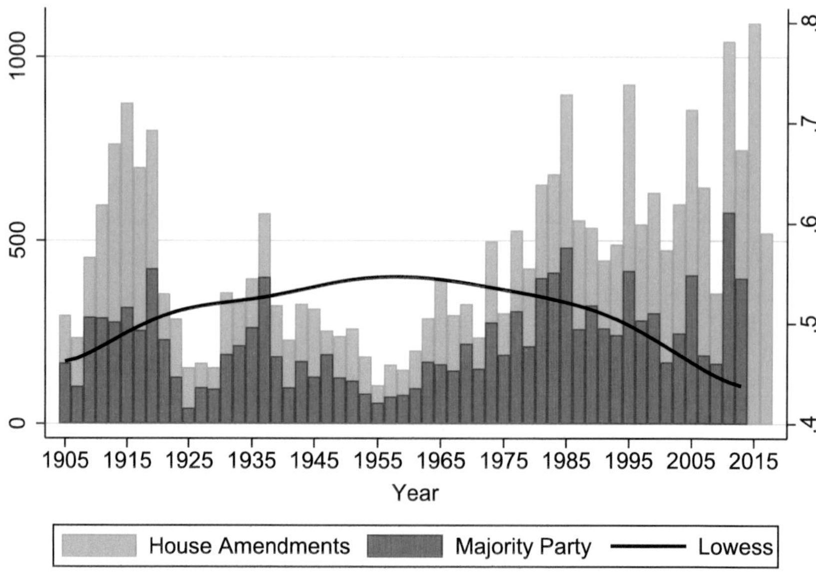

Figure D3. House Amendments by Party Status, 1905–2014

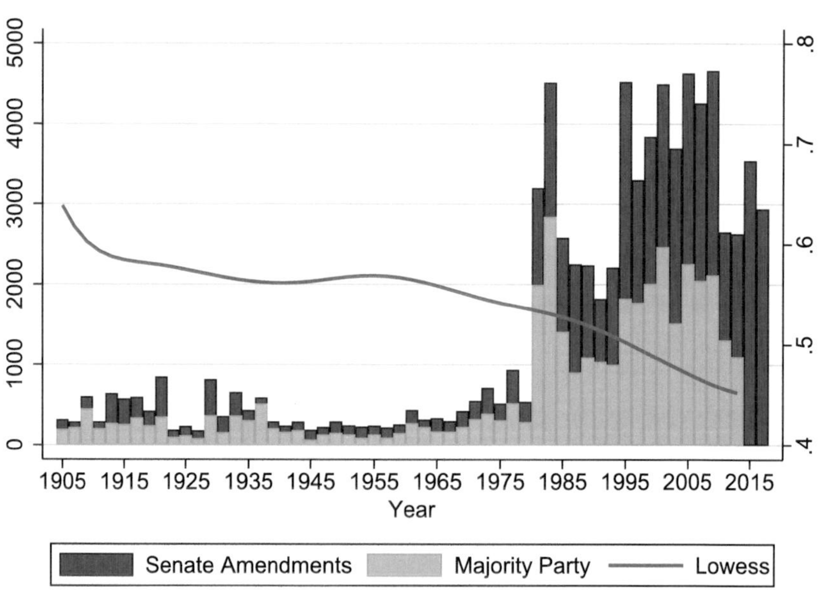

Figure D4. Senate Amendments by Party Status, 1905–2014

TABLE D1. House Amendments by Party Sponsor, 1905–2014

All Sponsors	Offered	Recorded	Percent
Majority Party	15,154	3,280	21.65%
Minority Party	13,663	4,107	30.01%
Total	28,817	7,387	25.73%

TABLE D2. Senate Amendments by Party Sponsor, 1905–2014

All Sponsors	Offered	Recorded	Percent
Majority Party	24,178	4,727	19.55%
Minority Party	18,476	5,894	31.90%
Total	28,817	10,621	24.90%

restrict the data to amendments receiving recorded votes. Tables D.1 and D.2 pool all non-committee amendments that received floor consideration in the House and the Senate.

As the tables demonstrate, there is about a 10% bias toward minority-party amendments in terms of which receive recorded votes. Restricting the data to the post-reform congresses yields a more pronounced split. For those congresses there is about a 15% bias toward minority-party amendments (pooling the House and the Senate).

Notes

Chapter 1

1. See Farrand (1966, 255).

2. "John Jay to Jesse Root," August 31, 1779, *Letters of Delegates to Congress*, 25:660.

3. The measure was unveiled to the public via the website readthebill.gop on March 6. The bill was formally introduced in the House as H.R. 1628 on March 20.

4. On March 22, the House adopted both the previous question motion and H.Res. 221, which allowed consideration of H.Res. 228. The previous question motion was adopted on a pure party-line vote, 233–185, and the rule by 227–189 vote with only four Republicans voting no. On March 24, the House adopted the previous question motion on H.Res. 228 on another party-line vote, 236–186. The rule was then adopted 230–194 with six Republican nays.

5. The drafting of the measure was largely done behind the scenes. Once released, the bill was quickly opposed by interest groups representing hospitals, doctors, and nurses, as well as powerful interest groups that support patient interests, including the AARP (Goodnough et al. 2017). They were joined by many conservative interest groups, including Heritage Action for America, the Cato Institute, and FreedomWorks (Weigel 2017).

6. The Senate cast 12 votes on H.R. 1628—eight on procedural matters and four on amendments—with 590 of the 623 votes by Republican senators supporting their party's position (or 94.7%). The Senate adopted a motion to proceed to H.R. 1628 on July 25 by a 50–50 vote, with Vice President Mike Pence (R-IN) casting a tie-breaking vote in favor. It then defeated a motion to waive the Budget Act on a full-text substitute amendment that would have provided a "clean repeal" of the ACA by a 57–43 vote (Kaplan 2017). A substitute sponsored by Sen. Rand Paul (R-KY) that would have repealed the ACA, but after a two-year delay, was defeated 55–45 (Sof-

fen and Schaul 2018). Two motions to commit with instructions offered by Sens. Joe Donnelly (D-IN) and Bob Casey (D-PA) were then rejected on straight party-line votes. Another motion to waive the Budget Act to consider an amendment, this one by Sen. Dean Heller (R-NV) that would have encouraged senators to commit to Medicaid expansion, was rejected. Heller's motion to waive failed overwhelmingly 90–10 (Turman 2017). Sen. Steve Daines (R-MT) offered an amendment that attempted to put Democrats on the record as supporting "single-payer health care," but Democrats did not bite, with the amendment failing 57–0 and 43 Democrats voting "present" (Foran 2017). The Senate rejected a motion to waive, 50–50, on an amendment by Sen. Luther Strange (R-AL). It then rejected a motion to commit with instructions by Senate Minority Leader Chuck Schumer (D-NY), 57–43. It adopted, on a straight party-line vote, a Heller amendment repealing the "Cadillac tax" on employer-based health premiums (Messerly and Snyder 2017). A fourth motion to commit, offered by Sen. Patty Murray (D-WA), was then rejected on a party-line vote. Finally, the Senate Republican substitute, dubbed the "skinny bill," was dramatically defeated 51–49, with Sens. Susan Collins (R-ME), Lisa Murkowski (R-AK), and John McCain (R-AZ) joining all Democrats in opposition (Eilperin et al. 2017).

7. Despite the defeat of the AHCA, Republicans remained highly unified on healthcare votes during the 115th Congress. In six procedural votes in the House, Republicans cast 1,396 "yea" votes, with only 12 "nays," giving voters the impression that Republicans vote together on healthcare 99.25% of the time.

8. Such "post hoc" adjustments in scheduling have become commonplace in the contemporary Congress. Newspaper sources highlighted at least 17 measures pulled from the House floor or rescheduled after adjustments were made during the three congresses that preceded the AHCA.

9. US Constitution, Article I, Section 5.

10. "One fifth of those Present" means that the support of at least one-fifth of number of members needed to reach a quorum are required before a vote can be recorded. As an example, 51 senators are needed to reach a quorum in the Senate, so the support of 11 senators (one-fifth of 51) is needed to allow a recorded vote.

11. "John Jay to Jesse Root," August 31, 1779, *Letters of Delegates to Congress*, 25:660.

12. As we discuss in later chapters, some of this work suggests this accountability does not hold across all voters (Crespin 2010; Clinton 2006; Deckard 1976).

13. As we discuss in Chapter 2, procedural rules promoting recorded voting were one of the few legislative procedures that were not adopted from the British Parliament. While the practice of publicizing how legislators voted occurred on rare occasion in 17th- and 18th-century Great Britain, it was not regularly employed by the House of Commons until 1836 (Bryce 1889; Luce 1922).

14. Not all votes can be paired with laws. For example, votes on nominations or pure procedural motions like adopting the House journal were omitted.

15. The University of Georgia Congress Project's website can be found at www.thecongressproject.com.

16. First, the data collection process is especially labor intensive. Coding all

amendments in a specific Congress is a massive undertaking. Completing a dataset that spanned a large number of congresses would require resources we simply do not have at this point. Second, utilizing important legislation helps minimize biases stemming from the large amount of trivial legislation the Congress produces (Clinton and Lapinski 2006). This allows us to ensure a certain level of salience.

17. We note, as discussed in Appendix B, that each individual enactment may include multiple bills. For example, Mayhew's (1991) list of "landmark bills" is included in our list. In it, he includes the Higher Education Act of 1972, a measure considered and adopted in the 92nd Congress. That measure was not only covered by the enacted bill, S. 659, but a House companion, H.R. 7248, and another Senate bill, S. 1557, which passed the Senate separately but was folded into S. 649 in the House.

Chapter 2

1. *Congressional Record*, 114th Congress, September 28, 2015, H6376.

2. It should be noted that the constitutional provision for recorded roll call voting does not apply to amendment voting within the Committee of the Whole in the House, which developed its own separate procedures.

3. The Founders also saw it fit to mandate that the yeas and nays be called on all votes to override presidential vetoes in Article 1, Section 7, Clause 2.

4. Luce (1922, 356) notes that "the Pennsylvania assembly in 1703 provided a rule that questions put to a vote would be answered by Members standing up, and saying Yea or Nay." In 1776, the Pennsylvania Constitution provided for yeas and nays upon the request of any two members. Luce also reported instances of recorded voting in New York. In his opposition toward the yeas and nays clause at the Constitutional Convention, Nathaniel Gorham cited problems caused by the practice in Massachusetts.

5. The full article specified: "The congress of the united states shall have power to adjourn to any time within the year, and to any place within the united states, so that no period of adjournment be for a longer duration than the space of six Months, and shall publish the Journal of their proceedings monthly, except such parts thereof relating to treaties, alliances or military operations, as in their judgment require secrecy; and the yeas and nays of the delegates of each State on any question shall be entered on the Journal, when it is desired by any delegate; and the delegates of a State, or any of them, at his or their request shall be furnished with a transcript of the said Journal, except such parts as are above excepted, to lay before the legislatures of the several states." The first recorded vote in the Confederation Congress was a 1777 vote on whether to restore General Benedict Arnold's rank. It failed (Luce 1922, 357).

6. Prior to 1777, neither state nor individual voting records were kept. In August 1777, the rules provided that the yeas and nays would be provided if required by any state. This was later amended to allow any member. After a recorded vote request killed a motion that had previously passed by voice vote, the provision was altered again to require that a request for the yeas and nays must be made prior to the question being taken (Jillson and Wilson 1994).

7. Specifically, Rush, who would claim authorship of the letter in a subsequent letter to John Adams, wrote, "Let us read something more than 'Yeas' and 'Nays' and questions for recommitting and postponing business in your Journals. Your money—your money—demands every thought and every hour" (Butterfield 1951, 235).

8. "Jesse Root to John Jay," July 19, 1779, *Letters of Delegates to Congress*, 25:657.

9. Journals of the Continental Congress, 1774–1789, May 4, 1781, 480.

10. "John Jay to Jesse Root," August 31, 1779, *Letters of Delegates to Congress*, 25:660.

11. "Henry Laurens' Notes of Debates," April 30, 1779, *Letters of Delegates to Congress*, 12:409.

12. In February 1780, Gerry made a motion to recommit part of a report with instructions it be amended to reduce the amount of supplies and money requested of Massachusetts. This was ruled out of order by the presiding officer. Gerry, who was upset by the ruling, appealed and asked for a recorded vote on his appeal. The recorded vote request was denied by the presiding officer, a decision that outraged Gerry. The presiding officer, apparently relying on the ambiguity of what constitutes a "question" as specified by the rule, determined it was not in order to request the yeas and nays on a question of order. Gerry refused to return to the Continental Congress until the ruling was reversed and his request for the yeas and nays was honored. He argued that the right to the yeas and nays was of essential interest to the public, as the Congress adopted the yeas and nays clause without a sufficient second to provide members "an opportunity [to demonstrate their] conduct to his constituents" (Billias 1976, 86). The ruling was not reversed, and despite his reelection in 1871, Gerry did not resume his seat in Congress until August 1783 (Austin 1828; Billias 1976).

13. Jillson and Wilson (1994, 85) note that "while it would be too much to say that by the early 1780s men stayed away from the Congress to avoid serving as president . . . or declined to serve when elected . . . to avoid being rendered mute, it is safe to say that prominent men found other things to do while lesser men held the chair."

14. Cushing (1856, 530) continues, noting that "in many cases, a proposition was held to be divisible in which some of the members, if adopted, would require the addition of formal or technical words—by the clerk, to make them into distinct propositions. In others, again, propositions were held to be divisible, the second member of which was a mere qualification of the first, and recorded on the journal to have failed, of course, without a question, in consequence of the failure of the first."

15. See Jillson and Wilson (1994, 150–153).

16. The Articles did not have an explicit quorum provision comparable to the US Constitution. Instead, Article IX specified that "the yeas and nays of the delegates of each State, on any question, shall be entered on the Journal, when it is desired by any delegate."

17. The yeas and nays provision of the journal clause was included in Charles Pinckney's plan, though without the sufficient second clause. When the Committee on Detail reported the clause on August 6, the sufficient second clause (specifying one-fifth) was included.

18. This was opposed by Morris, who, ironically, felt it would lead to a filling of the journals.

19. As we discuss later, roll call voting on nominations in the Senate has an especially complex history.

20. Since 1640, the House of Commons has required a quorum of 40 members for business to be conducted. It is unclear why that number was selected (Luce 1922).

21. US Constitution, Article 1, Section 5, Clause 1. Discussion of the provision occurred primarily on August 10, 1787. A proposal by Morris to fix a quorum at 33 members of the House and 14 in the Senate was defeated by a vote of 9 to 2. An amendment by Madison to add language at the end of the clause passed unanimously. The added language read, "and may be authorized to compel the attendance of absent members in such manner and under such penalties as 'each House may provide'" (Farrand 1966, 245–246). The amended clause then passed via voice vote.

22. US Constitution, Article 1, Section 2, Clause 2. Some discussion occurred over a Madison amendment to the second part of the clause. It originally provided each House may also "punish its Members for disorderly behavior; and may expel a member." Madison, concerned a bare majority of a quorum could abuse the expulsion requirement, proposed an amendment that added "with the concurrence of 2/3." It was adopted unanimously (Benton 1986, 672–673).

23. US Constitution, Article 1, Section 2, Clause 4. See Lynch et al. (2018) for a more detailed discussion of this clause and its effect on the development of the Senate.

24. The Court declared that "the General Assembly has failed to adhere to the mandates of accountability and transparency that the Constitution requires when the General Assembly exercises the legislative taxing authority permitted by the Constitution" (*Marshall v. Northern Virginia Transportation Authority*).

25. Some state constitutions, like Montana's, mandate recorded votes on "each substantive question" in both the legislature and in committees (Vermeule 2004).

26. Likewise, the rules of the US Senate provide for mandatory recorded votes on motions to invoke cloture.

27. See National Conference of State Legislatures. 2002, *Inside the Legislative Process*, http://www.ncsl.org/research/about-state-legislatures/inside-the-legislative-process.aspx#FloorAction

28. There is also considerable variance between countries and US state legislatures. For example, the rules of the Canadian House and Senate have provided for the yeas and nays since its inception in 1867. The Canadian House of Commons requires a recorded vote if "demanded by five members" and the Senate upon the demand of "two senators" (Bourinot 1884). In the British House of Commons, a recorded teller vote can be requested by any one member. And Carey (2003, 197) notes that all Latin American legislatures have rules providing for roll call votes "under certain conditions, generally at the request of the chamber leadership (mesa directiva or directorio), by consensus of the leadership of the various parties (bancadas, fracciones, grupos), or by petition of some qualified quorum" (one-fifth, one-fourth, one-third, or one-half of the membership or of those present).

29. The Indiana Constitution specifies, "Two-thirds of each House shall constitute a quorum to do business." Oregon, Tennessee, and Texas also require two-thirds standards for quorums (Squire and Moncrief 2015).

30. In the absence of the recorded voting provision, the chamber, presumably operating under the assumption of a quorum, could pass such a measure by an unrecorded vote. See Wisconsin Constitution, Article VIII, Section 8.

31. See Jenkins and Stewart (2013) for more on the development of the speaker.

32. Anzia and Jackman (2013) found that majority-party roll rates in state legislatures are partially conditioned by the party's control over the appointment of committee members and chairs, as well as rules mandating committees hold hearings on bills. In 95 out of 99 state legislative chambers, the majority-party committee members and chairs were appointed by the majority party (the leader, the majority caucus, or a committee on committees). Similar findings can be found in comparative politics. For example, Doring (2001) reports high levels of variation among procedures providing for committee autonomy from the parent chamber among Western European countries. Countries with less committee autonomy and more centralized agenda control passed more complex legislation and featured more conflict. For work demonstrating the policy impact of party control over appointments, see Cox and McCubbins (2005) and Heath et al. (2005).

33. Disappearing quorums were of particular concern for Reed, who was elected speaker with 166 votes—the exact number required for a quorum to be present. A Republican member died shortly after Reed's election, leaving the party one member shy of a quorum (McCall 1914). The constitutionality of Reed counting members to determine a quorum was later upheld by the Supreme Court in *United States v. Ballin* (1892). The ruling essentially upheld the ability of each chamber of Congress to determine whether a majority is present for the purpose of determining whether a quorum exists.

34. This was the first ruling of a particularly significant nature. However, Reed had issued several mildly controversial procedural rulings earlier in the month of January.

35. Consult Figures A.1 and A.2 in Appendix A for a full time series of House and Senate roll calls per congress. These figures demonstrate an increase in roll call votes in both chambers in the years leading up to the Civil War, though not to the extent observed in the contemporary era.

36. Cruz went on to argue, "What does 'denying a second' mean? Denying a recorded vote. Why is that important? When you are breaking the commitments you have made to the men and women who have elected you, the most painful thing in the world is accountability. When you are misleading the men and women who showed up to vote for you, you don't want sunshine making clear that you voted no. A recorded vote means each Senator's name is on it" (*Congressional Record,* 114th Congress, September 28, 2015, H6376).

37. This was the second time in the 114th Congress Cruz had been denied a sufficient second. He and Sen. Mike Lee (R-UT) had been blocked in July when they sought to offer amendments in the third-degree. Such amendments were long barred by Senate rules. Cruz and Lee unsuccessfully sought roll call votes on their appeals of the chair's rulings that the amendments were out of order (Lesniewski 2015a). Cruz's troubles likely stemmed from his well-established poor relationship with Majority Leader Mitch McConnell (R-KY) and the bulk of the Republican caucus. He had

famously called McConnell a "liar" on the floor and sarcastically complimented him for being a "very effective Democratic leader" (Everett 2015b).

38. Attendance was calculated by taking the total number of votes cast and dividing them over the total number of votes cast plus missing votes as presented by Poole and Rosenthal (2007). Members who cast "paired" votes are coded as attending. Senate attendance is comparable during this period. Consult Figures A.3 and A.4 in Appendix A for Senate and House attendance from 1860 to 2013.

39. For example, Sen. Boies Penrose (R-PA) and Sen. John Sharp Williams (D-MS) were paired for several congresses. Penrose died in 1921. Upon learning this, Williams approached Sen. James Watson (R-IN), informing him, "Jim, Penrose is dead, my pair is going, and I've to have another one. I don't want any confounded mugwump for my pair. I want just as much of a reactionary as I can find. I want a man who for thirty years, by neither direction nor indirection, has ever been right on any public question, and, by golly, you're my man!" Williams and Watson remained paired throughout the rest of the Mississippian's time in the Senate (Osborn 1943, 386).

40. See also "House Votes to Give Navy $396,000,000," *New York Times*, April 29, 1921.

41. Blanton had used the word "damn" during debate on the congressional floor in October. Since this was considered an inappropriate curse word, a resolution expelling him from the House was introduced. While many anticipated Blanton would apologize, he instead gave an hour-and-half-long speech defending himself, declaring that "the man who is not afraid to lose his own head does not consider his political head" (*Congressional Record*, 67th Congress, October 27, 1921, 6886). His defense was largely led by the noted parliamentarian Rep. Robert Luce (R-MA). A Republican, Luce announced it was difficult to defend Blanton but he felt duty-bound to oppose expulsion, which he felt was too extreme an option. Luce argued, "A seemingly righteous precedent set now may be turned to unrighteous ends next year" (*Congressional Record*, 67th Congress, October 27, 1921, 6890). After the expulsion resolution was defeated, Blanton was unanimously censured. Blanton would faint on the floor afterward (Stevens 1982; Fishbein 2018).

42. The amendment data are discussed in greater detail in Appendix D. As we explain in the appendix, amendment data from the 97th Congress on were downloaded from Congress.gov using govtrack and coded for vote type. Hence, manual coding of failed vote requests was not feasible.

43. See *Rules of the U.S. Senate*, Rule XXII.

44. See *Rules of the U.S. House*, Rule XX, Clause 10.

Chapter 3

1. Committee consideration also included a vote on a Democratic Party amendment offered by Rep. Lois Capps (D-CA). Her amendment sought to strike the usage of the Prevention and Public Health Fund established by the Affordable Care Act as a funding source for H.R. 1549. It was also defeated on a party-line vote.

2. Structured rules allow the House Rules Committee to choose which proposed

amendments to a bill are to be allowed consideration on the House floor. A further discussion of structured rules is located in Chapter 4. This rule provided for consideration of two amendments—one offered by Pitts and one offered by Rep. Julia Brownley (D-CA). The Pitts amendment would provide states with a block grant to fund state high-risk pools. Republicans argued this would provide Americans with a preexisting condition with an "escape valve" from the "train wreck" created by the ACA (*Congressional Record*, 113th Congress, April 24, 2013, H2269). Brownley's amendment called for the secretary of Health and Human Services to submit a report to Congress on the effect of the act (see House Report 113-46, 113th Congress).

3. Rep. Louise Slaughter (D-NY) argued that "given the fact that not a single Republican voted for the Affordable Care Act, it seems incongruous to me that they are now here today with great bleeding-heart concerns about the people with previous conditions that keep them from being insured" (*Congressional Record*, 113th Congress, April 24, 2013, H2268).

4. The vote to order the previous question on the rule passed 228–192, with only one Democrat, Rep. Jim Matheson (D-UT), joining all voting Republicans in support. H.Res. 175 passed 225–189, with only Tea Party conservative Rep. Matt Salmon (R-AZ) joining all voting Democrats in opposition.

5. Democrats were aware of this as well. Rep. Louise Slaughter (D-NY) stated, "In news reports earlier this morning, we were told that today's bill, dubbed by reporters as 'CantorCare,' may even be pulled before it gets a vote. One Member of the majority was purported to say that today's bill does nothing but shift money from a program he doesn't support to another program he doesn't support" (*Congressional Record*, 113th Congress, April 24, 2013, H2268). Hoyer commented that the bill "deeply divided the Republican Party" (*Congressional Record*, 113th Congress, April 24, 2013, H2270).

6. The rule, H.Res. 215, was adopted after two almost perfect party-line votes. The vote to order the previous question on the rule passed 228–193, with only one Democrat, Rep. Jim Matheson (D-UT), joining all voting Republicans in support. H.Res. 215 passed 226–192, with Matheson and Rep. Mike McIntyre (D-NC) joining the Republicans. Matheson and McIntyre also accounted for the only Democratic votes in favor of H.R. 45.

7. In the 112th Congress, Heritage included passage of H.R. 2, H.R. 358, H.R. 1217, and H.R. 6079 in its scorecard. In the 113th, it scored H.R. 7, H.J.R. 59, and the Republican Study Committee's (RSC) substitute budget amendment to H.C.R. 96. H.J.R. 59, a continuing resolution that fully repealed the ACA, was eventually enacted into law, but only after the ACA repeal was dropped. Similarly, the Club for Growth scored passage of H.R. 2, the RSC's substitute budget amendment to H.C.R. 112, H.R. 1173, and H.R. 6079 in the 112th Congress, and H.J.R. 59, H.R. 2667, Bachman's H.R. 45, and H.R. 3522 in the 113th. H.R. 1173 repealed the CLASS program of the ACA and was folded into another bill and eventually enacted. Another conservative interest group, the Chamber of Commerce, scored passage of H.R. 2, H.R. 1173, and H.R. 436 in the 112th Congress and H.R. 2667 and H.R. 4414 in the 113th Congress. See https://heritageaction.com/scorecard/votes; https://www.clubforgrowth.org/scorecards/; https://www.uschamber.com/report/how-they-voted-2014-house#4

8. Matthews and Stimson (1975), who reported that nearly 80% of members did not think voters were aware of their voting record in Congress, also report that members believed that one or two bad votes could hurt them. These members complained that identifying which votes those would be was extremely difficult.

9. Data from roll call voting in state legislatures also show that roll calls do not have meaningful electoral consequences (Rogers 2017).

10. Legislators can sometime avoid needing to explain a vote by simply not taking one. President Obama was criticized when he was running for president for the "nearly 130" times he voted "present" while an Illinois state senator, allowing him to avoid voting either for or against a variety of issues (Hernandez and Drew 2007).

11. Such "pay raise" ads are common for members of both parties. See advertisements attacking former Rep. Charlie Bass (R-NH), Sen. Sherrod Brown (D-OH), and Sen. Roy Blunt (R-MO). *PolitiFact*'s Truth-O-Meter rated the claims Perdue made in his "pay raise" ad as "mostly false." See www.politifact.com/georgia/statements/2014/jul/11/david-perdue/perdue-pay-raise-claim-falls-short/

12. Pelosi was frequently employed in campaign advertisements, even in the absence of roll call votes. For example, Republicans prominently featured Pelosi in a series of ads attacking the Democratic candidate Jon Ossoff in a 2017 Georgia special election. These ads asserted Ossoff would be a "rubber-stamp" for Pelosi's liberal policies (Schneider 2017).

13. Barber, Canes-Wrone, and Thrower (2017) report that individual donors are significantly more likely to donate to a senatorial campaign if the senator voted with them on roll call votes. Bonica (2014) argues that donors give to members who match them ideologically. And Stratmann (2002, 345) finds that "evidence that changes in contribution levels determine changes in roll call voting behavior, that contributions from competing groups are partially offsetting, and that junior legislators are more responsive to changes in contribution levels than are senior legislators." However, the evidence here does not conclusively support the idea that outside groups "buy votes." For example, Barber (2016) argues influence is conditional on donor type. PACs tend to support more moderate members and individual donors more extreme members. Examining aggregate ideology, McCarty, Poole, and Rosenthal (2008) find no relationship between a House member's extremity and the total amount raised from individual donors. Other work finds no relationship between outside group donations and member votes on roll calls (Wright 1985). This does not mean outside groups do not influence member behavior—especially ideologically extreme members—it just occurs earlier in the legislative process (Denzau and Munger 1986; Hall and Wayman 1990).

14. Boehner had argued that the 16-day shutdown in October 2013 was influenced by Heritage Action and the Club for Growth "key voting" certain proposals (Kane and O'Keefe 2013). Several months earlier, Boehner was forced to pull a special rule providing for consideration of his "Plan B" proposal to deal with the expiring Bush tax cuts and mandatory cuts in government spending after both groups urged members to vote no (Logiurato 2012; Weisman 2012).

15. Not all votes can be paired with bills. For examples, votes on nominations or pure procedural motions like adopting the House journal were omitted.

16. Jessee and Theriault (2014) cleverly control for the potential that increased party-line voting on procedural matters is caused by member attitudes on the substance of the bill. However, they lacked the data to examine the type of procedure employed.

17. Both the DREAM Act and a provision repealing "Don't Ask, Don't Tell" were initially considered in the Senate as part of the Ike Skelton National Defense Authorization Act for Fiscal Year 2011 (H.R. 6523, 111 P.L. 383). Cloture on the motion to proceed to the bill failed by a vote of 56–43 on September 21, 2010. On December 9, a second cloture vote on the motion to proceed failed, this time by a vote of 57–40. The Defense Authorization Act was eventually adopted without the DREAM Act and Don't Ask, Don't Tell, the latter of which was adopted separately on December 18th (H.R. 2965, 111 P.L. 321). The DREAM Act was considered separately on two additional occasions, but failed both times. On December 9, S. 3992 was tabled 59–40. On December 18, cloture on the motion to concur in the House amendment to the Senate amendment to H.R. 5281 was defeated 55–41.

Chapter 4

1. *Congressional Record*, 111th Congress, September 29, 2010, 17030.

2. Quoted in Oleszek and Oleszek (2012, 261).

3. It was named after Detective James Zadroga, believed to be the first 9/11 first responder to die from inhaling dust at Ground Zero (Nelson 2009). The measure had been introduced and not acted upon in both the 109th and 110th Congresses. Maloney stated her intent with the law when she said that "the legislation would provide medical care and compensation for those who are sick with World Trade Center (WTC) illnesses, including first responders who came to New York from every state and nearly all Congressional districts in the nation" (*Congressional Record*, Extensions of Remarks, 111th Congress, February 4, 2009, E201).

4. A multi-measure or "grab-bag" rule, H.Res. 1674 also provided for consideration of the Currency Reform for Fair Trade Act (H.R. 2378) and the Intelligence Authorization Act for Fiscal Year 2010 (H.R. 2701).

5. *Congressional Record*, 111th Congress, September 29, 2009, H7221.

6. See the motion to recommit subsection for further details on the procedure.

7. Four Republicans joined all but 14 Democrats in voting no.

8. The bill would eventually pass the Senate, but only after a cloture motion on a motion to proceed failed 57–42. In response to the defeat of the cloture motion and additional threats by opponents, Senate supporters cut the total cost of the measure from $7.4 billion to $4.2 billion and dropped the controversial offset provision. On December 22, a substitute amendment to H.R. 847 was adopted, and the amended bill passed by unanimous consent. The House then passed the bill later that night, by a vote of 206–60, and it was signed into law by the president on January 2, 2011 (111 P.L. 347).

9. For example, Democrats featured Zadroga's father in a 2016 ad attacking Rep.

Scott Garrett (R-NJ) for being the only member of the New Jersey delegation to vote against the act in 2010. Garrett had voted for it in September, but voted against the motion to suspend the rules the bill was first considered under, voted against passage in July, and supported all three Republican procedural motions (Sanchez 2016).

10. See *Congressional Record,* 111th Congress, September 29, 2010, 16997.

11. *Congressional Record,* 100th Congress, October 29, 1987, 29920. In contrast, the minority leader, Bob Michel (R-IL) asserted, "There was no reason to gloat over our victory." Michel then went on to chastise Wright for his "parliamentary trickery." (*Congressional Record,* 100th Congress, October 29, 1987, 30227).

12. The new rule included language that would strip a controversial welfare provision from the bill.

13. It was signed into law on December 22, 1987 (100 P.L. 203).

14. Rep. Dick Cheney (R-WY) bemoaned that "there's no sense of comity left" (Barry 2015, 2). Conservative Democrats blamed Gingrich's speech for their shift on the measure. *CQ Almanac* (1987) reports, "Many of these were so angry with Gingrich's outburst, that they changed course, helping Wright win an important procedural vote that brought the legislation to the floor. Most dissidents later voted against passage, however. One of the leaders of the House Southern Democrats, Buddy MacKay (D-FL), told Gingrich that his speech "is one of the most destructive things that could have happened today." See "Reconciliation Bill Raises Taxes, Cuts Spending," *CQ Almanac,* 1987.

15. Cox and Poole (2002) find increased party effects on procedural votes—such as votes on special rules or chamber organization. Crespin (2010) shows that members are responsive to party pressure on procedural votes under varying circumstances. Additionally, Roberts (2005) finds elevated party pressure on another procedural tool, the motion to recommit.

16. A second, somewhat complimentary explanation is that there are macro-level partisan benefits for members asked to cast these tough votes. These benefits largely stem from a party's ability to stay in control of the chamber. For example, members may be rewarded with favorable committee assignments, which can lead to increased credit-claiming opportunities (Aldrich and Rohde 2000; Cox and McCubbins 2005). The majority party is also in a stronger position to distribute pork-barrel projects to legislators. Jenkins and Monroe (2012a, 2012b) have found that members asked to cast difficult votes on procedural matters are disproportionately likely to receive high compensation to congressional campaigns. Lynch, Madonna, and Roberts (2016) argue that majority-party leaders allow moderates to make amendments to bills as a form of compensation. Finally, there are collective benefits accrued through the maintenance of a favorable partisan "brand name" (Cox and McCubbins 2007; Monroe and Robinson 2008).

17. However, the decision not to maximize their policy benefits can be consequential. Scholars note that the possibility of net policy loss certainly exists. Cox and McCubbins argue, "The only downside to cartelizing is that consistently centrist members may suffer a net policy loss from the majority's veto. This loss must be coun-

terbalanced by office and distributive benefits in order to secure the centrists support" (2005, 46).

18. Other recent cases featuring "pay raise" accusations include the 2012 Montana Senate race, the 2016 Missouri Senate general election, the 2012 Ohio Senate general election, the Virginia Senate general election, the 2014 Iowa Fourth House District general election, the 2014 Kentucky Senate general election, the 2012 Georgia 14th House District Republican election, the 2010 Florida gubernatorial election, the 2014 Mississippi Republican Senate primary election, the 2012 Florida 22nd House District general election, and the 2012 Florida Republican Senate primary election.

19. A *PolitiFact* assessment of Rigell's ad can be found at https://www.politifact.com/virginia/statements/2010/oct/25/scott-rigell/nye-voted-lockstep-nancy-pelosi-83-percent/

20. Specifically, Republicans had been using a modified version of a motion to recommit with instructions that included the word "promptly." Democrats barred usage of the word "promptly" for the traditional "forthwith" in motions to recommit with instructions. This technique allowed the minority to offer an amendment while simultaneously sending the bill back to committee. In essence, this combined the best elements of both types of motions to recommit—it allowed a vote on an amendment that the minority could use in a 30-second attack ad (Ornstein 2010) while also essentially killing the bill. In opposing the rule change, Rep. Dave Dreier (R-CA), the ranking Republican on the Rules Committee, asserted, "Mr. Speaker, process is substance" (*Congressional Record*, 111th Congress, January 6, 2009, 14).

21. As discussed in Chapter 2, legislative process is dictated by both exogenously and endogenously designed rules. While we have conceded exogenous rules are generally more difficult to alter than those endogenously determined by the chamber, it is important to note there are limitations to viewing rules dichotomously. First, rules placed on chambers exogenously through things like constitutions often contain ambiguities. For instance, the quorum rule in the US Constitution did not specify how a quorum would be counted or how business would be defined. As a result of these ambiguities, majorities can occasionally bypass exogenously determined rules.

Second, scholars frequently underestimate the transaction costs required to alter endogenously set rules. Changing standing rules takes time that could be spent on enacting policies. For example, in the 87th and 88th Congresses, Majority Leader Mike Mansfield (D-MT) persuaded Senate Democrats supporting civil rights legislation to back off from an effort to decrease the cloture threshold. Unwilling to sacrifice incoming President John F. Kennedy's legislative agenda, he argued that "we ought to face up to the realities of the situation and recognize that the Democratic President will have a program he will want to put through" (Bell 1960). In addition to taking up time, rules reforms invite increased scrutiny from the minority and the media.

22. For example, during consideration of the Serve America Act (H.R. 1388), a motion to recommit with instructions was offered by Rep. Virginia Foxx (R-VA). The motion sought to amend the bill to prohibit participants in national service programs from attempting to influence legislation, engage in protests, boycotts, or strikes, or assist union efforts (Adofo and Gensheimer 2009). The bill manager, Rep. George

Miller (D-CA), announced his support for the motion and it was adopted 318–105. The bill then passed the House, 321–105.

Miller argued, "I think, as we have only seen it for a few minutes, I think most of the motion to recommit is, in fact, already covered in statutes, regulations and the grant agreements that are issued. We are well aware of these issues. The Members on both sides of the aisle have spoken to them, and they have offered statutes, not only in this act, but in other acts, making sure that people who get these grants don't engage in activities that they should not be. So we plan to accept this amendment. I appreciate the gentlewoman offering it, and we will take it to conference" (*Congressional Record*, 111th Congress, March 18, 2009, H3606).

23. This includes omnibus lawmaking and the usage of vehicles. Additionally, in the 1980s and early 1990s, the House Rules Committee issued a number of restrictive special rules barring the minority from offering a motion to recommit. In 1995, the new Republican majority added language to the House standing rules barring the Rules Committee from doing this in the future (Lynch et al. 2016).

A second potential reason for the motion to recommit's stability stems from limitations in our data. It is likely that over our time series the usage of the motion to recommit has shifted from straight motions to recommit, to motions to recommit with instructions. Unfortunately, our expanded roll call data do not distinguish between motions to recommit and motions to recommit with instructions. However, our amendment dataset presented in Chapter 5 does distinguish between the two, albeit with a more limited time series.

24. They also can lead to additional roll calls on other procedural votes. An example of this occurred during consideration of H.R. 2, a bill increasing the minimum wage, in the 110th Congress (2007–2008). Republicans forced roll calls on two motions to commit the rule (H.Res. 6, which also provided for the rules of the 110th Congress), a point of order regarding the germaneness of a motion to recommit H.R. 2 and another roll call on a second motion to recommit H.R. 2. These motions were all tied to substantive proposals providing small business tax breaks. Electorally vulnerable Republicans, like Heather Wilson (R-NM) and Christopher Shays (R-CT), then highlighted Democratic votes against small businesses while speaking on the measure.

25. Dalzell would go on to characterize the minority's actions as "childish, imbecile [and] a disgrace to grown men of full stature." He then introduced several rules curtailing the minority's ability to delay chamber business (see "Defeat for Minority," *Washington Post*, April 5, 1905).

26. The point is reported in Hudiburg (2018). Multiple anonymous staff members have reiterated to us this has been the motivation for their members requesting journal votes as well.

27. Additionally, roll calls on previous question motions are increasingly likely to yield party votes when compared to special rule votes. Looking across the three eras: 81% of previous question roll calls in Era 1 were party votes (compared to 74% of special rules votes); 63% of previous question motions in Era 2 were party votes (compared to 41% of special rules votes), and 96% of previous question votes in Era 3 were party votes (compared to 68% of special rule votes).

28. If they did, they would likely pass the legislation via suspension.

29. The term appeared to originate during consideration of one such rule, H.Res. 294 in the 102nd Congress (1991–1992). The Rules Committee ranking member, Dave Dreier (R-CA), asserted he had heard Speaker Tom Foley (D-WA) use the term to describe the rule. Rep. Bob Walker (R-PA) expressed gleeful shock on the floor upon learning this was not "a term [Republicans] are making up on this side in order to talk about this rule" (*Congressional Record*, 102nd Congress, November 23, 1991, 34183).

Rep. Bob McEwen (R-OH) played off the term earlier in the debate, noting that "martial law is a temporary rule imposed by military authorities on the civilian population in time of war or when civil authority has broken down. Mr. Speaker, I do not know exactly whether the majority leader is saying by this resolution that it considers the House to be in a state of war or simply that the leadership's civil authority has been destroyed. But in either case, I strongly oppose this military edict from on high" (*Congressional Record*, 102nd Congress, November 23, 1991, 34180).

30. Historically, much of the Senate's business was governed by unanimous consent agreements. These agreements frequently specify the length of debate and the number and quantity of amendments offered (Ainsworth and Flathman 1995; Oleszek et al. 2016). They often are the result of lengthy negotiations among party leaders, committee chairs, and other key senators.

31. See Chapter 5 for a description of filling the amendment tree.

32. The motion to table was made non-debatable sometime between 1828 and 1841. Even after Senate practice had dictated that it was non-debatable, there was much ambiguity as to whether it was in order on an appeal. In 1841, the Senate overruled a decision by Sen. Willie Mangum (W-NC), declaring that it was (*Congressional Globe*, 27th Congress, August 7, 1841).

33. Sen. Robert Byrd (D-WV) viewed the coverage factor as a key component to the motion's value. He argued, "A motion to table is a procedural motion. It obfuscates the issue, and it makes possible an explanation by a senator to his constituents, if he wishes to do, that his vote was not on the merits of the issue. He can claim that he might have this or he might have voted that way, if the Senate had voted up or down on the issue itself" (quoted in Tiefer 1989, 658). The explosion in the usage of the motion is frequently credited to Byrd (Smith et al. 2013).

34. McConnell responded by noting that the Senate voted on more amendments in January 2015 than all of 2014 (Lesniewski 2015b).

35. We took our expanded roll call dataset and collapsed it to the bill level by vote type. We then merged it into our important enactment dataset. This allows us to evaluate important legislation that received any recorded votes. This was the case for 392 of the 2,036 enactments in our data. Figure 4.2 plots the average number per enactment by Congress, excluding lopsided votes, failed enactments, and simple resolutions. For an examination on the likelihood an enactment receives at least one final passage vote, consult Appendix B's Figures B.4 and B.5.

36. For a separate breakdown by chamber, consult Appendix B's Figures B.6 and B.7.

37. There are 108 observations in our first five congresses and 189 in the last five.

This statistic follows Figure 4.2 in excluding lopsided votes, failed enactments, and simple resolutions.

38. Many of the early enactments not brought to the floor through restrictive rules were brought using either unanimous consent, suspension of the rules, or Calendar Wednesday. Calendar Wednesday isn't used in the modern era. However, a number of important measures were considered under the procedure throughout the history of Congress, for example, the Mann Act in 1910 and, perhaps most notably, the 19th Amendment in the 66th Congress. It is still provided for in Rule XV, Clause 6, "Calendar Call of Committees, Wednesdays" of the House rules. The rule allows committees to call up non-privileged bills directly from the Union calendar. It provided for two hours of debate, equally divided, on a bill called up under the procedure. Calendar Wednesday was adopted at the end of the 60th Congress after pressure from rank-and-file members who resented the power held by the "Czar" speakers, Thomas Brackett Reed (R-ME) and "Uncle" Joe Cannon (R-IL). The idea was that it would allow committees to bypass centralized speaker and Rules Committee power (Jones 1968).

39. These numbers exclude appropriation bills and House and Senate simple resolutions.

40. For more on this, see Figure A.5 in Appendix A.

41. See, for example, Hulse 2019; McPherson 2019.

Chapter 5

1. Quoted in Quirk and Hinchcliffe (1998).

2. *Congressional Record*, 111th Congress, March 24, 2010, S1942.

3. None of Flake's amendments came close to passing. The most popular of these amendments failed on a 342 to 118 vote. None of his other amendments garnered 100 votes.

4. Two of the House roll calls were on ordering the previous question motion on a special rule, two on the rules themselves, 13 on amendments, one on a motion to recommit with instructions, one on final passage, and one on a motion to concur in the Senate amendment with an amendment. In the Senate, 10 roll calls were on amendments, two were on motions to waive the Budget Act, one on final passage, one on a motion to concur in the House amendment with an amendment, and one on a motion to concur in the House amendment.

5. The Naval Appropriations Act of 1909 was a highly salient measure. Clinton and Lapinski (2006) list it as the fifth most influential measure of the 60th Congress. In total, there were 16 roll calls related to the bill—12 in the House, four in the Senate. All four Senate roll calls dealt with amendments. In the House, six of the roll calls related to two special rules, one related to suspension of the rules, one to final passage, one on a motion to disagree with the Senate, and three on the motion to resolve in the Committee of the Whole. While not comparable to H.R. 3326 in 2009, this is an elevated roll call total that coincided with a deliberate minority-party strategy to delay this bill by forcing a high number of roll calls (Sala 2002).

6. Filling the amendment tree is a procedure used almost exclusively in the Senate. In both chambers only a certain number of amendments can be pending simultaneously. To block unfavorable amendments, majority leaders will use their right of first recognition to offer a series of amendments until all the available amendment slots are filled. If a cloture motion is successful, further amending is then cut off. Most scholarly and journalistic accounts credit the procedure to former Senate Majority Leader Robert Byrd (D-WV). The technique was then employed by his Republican successors, Majority Leaders Howard Baker (R-TN) and Robert Dole (R-KS). Dole noted that he "never knew what 'filling the tree' was until I tried it, but it turned out to be pretty good" (Weisman 2012). During a debate over the procedure in 1999, Byrd, who served as majority leader from 1977 to 1981 and from 1987 to 1989, was uncertain as to whether he deserved the credit or not, stating, "I may have been the first one to fill up the tree in my service in the Senate—I am not sure—I did do that on a few occasions, but only on a very few occasions" (*Congressional Record*, 106th Congress, July 26, 1999, S9205).

7. McConnell, criticizing Reid, claimed he would "treat senators with respect" and "work harder and accomplish more" and added that the "Senate can be returned to the place of great debates, contentious debates, but where you can still get outcomes on things where you have at least 60 senators" (Hulse 2014).

8. See also Pierce (2010).

9. Sen. Ben Nelson (D-NE) and Sen. Evan Bayh (D-IN) joined all voting Republicans in opposition to the tabling motion.

10. *FactCheck* called a similar ad attacking Sen. Patty Murray (D-WA) "bogus" (Kiely 2010). And *PolitiFact* rated a similar ad attacking Rep. Ed Perlmutter (D-CO) as "pants-on-fire," for similar reasons, in addition to Perlmutter being in the House, which did not vote directly on Coburn's amendment (Holan 2010).

11. Reid himself aggressively criticized the practice of filling the amendment tree (see Smith 2014). He complained that Majority Leader Trent Lott (R-MS) filled up the amendment tree too frequently and argued the Senate must resist the urge to tell the minority "there is not much else you can do in terms of trying to constructively affect the legislative process" (*Congressional Record*, 106th Congress, July 26, 1999, S9200).

12. For example, Rep. Justin Amash (R-MI), a member of the conservative House Freedom Caucus, asserted that his objection to Boehner was not because he "isn't conservative enough" but rather because he "doesn't follow the process" (Sherman 2014). Boehner was elected speaker again in 2013, but with 14 Republican no votes (Weisman 2013b). Rep. Mark Meadows (R-NC) would later file two separate motions to vacate the chair, seeking to remove Boehner midway through the session. The first, filed in 2015, was not voted on before adjournment. In 2016, Boehner resigned prior to the end of the Congress (Dickinson 2015). Afterward, Boehner would call the House Freedom Caucus "anarchists" who "want total chaos" and dubbed their founding chairman, Rep. Jim Jordan (R-OH), a "legislative terrorist" (Alberta 2017).

13. Ryan stated, "We need to let every member contribute, not once they earn

their stripes, but now. . . . Let's open up the process. . . . In other words, we need to return to regular order" (Levy 2015). This pledge led conservative House Freedom Caucus members to support his speakership. Rep. Dave Brat (R-VA), while justifying his support for Ryan on a December 2015 budget deal, noted, "[Ryan] gained support because he has been credible on regular order" (Palmer and French 2015).

14. Unsurprisingly, this generated additional criticism from House Freedom Caucus members. Jordan suggested his problem with Boehner's use of the rules was that he barred conservative amendments (Sherman and Caygle 2016). Amash argued the House may have been "more open under Speaker Boehner," adding that Ryan's pledge to return to regular order should "result in all of the members [being able] to amend legislation" (Marcos 2017).

15. Such claims of "openness" go back even further. Similar reactions occurred to pledges in 2006 and 1994 (see Binder 2015).

16. All amendments adopted in the Committee of the Whole were considered by the full chamber later. Members could reserve the right to request a recorded vote on them after the Committee of the Whole dissolved.

17. Many members spoke in support. For example, Rep. John Emerson Moss (D-CA) stated, "There is a need to know how we vote in order that an honest evaluation of our effectiveness as a Representative may be made by the voters in the election" (*Congressional Record*, 91st Congress, July 27, 1970, 25804). As Lawrence (2018) notes, however, many reformers quickly came to regret the recorded voting change. An effort to increase the number needed for a sufficient second was introduced, but defeated, just four years later (Schickler 2001).

18. Some members did take issue with transparency reforms more broadly. The "Dean of the House," 82-year-old Emanuel Celler (D-NY), argued the "light of the publicity should not be focused on every nook and cranny" (Hunter 1970). Celler would be defeated in his next primary election.

19. Two amendments restricting closed rules were quickly dismissed on points of order (the House had adopted a special rule providing no amendments would be in order that altered committee jurisdiction). The first amendment, by Rep. Andrew Jacobs (D-IN), barred closed rules. In debate, Jacobs conceded majorities could vote those rules down. However, he argued the dichotomy they created was the equivalent of "saying when you are drowning, you can have a life raft only if you will agree to have a tiger on it" (*Congressional Record*, 91st Congress, July 29, 1970, 26415). A second amendment, by Rep. Charles Vanik (D-OH), sought to ensure members could cast separate votes on different sections on omnibus bills brought up under closed rules.

20. Drutman (2015b) suggests this increase in lobbying expenses was partially a response to the regulatory reforms of the 1970s.

21. These problems are also likely exacerbated by increased legislative complexity. As Curry (2015, 116) notes, "The indicators for each Congress show that, all else equal, the typical bill is becoming more complex with each passing Congress." This, he suggests, allows leadership to help "nudge" their rank-and-file members in a partisan direction on certain votes.

22. Neugebauer's amendment cut $13.5 billion from the $123.1 billion proposed in the original bill, and Jordan's proposed to reduce it by over $20 billion.

23. Cao's amendment required the Neighborhood Reinvestment Corporation to offer more frequent reports to Congress regarding their efforts to curb mortgage defaults. Schock's amendment proposed to make pre-home purchase counseling more available.

24. The 16 votes produced cut lines, as reported by voteview.com, with relatively vertical angles (the average absolute cutline angle was 73 degrees, approximately seven degrees higher than the average vote in the 111th Congress) indicating that splits followed those predicted by standard liberal/conservative ideological differences.

25. Some Republicans took to the floor to oppose Flake's earmark amendments. In opposition, Rep. Stephen LaTourette (R-OH) argued that "if this earmark thing was such a great idea and it really captured the hearts and minds of the American people and would do anything to reduce spending in a significant way, John McCain would be President of the United States today and we would have had a different budget resolution" (*Congressional Record*, 111th Congress, July 22, 2009, H8658).

26. Bryan Smith's primary challenge of Simpson received the support of several important conservative groups, including the Club for Growth. For a further discussion of Flake's amendments and how they were used in that primary contest see http://www.conservativeintel.com/2014/03/24/id02-congressman-makes-the-case-for-bringing-back-earmarks/, accessed August 15, 2017.

27. Hinchey and cosponsor Rep. Dana Rohrabacher (R-CA) had proposed the amendment to H.R. 2500, the 2002 Commerce, Justice, and State, the Judiciary, and Related Agencies Appropriations Act. After a brief discussion, he withdrew the amendment, stating, "I have determined over the course of the last few days that this House is not ready to vote on this issue at this moment. I wish it were" (107th Congress, *Congressional Record*, July 18, 2001, 13708).

28. First, the data collection process is especially labor intensive. Coding all amendments in a specific Congress is a massive undertaking, and completing a dataset that spanned a large number of congresses would require resources we simply do not have. Second, utilizing important legislation helps minimize biases stemming from the large amount of trivial legislation the Congress produces (Clinton and Lapinski 2006). This allows us to ensure a sufficient level of salience.

29. In an effort to make our data more useful for other scholars, student coders were tasked with coding a wide array of variables in addition to the "vote type." The data include information on, among other things, how the amendment was dispensed with (roll call vote, division, teller, voice, withdrawn, not voted on), whether it was offered by way of a motion to recommit, dispensed with by some other procedure (point of order, motion to table, failed cloture vote, etc.), whether it passed or failed, what it sought to amend (i.e., the bill, another amendment), who the sponsor of the amendment was, and if it was offered on behalf of a committee. A complete codebook can be found at thecongressproject.com.

30. Of these, 16,159 were committee amendments. Committee amendments are historically less controversial and often adopted with minimal debate. In the earlier congresses in our times series, a substantial number of amendments were sponsored by committees.

31. These percentages narrow if we exclude committee amendments.

32. Specifically, we took the absolute distance between each sponsor and the House or Senate median and ranked them in each congress, starting with the members closest to the median. Then, we divided that rank by the total number of members in each chamber in that congress.

33. Amendments that were not offered or considered on the floor are excluded.

34. The Senate used the Committee of the Whole until the 71st Congress (1929–1931), when the practice was abolished with respect to bills and joint resolutions. The Senate continued to utilize it with respect to treaties until the 99th Congress (1985–1987). However, recorded voting was allowed in the Senate Committee of the Whole.

35. Committee data were provided by Nelson (1994), Canon et al. (2002), and Stewart and Woon (2013).

36. This variable includes both floor leaders and whips. It was coded using Heitshusen (2017).

Chapter 6

1. See, for example, "Democracy in the House." *New York Times*, January 9, 2013; Klein (2012); Allen (2012); and Mann and Ornstein (2013).

2. In contrast, the 80th Congress, which President Truman famously dubbed "the Do-Nothing" Congress, enacted 906 public laws (Ornstein et al. 2019).

3. Lopsided votes are votes where 95% or more of members vote on the same side of an issue.

4. Notably, these numbers only account for votes on bills that became public law and not companion or related measures. It also includes votes on amendments to those bills that failed.

5. During the two congresses, there were 231 votes on motions to recommit in the House, all of which were party votes, as were all but one of the 380 recorded votes ordering the previous question motion and adopting special rules. In the Senate, all 63 failed motions to order cloture were party votes. In the 112th Congress, the Senate cast 82—or just over 15% of its votes—on nominations. In the 113th, more than 75% of the 657 roll calls taken in the Senate were on either procedural votes or nominations.

6. A bipartisan Senate coalition passed the pared-down $1 trillion physical infrastructure plan, named the Infrastructure Investment and Jobs Act, by a 69 to 30 vote. The House passed the bill with more limited Republican support on a 228 to 205 vote. President Biden signed the infrastructure act on November 15, 2021 (Tankersley 2021).

7. The bill passed the House on a 220 to 213 vote. All Democrats, except Rep.

Jared Golden (D-ME), voted for the measure and all Republicans voted against it. Golden voted no over concerns about increased state and local tax deductions that appeared in the bill (Cochrane and Weisman 2021).

8. While the bill includes $450 billion of new spending on climate and healthcare, tax increases and $80 billion to improve the IRS's enforcement capabilities included in the bill are estimated to substantially increase government revenue, meaning the overall package is estimated to reduce the federal deficit by approximately $300 billion over the next 10 years (Weiss 2022).

9. Interestingly, all 39 votes took place between late at night on August 6 and the afternoon of August 7. Most of the votes were part of what is known as a vote-a-rama. Vote-a-ramas occur just prior to the passage of a bill being considered via the reconciliation process and consists of a flurry of votes on amendments and motions to waive provisions required by the Byrd Rule. The *New York Times* describes a vote-a-rama as "a time-consuming exercise that has little impact on policy but keeps senators up through the night, ending only when they run out of steam for offering more amendments" (Lai 2022).

10. Of 10 votes where Democrats did not vote in a bloc, four consisted of Sen. Bernie Sanders (I-VT) voting yea for an amendment or motion to waive the Byrd Rule and all other senators voting no.

11. The amendment, which gained the support of seven Democrats and all 50 Republicans, altered the requirements that defined which type of corporations would have a new 15% corporate alternative minimum tax imposed on them (Ernst and Young 2022).

12. Greene forced a total of four roll call votes on adjournment during February and March 2021. According to the *Washington Post*, "Each time, the number of Republicans voting against her increased, including some of the chamber's most conservative members" (Sotomayor and DeBonis 2021).

13. Murkowski voted for the motion to discharge, cloture, and confirmation, but against the motion to proceed.

14. Given the difficulty of assessing what measures would/might have come to a vote if not for negative agenda control, we will focus our analysis on the addition of party-splitting votes.

15. Polarization rates are calculated by taking the absolute value of the difference between the mean Democratic and mean Republican Party member of a legislative chamber. See legacy.voteview.com/political_polarization_2015.htm for further discussion.

16. We estimate all W-NOMINATE scores using the wnominate R library with the polarity set using the most conservative House member identified by DW-NOMINATE scores. See cran.r-project.org/web/packages/wnominate/wnominate.pdf and Poole et al. (2011) for more on the wnominate R library.

17. Polarization rates are calculated by finding the difference between the mean Republican member's W-NOMINATE score and the mean Democratic member's W-NOMINATE score.

Chapter 7

1. "John Jay to Jesse Root," August 31, 1779, *Letters of Delegates to Congress*, 25:660.

2. Not all would agree with this decision. Thomas Jefferson famously called it "abominable" and further claimed, "Nothing can justify this example but the innocence of their intentions and ignorance of the value of public discussions" (Hoffman 1981, 22).

3. A good example of this is the 2015 denial of Ted Cruz's request for a recorded vote, discussed in Chapter 2.

4. CARES stands for the Coronavirus Aid, Relief, and Economic Security Act.

5. The *New York Times* would later report that at least two Republican House members donated to Massie's primary opponent in response to the episode (Edmondson 2020).

6. President Trump would sign the CARES Act into law later that day (116 P.L. 136). The House would revise its rules in response to the pandemic several months later on a party-line 217–189 vote (DeBonis 2020b). The most notable of these changes was a provision that allowed for "proxy voting." The coronavirus would eventually claim the lives of Rep. Ron Wright (R-TX) and Representative-elect Luke Letlow (R-LA).

7. Specifically, the vote was on a motion by Sen. Robert La Follette Jr. (R-WI) to concur in the House amendment to the Senate-passed bill.

8. In 1997, Congress, seeking to curb the growth in Medicare spending, created a payment formula called the Sustainable Growth Rate. The formula set yearly limits in how much Medicare can pay to doctors. When breached, the formula reduces fees paid in the following years for medical services. In order to make up for the reductions, doctors performed more procedures, driving up physician spending and requiring bigger cuts in fees. In order to deal with this compounding problem, Congress routinely passed a "fix" that would hold payments to physicians close to the current levels. In the absence of the fix, the formula would impose a substantial cut in payments to physicians, which could lead to many doctors refusing to see Medicare patients. Such short-term "doc fix" measures were controversial due to their high costs and comparatively minimal electoral benefit for members (Lesniewski 2015c; Haberkorn 2015; Newhauser and Fuller 2014).

9. For example, the Republican Doctors Caucus announced its opposition to the doc fix bill, but leadership cleared the tactic of passing the measure by voice vote with them before doing so. Reps. John Fleming (R-LA) and Michael Burgess (R-TX), both members of the Republican Doctors Caucus, would have voted no on a recorded vote. However, they expressed that a bigger problem would be letting the doc fix expire. As Burgess put it, "[I opposed the bill] but not enough to stop it" (Haberkorn and Sherman 2014).

10. This was based on a vote against H.R. 5325, an appropriations bill that included a pay freeze for representatives. As Kirkpatrick's campaign pointed out, McCain had voted against a similar bill the previous year. Other cases include the 2014 Georgia

Senate Republican primary election in 2014; the 2016 Missouri Senate general election; the 2012 Ohio and Virginia Senate general election; the 2014 Iowa Fourth House District general election; 2014 Kentucky Senate general election; the 2012 Georgia 14th House District Republican election; the 2010 Florida gubernatorial election; the 2014 Mississippi Republican Senate primary election; the 2012 Florida 22nd House District general election; and the 2012 Florida Republican Senate primary election.

11. From July 4, 2010, to April 11, 2018, we found 243 statements related to a member's "voting record." Of these, 30 were rated as "true," 46 as "mostly true," 41 as "half-true," 63 as "mostly false," 45 as "false," and 18 as "pants on fire."

12. See *Brown v. Hartlage*, 456 U.S. 45 (1982).

13. The bill was originally titled the Generations Invigorating Volunteerism and Education Act, or GIVE Act.

14. Of the 1,246 roll call votes ordering the previous question motion from the 59th Congress to the 115th Congress, 1,089 were requested by members of the minority party. That is just under 90% of recorded votes of previous question motions. As discussed in Chapter 4 and Appendix D, these patterns are comparable to roll call data on the underlying rules as well.

15. H.R. 2872 was passed in the Senate on a 77–18 vote on January 18. It passed the House the same day on a 314–108 vote. President Biden the bill into law on January 19, just in time to avoid a shutdown. S. 788, the Duck Stamp Modernization Act of 2023, a bill with language almost identical to that of the original H.R. 2872, passed the House and Senate and became 118 P.L. 25.

16. While the literature on transparency and legitimacy is an interesting one, an examination of the changing roll call record and its influence on legitimacy is beyond the scope of this project.

Appendix B

1. In previous working papers, our discussion included the broader data collection project. This included lists of landmark legislation and amendment data going back to the 45th Congress (1877–1878). In total, it included data on 2,322 enactments across 69 congresses. While those data and discussion are still available, they were not continuous across the time series. Accordingly, we have focused our discussion here on the data employed throughout the book, which stem from the 59th Congress (1905–1906) to the 113th Congress (2013–2014).

2. Sweep One relied on newspaper articles in the *New York Times* and *Washington Post* after legislation at the end of a Congress. They were supplemented by "books or articles that discuss the overall legislative records of particular Congresses" (Mayhew 1991, 39). Mayhew then relied on the authors' judgments of whether the law was important or not. This resulted in 211 enactments. Noting that the authors of the contemporaneous articles used in Sweep One were "generalists," Mayhew (1991, 44) sought to compliment his list of landmark laws by using sources generated by experts.

These policy experts were distributed across substantive areas, and their works were written well after the legislation was adopted. The Sweep Two list included 147 enactments included in Sweep One and added 56 new measures.

3. Expanding beyond the contemporaneous versus retrospective rating debate, Binder (1999 2003) focused on the relative success of a Congress to measure its effectiveness. She argued that tests of divided government using only landmark legislation were biased because they ignored public demand for such bills. To correct this, she employed a new measure of the public's demand for legislation, derived from contemporaneous newspaper accounts. She found that unified government is more responsive to the public and successful at producing landmark laws. Other work tested Mayhew's claim using a range of lists. Krehbiel (1998) reports that legislative success hinges on the support of "pivotal" legislators identified by institutionally defined decision rules, as opposed to partisan control. And Coleman (1999) finds that unified government leads to more legislative productivity and greater responsiveness to the public's mood. See also Baumgartner and Jones (2003). More recently, Ansolabere, Palmer, and Schneer (2018) employ a newly created list of 1,040 landmark laws from 1789 to 2010 and find that unified government results in one fewer law per congress.

4. Grant and Kelly (2008) took a different approach. Instead of examining productivity at the statute level, they combined a number of factors to create one macro-level variable for each congress.

5. Political scientists have focused on three particular limitations of lists of landmark legislation. The first is the choice of whether to use either or both retrospective or contemporaneous sources (see the above exchange between Mayhew 1991, 1993, 2005 and Howell et al. 2000 and Kelly 1993a). The second is the length of the time series. Generally, lists with longer time series have been employed to test the effects of institutions on congressional performance. Employing Petersen's (2001) list, Wawro and Schickler (2004, 2006) report that the adoption of a formal cloture rule in the Senate led to greater consensus building as evidenced by larger enacting coalitions. Madonna (2011) argues this result is spurious. And finally, there are changes in legislative process. Using raw counts of laws (even landmark laws) produced introduces bias, as modern legislation is longer and has a farther reaching policy impact (Straus 2014). Moreover, without controlling for content, it is impossible to separate major titles from larger laws even when it makes theoretical sense to do. As a result, the Civil Rights Acts of 1957 and 1964 are counted equally as landmark laws, even though the former was roundly viewed as ineffective.

6. As detailed in Appendix D, we have collected data on all amendments offered from the 97th Congress (1979–1980) to the 113th Congress (2013–2014). However, for comparison purposes, we have restricted these data to only amendments to landmark and appropriation bills.

7. For a discussion on the use of vehicles and tracking the origins of a policy see Wilkerson et al. (2015).

8. It was 2 in the 91st–96th, 105th, and 110th Congresses.

Appendix C

1. The full Roberts (2010) dataset extends from 1881 to 1937. From 1905 on we merged in roll call vote numbers when appropriate and added resolution numbers when available. We also added the text of the rules. We thank Jason Roberts for making these data available.

2. "Floor consideration" was defined to include any resolution that received at least one vote (either recorded or not). This could include rules subjected to failed motions to discharge, those defeated on the House floor, or those considered under suspension.

3. Information is available on the additional 167 resolutions during that period that were later excluded on the basis of not receiving floor consideration or not constituting a special rule.

4. Information on our important legislation dataset ("Important Legislation, 45th (1877–1879)–113th (2013–2014) Congresses") can be found here: thecongressproject.com/data-and-links

5. Stiglitz's data are restricted to rules subject to recorded votes and covers the 98th Congress (1983–1984) through the 109th Congress (2005–2006).

6. For example, H.Res. 477 in the 112th Congress provided three separate structured rules for H.R. 527, H.R. 3010, and H.R. 3463.

7. He went on to say, "What the majority has done once again is to waive the rules of the House for the majority product, but then refuse to waive those same rules for amendments that the minority wishes to offer. In my view, that is a gutless way to legislate. It is an unfair way to legislate. It does discredit to this House and discredit to those who impose those kinds of rules. And to suggest that this is an open rule, implying, somehow implying that this is business as usual, if this is business as usual, I think the American public would hang their heads when they understand it" (*Congressional Record*, 108th Congress, September 4, 2003, 21149).

8. This can also be waived by two-thirds vote.

9. In opposing the rule allowing the House to entertain the motion to suspend, Rep. Lincoln Diaz-Balart (R-FL) argued the bill did not go far enough. He complained, "Although I support the bills we will consider today, I find it quite unfortunate the way in which the majority leadership has decided to handle this scandal. The heavy-handed process they are using will block all Members of this House from offering amendments. It will also block every procedural right the minority has to shape legislation, including the motion to recommit. It will even limit debate on this important issue to a total of 40 minutes" (*Congressional Record*, 111th Congress, March 19, 2009, 8096). In another instance, minority-party Democrats criticized the usage of suspension rules because they enabled the majority to bypass committees. Rep. Joe Moakley (D-MA) argued, "These suspension rules are part of a pattern of bypassing the committee process that my Republican colleagues have turned into a state-of-art form. I just cannot support this rule that will make it even easier for my colleagues on the Republican side to bypass committees and rush bills to the floor with only 1 hour's notice" (*Congressional Record*, 106th Congress, November 16, 1999, 29832).

10. The resolution ID variable (or "rid") is unique, seven- or eight-digit ID number for each resolution. The first two or three numbers correspond to the Congress, the fourth is a "3" denoting this is a House resolution. The last four digits refer to the resolution number. So if a resolution has a rid of 6530440 it is referring to H.Res. 440, a resolution considered in the 65th Congress. For 13 resolutions (four in the 59th Congress, seven in the 60th Congress, one in the 61st Congress, and one in the 68th Congress) no resolution number could be identified. These resolutions were assigned resolution numbers starting with 9000 in each congress.

Appendix D

1. The broader dataset included an additional 6,083 amendments considered prior to the 59th Congress and 26,048 amendments considered from the 97th Congress (1981–1982) to the 113th Congress (2013–2014). The latter were excluded from the dataset as they were not filed to measures included in our important bill dataset.

2. For example, in the 84th Congress (1955–1957), Sen. Prescott Bush (R-CT) moved "to lay on the table the amendment on page 3, line 10" (*Congressional Record*, 84th Congress, July 22, 1956, 10831). In this case, Bush would be listed as the tabling motion sponsor.

3. As was the case with the amendment sponsor variable, in the rare instance multiple members requested the yeas and nays, only the first member is coded as the member requesting the yeas and nays. Additional members are listed in the notes section.

References

Achen, Christopher H., and Larry M. Bartels. 2017. *Democracy for Realists: Why Elections Do Not Produce Responsive Government*. Princeton, NJ: Princeton University Press.

Adler, E. Scott, and John Wilkerson. 2019. *Congressional Bills Project: 1945–2014*, NSF 00880066 and 00880061. http://congressionalbills.org/

Adofo, Adjoa, and Lydia Gensheimer. 2009. "Volunteerism Measure Advances in Both Chambers." *CQ Online*, March 18.

Ainsworth, Scott, and Marcus Flathman. 1995. "Unanimous Consent Agreements as Leadership Tools." *Legislative Studies Quarterly* 20(2): 177–195.

Alberta, Tim. 2017. "John Boehner Unchained." *Politico*, December 2017. https://www.politico.com/magazine/story/2017/10/29/john-boehner-trump-house-republican-party-retirement-profile-feature-215741

Aldrich, John H., Jacob M. Montgomery, and David B. Sparks. 2014. "Polarization and Ideology: Partisan Sources of Low Dimensionality in Scaled Roll Call Analysis." *Political Analysis* 22(4): 435–456.

Aldrich, John H., and David W. Rohde. 2000. "The Consequences of Party Organization in the House: The Role of the Majority and Minority Parties in Conditional Party Government." In *Polarized Politics: Congress and the President in a Partisan Era*, ed. Jon R. Bond and Richard Fleisher, 31–72. Washington, DC: CQ Press.

Alexander, DeAlva Stanwood. 1916. *History and Procedure of the House of Representatives*. New York, NY: Houghton Mifflin Company.

Allen, Jonathan. 2012. "112th Congress: The Worst Ever?" *Politico*, January 20. https://www.politico.com/story/2012/01/the-worst-ever-071496

Alston, Lee J., Jeffery A. Jenkins, and Tomas Nonnenmacher. 2006. "Who Should Govern Congress? Access to Power and the Salary Grab of 1873." *Journal of Economic History* 66(3): 674–706.

Alvarez, R. Michael, and Paul Gronke. 1996. "Constituents and Legislators: Learning About the Persian Gulf War Resolution." *Legislative Studies Quarterly* 21(1): 105–127.

Andrejevic, Mark. 2013. *Infoglut: How Too Much Information Is Changing the Way We Think and Know*. New York, NY: Routledge.

Ansolabehere, Stephen, and Philip E. Jones. 2010. "Constituents' Responses to Congressional Roll Call Voting." *American Journal of Political Science* 54(3): 583–597.

Ansolabehere, Stephen, Maxwell Palmer, and Benjamin Schneer. 2018. "Divided Government and Significant Legislation: A History of Congress from 1789 to 2010." *Social Science History* 42(1): 81–108.

Ansolabehere, Stephen, James M. Snyder Jr., and Charles Stewart III. 2001. "The Effects of Party and Preferences on Congressional Roll-Call Voting." *Legislative Studies Quarterly* 26(4): 533–572.

Anzia, Sarah F., and Molly C. Jackman. 2013. "Legislative Organization and the Second Face of Power: Evidence from US State Legislatures." *Journal of Politics* 75(1): 210–224.

Arnold, R. Douglas. 1990. *The Logic of Congressional Action*. New Haven, CT: Yale University Press.

Ashdown, Gerald G. 2012. "Distorting Democracy: Campaign Lies in the 21st Century." *William and Mary Bill of Rights Journal* 20(4): 1085–1113.

Austin, James. 1828. *The Life of Elbridge Gerry*. Carlisle, MA: Applewood Books.

Bade, Rachel, Kyle Cheney, and John Bresnahan. 2017. "GOP's Bold Prediction: Obamacare Repeal Will Pass This Month." *Politico*, March 3. https://www.politico.com/story/2017/03/house-leaders-obamacare-repeal-pass-month-235623

Badertscher, Nancy. 2014. "Perdue Pay Raise Claim Fall Short." *PolitiFact*, July 11. http://www.politifact.com/georgia/statements/2014/jul/11/david-perdue/perdue-pay-raise-claim-falls-short/

Bafumi, Joseph, and Michael C. Herron. 2010. "Leapfrog Representation and Extremism: A Study of American Voters and Their Members in Congress." *American Political Science Review* 104(3): 519–542.

Ball, Molly. 2013. "The Fall of the Heritage Foundation and the Death of Republican Ideas." *The Atlantic*, September 25. https://www.theatlantic.com/politics/archive/2013/09/the-fall-of-the-heritage-foundation-and-the-death-of-republican-ideas/279955/

Barber, Michael J. 2016. "Donation Motivations: Testing Theories of Access and Ideology." *Political Research Quarterly* 69(1): 148–159.

Barber, Michael J., Brandice Canes-Wrone, and Sharece Thrower. 2017. "Ideologically Sophisticated Donors: Which Candidates Do Individual Contributors Finance?" *American Journal of Political Science* 61(2): 271–288.

Barr, Andy. 2010. "Angle Ad: He Gives Predators Viagra." *Politico*, September 7. https://www.politico.com/story/2010/10/angle-ad-he-gives-predators-viagra-043282

Barron-Lopez, Laura. 2015. "Keystone Marathon Begins in the Senate." *The Hill*, January 21.

https://thehill.com/policy/energy-environment/230110-keystone-marathon-begins-in-senate/amp/

Barry, John M. 2015. "The House of Jim Wright." *Politico*, May 7. https://www.politico.com/magazine/story/2015/05/the-house-of-jim-wright-117718?o=1

Bateman, David A., Joshua D. Clinton, and John S. Lapinski. 2017. "A House Divided? Roll Calls, Polarization, and Policy Differences in the U.S. House, 1877–2011." *American Journal of Political Science* 61(3): 698–714.

Baumgartner, Frank R., and Bryan D. Jones. 2003. "Representation and Agenda Setting." Paper presented at the Annual Meeting of the American Political Science Association, Philadelphia.

Bawn, Kathleen, David Karol, Seth Masket, Hans Noel, and John Zaller. 2012. "A Theory of Political Parties: Groups, Policy Demands and Nominations in American Politics." *Perspectives on Politics* 10(3): 571–597.

Beeman, Richard. 2010. *Plain, Honest Men: The Making of the American Constitution*. New York, NY: Random House.

Bell, Jack. 1960. "Mansfield Urges Liberal Democrats to Sidetrack Attacks on Filibuster." *Washington Post*, December 12.

Benton, Wilbourn E. 1986. *Drafting the US Constitution*. Vol. 2. College Station, TX: Texas A&M Press.

Berkin, Carol. 2002. *A Brilliant Solution: Inventing the Constitution*. New York, NY: Harcourt.

Bever, Lindsey. 2017. "Anthony Weiner Pleaded Guilty to 'Sexting' a Teen Girl. Then His Estranged Wife Filed for Divorce." *Washington Post*, May 19. https://www.washingtonpost.com/news/post-nation/wp/2017/05/19/anthony-weiner-disgraced-former-congressman-expected-to-plead-guilty-today-in-sexting-case-involving-minor/?utm_term=.f0d060d45fd9

Bianco, William T., David B. Spence, and John D. Wilkerson. 1996. "The Election Connection in the Early Congress: The Case of the Compensation Act of 1816." *American Journal of Political Science* 40(1): 145–171.

Billias, George Athan. 1976. *Elbridge Gerry: Founding Father and Republican Statesman*. New York, NY: McGraw-Hill.

Binder, Sarah A. 1997. *Minority Rights, Majority Rule*. New York, NY: Cambridge University Press.

Binder, Sarah A. 1999. "The Dynamics of Legislative Gridlock." *American Political Science Review* 93(3): 519–533.

Binder, Sarah A. 2003. *Stalemate: Causes and Consequences of Legislative Gridlock*. Washington, DC: Brookings Institution Press.

Binder, Sarah A. 2010. "A Primer on Self-Executing Rules." *Brookings*, March 17. https://www.brookings.edu/articles/a-primer-on-self-executing-rules/

Binder, Sarah A. 2015. "Why Can't Mitch McConnell Keep His Promises?" *Washington Post*, Monkey Cage, May 26. https://www.washingtonpost.com/news/monkey-cage/wp/2015/05/26/why-cant-mitch-mcconnell-keep-his-promises/?utm_term=.e199616315bc

Binder, Sarah A., and Frances E. Lee. 2016. "Making Deals in Congress." In *Political Negotiation: A Handbook*, ed. Jane Mansbridge and Cathie Joe Martin, 54–72. Washington, DC: Brookings Institution Press.

Black, Duncan. 1948. "On the Rationale of Group Decision-Making." *Journal of Political Economy* 56(1): 23–34.

Blake, Aaron. 2016. "The 'Do-Nothing Congress' Graduates to the 'Do-Nothing-Much Congress.'" *Washington Post*, December 20. https://www.washingtonpost.com/news/monkey-cage/wp/2014/02/13/polarization-in-congress-has-risen-sharply-where-is-it-going-next/?utm_term=.8de6dcd2e70b

Bluestein, Greg. 2014. "David Perdue Dubs Himself 'True Conservative' in Jack Kingston Attack Ad." *Atlanta Journal Constitution*, June 18. http://politics.blog.ajc.com/2014/06/18/david-perdue-dubs-himself-true-conservative-in-attack-ad-slamming-kingston/

Bonica, Adam. 2014. "Mapping the Ideological Marketplace." *American Journal of Political Science* 58(2): 367–386.

Bourinot, John George. 1884. *Parliamentary Procedure and Practice: With an Introductory Account of the Origin and Growth of Parliamentary Institutions in the Dominion of Canada*. Montreal, Canada: Dawson Brothers.

Bovitz, Gregory L., and Jamie Carson. 2006. "Position-Taking and Electoral Accountability in the U.S. House of Representatives." *Political Research Quarterly* 59(2): 297–312.

Brady, David W., Brandice Canes-Wrone, and John F. Cogan. 2000. "Differences in Legislative Voting Behavior Between Winning and Losing House Incumbents." In *Continuity and Change in House Elections*, ed. David W. Brady, John F. Cogan, and Morris P. Fiorina, 178–192. Palo Alto, CA: Stanford University Press.

Brady, Jessica, and John Stanton. 2011. "Boehner Delays Vote, Considers Changes to Debt Bill." *Roll Call*, July 28. http://www.rollcall.com/news/mccarthy_house_wont_vote_thursday_night_debt_plan-207821-1.html

Brandeis, Louis D. 1913. "What Publicity Can Do." *Harper's Weekly*, December 20.

Broder, David S. 1970. "Ending Secrecy in House Voting." *Washington Post*, July 9.

Broockman, David E., and Christopher Skovron. 2018. "Bias in Perceptions of Public Opinion Among Political Elites." *American Political Science Review* 112(3): 542–563.

Bryce, James. 1889. *The American Commonwealth*. Vol. 1. New York, NY: Macmillan.

Bump, Philip. 2014. "The 113th Congress Is Historically Good at Not Passing Bills." *Washington Post*, July 13. https://www.washingtonpost.com/news/the-fix/wp/2014/07/09/the-113th-congress-is-historically-good-at-not-passing-bills/

Burnett, Edmund Cody. 1941. *The Continental Congress: A Definitive History of the Continental Congress from Its Inception in 1774 to March 1789*. New York, NY: W.W. Norton.

Butterfield, L. H. 1951. *Letters of Benjamin Rush*. American Philosophical Society: Philadelphia, PA. https://archive.org/stream/in.ernet.dli.2015.475745/2015.475745.Leters-Of_djvu.txt

Canes-Wrone, Brandice, David W. Brady, and John Cogan. 2002. "Out of Step, Out of

Office: Electoral Accountability and House Members' Voting." *American Political Science Review* 96(1): 127–140.

Canon, David, Garrison Nelson, and Charles Stewart. Historical Congressional Standing Committees, 1st to 79th Congresses, 1789–1947. http://web.mit.edu/17.251/www/data_page.html#1

Carey, John M. 2003. "Discipline, Accountability, and Legislative Voting in Latin America." *Comparative Politics* 35(2): 191–211.

Carey, John M. 2007. "Competing Principals, Political Institutions, and Party Unity in Legislative Voting." *American Journal of Political Science* 51(1): 92–107.

Carlson, Peter. 1986. "Is Bob Walker the Most Obnoxious Man in Congress." *Washington Post*, September 6. https://www.washingtonpost.com/archive/lifestyle/magazine/1986/09/07/is-bob-walker-the-most-obnoxious-man-in-congress/e9d4d1e0-3b5a-46a1-a244-8d9548fa7ff2/

Carroll, Royce A., and Keith T. Poole. 2014. "Roll-Call Analysis and the Study of Legislatures." In *The Oxford Handbook of Legislative Studies*, ed. Shane Martin, Thomas Saalfeld, and Kaare Strøm, 103–125. Oxford, United Kingdom: Oxford University Press.

Carruba, Clifford J., Matthew Gabel, Lacey Murrah, Ryan Clough, Elizabeth Montgomery, and Rebecca Schambach. 2006. "Off the Record: Unrecorded Legislative Votes, Selection Bias and Roll-Call Vote Analysis." *British Journal of Political Science* 36(4): 691–704.

Carson, Jamie L., Michael Crespin, and Anthony Madonna. 2014. "Partisan Signaling and Agenda Control in the U.S. House of Representatives." *Political Research Quarterly* 67(4): 729–742.

Carson, Jamie L., and Erik J. Engstrom. 2005. "Assessing the Electoral Connection: Evidence from the Early United States." *American Journal of Political Science* 49(4): 746–757.

Carson, Jamie L., Michael S. Lynch, and Anthony J. Madonna. 2011. "Coalition Formation in the House and Senate: Examining the Effect of Institutional Change on Major Legislation." *Journal of Politics* 78(4): 1125–1138.

Carson, Jamie L., Anthony J. Madonna, and Mark E. Owens. 2016. "Regulating the Floor: Tabling Motions in the U.S. Senate, 1865–1945." *American Politics Research* 44(1): 56–80.

Carson, Jamie L., Mark E. Owens, and Anthony J. Madonna. 2013. "Partisan Efficiency in an Open-Rule Setting: The Amending Process in the U.S. Senate, 1865–1946." *Congress & the Presidency* 40(2): 105–128.

Chandler, William M., Gary W. Cox, and Mathew D. McCubbins. 2006. "Agenda Control in the Bundestag, 1980–2002." *German Politics* 15(1): 27–48.

Clausen, Aage. 1973. *How Congressmen Decide: A Policy Focus*. New York, NY: St. Martin's Press.

Clinton, Joshua D. 2006a. "Lawmaking and Roll Calls." *Journal of Politics* 69(2): 457–469.

Clinton, Joshua D. 2006b. "Representation in Congress: Constituents and Roll Calls in the 106th House." *Journal of Politics* 68(2): 397–409.

Clinton, Joshua D., and John Lapinski. 2006. "Measuring Legislative Accomplishment, 1877–1994." *American Journal of Political Science* 50(1): 232–249.

Clinton, Joshua D., and John Lapinski. 2008. "Laws and Roll Calls in the U.S. Congress, 1889–1994." *Legislative Studies Quarterly* 33(4): 511–542.

Cochrane, Emily. 2022. "Senate Passes Climate, Health, and Tax Bill, with All Republicans Opposed." *New York Times*, August 7. https://www.nytimes.com/2022/08/07/us/politics/climate-tax-bill-passes-senate.html?searchResultPosition=7

Cochrane, Emily, and Jonathan Weisman. 2021. "House Narrowly Passes Biden's social Safety Net and Climate Bill." *New York Times*, November 19. https://www.nytimes.com/2021/11/19/us/politics/house-passes-reconciliation-bill.html

Coleman, John J. 1999. "Unified Government, Divided Government, and Party Responsiveness." *American Political Science Review* 93(4): 821–835.

Cooter, Robert D., and Michael D. Gilbert. 2010. "A Theory of Direct Democracy and the Single Subject Rule." *Columbia Law Review* 110(3): 687–730.

Costa, Robert, and Paul Kane. 2014. "House GOP Pulls Border Bill Rather Than See It Defeated." *Washington Post*, July 31. https://www.washingtonpost.com/news/post-politics/wp/2014/07/31/at-11th-hour-house-gop-poised-to-pass-border-bill/?utm_term=.8668cc1087ef

Cox, Gary W. 2000. "On the Effects of Legislative Rules." *Legislative Studies Quarterly* 25(2): 169–192.

Cox, Gary W., William B. Heller, and Mathew D. McCubbins. 2008. "Agenda Power in the Italian Chamber of Deputies, 1988–2000." *Legislative Studies Quarterly* 33(2): 171–198.

Cox, Gary W., Thad Kousser, and Mathew D. McCubbins. 2010. "Party Power or Preferences? Quasi-Experimental Evidence from American State Legislatures." *Journal of Politics* 72(3): 799–811.

Cox, Gary W., and Mathew D. McCubbins. 2005. *Setting the Agenda: Responsible Party Government in the U.S. House of Representatives*. New York, NY: Cambridge University Press.

Cox, Gary W., and Mathew D. McCubbins. 2007. *Legislative Leviathan: Party Government in the House*. 2nd ed. New York, NY: Cambridge University Press.

Cox, Gary W., and Keith T. Poole. 2002. "On Measuring Partisanship in Roll Call Voting: The U.S. House of Representatives, 1877–1999." *American Journal of Political Science* 46(3): 477–489.

Crespin, Michael H. 2010. "Serving Two Masters: Redistricting and Voting in the U.S. House of Representatives." *Political Research Quarterly* 63(4): 850–885.

Crespin, Michael H., Anthony J. Madonna, Joel Sievert, and Nathaniel Ament-Stone. 2015. "Coordination, Not Coercion: Party Policy Committees and Collective Action in the United States Senate." *Social Science Quarterly* 96(1): 34–48.

Crespin, Michael H., and David W. Rohde. 2010. "Dimensions, Issues and Bills: Appropriations Voting on the House Floor." *Journal of Politics* 72(4): 976–989.

Crespin, Michael H., and David W. Rohde. 2016. *PIPC Votes*. University of Oklahoma.

Crosson, Jesse M. 2019. "Stalemate in the States: Agenda Control Rules and Policy Output in American Legislatures." *Legislative Studies Quarterly* 44(1): 3–33.

Curry, James M. 2015. *Legislating in the Dark: Information and Power in the House of Representatives*. Chicago, IL: University of Chicago Press.

Curtin, Deirdre and Albert Meijer. 2006. "Does Transparency Strengthen Legitimacy? A Critical Analysis of European Union Policy Documents." *Information Polity* 11(1): 109–122.

Cushing, Luther Stearns. 1856. *Elements of the Law and Practice of Legislative Assemblies in the United States of America*. Boston, MA: Little, Brown.

Dancey, Logan, and Geoffrey Sheagley. 2013. "Heuristics Behaving Badly: Party Cues and Voter Knowledge." *American Journal of Political Science* 57(2): 312–325.

Davey, Monica. 2011. "Democrats Missing, Wisconsin Vote on Cuts Is Delayed." *New York Times*, February 17. https://www.nytimes.com/2011/02/18/us/18wisconsin.html

Davidson, Roger H., Walter J. Oleszek, Francis E. Lee, and Eric Schickler. 2013. *Congress and Its Members*. Washington, DC: CQ Press.

Davis, Julie Hirschfeld, and Maggie Haberman. 2017. "In Dropping Health Vote, Trump Swallowed Need for a Showdown." *New York Times*, March 24. https://www.nytimes.com/2017/03/24/us/politics/trump-white-house-health-care.html

DeBonis, Mike. 2015. "Paul Ryan Pledges to Reform the House. Just like John Boehner Did." *Washington Post*, November 5. https://www.washingtonpost.com/news/powerpost/wp/2015/11/05/paul-ryan-pledges-to-reform-the-house-just-like-john-boehner-did/?utm_term=.f561e7536566

DeBonis, Mike. 2020a. "Rep. Massie, Opponent of $2.2 Trillion Spending Bill, Forces House Colleagues Back to D.C." *Washington Post*, March 27. https://www.washingtonpost.com/politics/republican-rep-massie-ratchets-up-his-obstinance-forces-house-colleagues-back-to-dc/2020/03/27/ddf94734-7028-11ea-b148-e4ce3fbd85b5_story.html

DeBonis, Mike. 2020b. "House Changes Its Rules During Pandemic, Allowing Remote Voting for the First Time in Its 231-year History." *Washington Post*, May 15. https://www.washingtonpost.com/politics/house-poised-to-adopt-historic-changes-allowing-remote-voting-during-pandemic/2020/05/15/b081d9f2-96ab-11ea-91d7-cf4423d47683_story.html

DeBonis, Mike, Ed O'Keefe, and Robert Costa. 2017. "GOP Health-Care Bill: House Republican Leaders Abruptly Pull Their Rewrite of the Nation's Health-Care Law." *Washington Post*, March 24. https://www.washingtonpost.com/powerpost/house-leaders-prepare-to-vote-friday-on-health-care-reform/2017/03/24/736f1cd6-1081-11e7-9d5a83e627dc120_story.html?utm_term=.1354033b9c2f

Deckard, Barbara Sinclair. 1976. "Electoral Marginality and Party Loyalty in House Roll Call Voting." *American Journal of Political Science* 20(3): 469–481.

Den Hartog, Chris, and Nathan Monroe. 2011. *Agenda Setting in the U.S. Senate: Costly Consideration and Majority Party Advantage*. New York, NY: Cambridge University Press.

Denzau, Arthur T., and Michael C. Munger. 1986. "Legislators and Interest Groups: How Unorganized Interests Get Represented." *American Political Science Review* 80(1): 89–106.

Devol, George H., 1887. *Forty Years a Gambler on the Mississippi*. Cincinnati, OH: Devol and Haines.

Devroy, Ann. 1994. "All-Out Assault Snuffs 11th-Hour Threat." *New York Times*, August 22.

Dickinson, Tim. 2015. "Meet the Right-Wing Rebels Who Overthrew John Boehner." *Rolling Stone*, October 6. http://www.rollingstone.com/politics/news/meet-the-right-wing-rebels-who-overthrew-john-boehner-20151006

Dinan, John. 2014. *The Virginia State Constitution*. 2nd ed. New York, NY: Oxford University Press.

Döring, Herbert. 2001. "Parliamentary Agenda Control and Legislative Outcomes in Western Europe." *Legislative Studies Quarterly* 26(1): 145–165.

Doudna, Michael. 2018. "Absent Alabama Legislators Sometimes Still Cast Votes." *WSFA News*, February 16. http://www.wsfa.com/story/37527111/absent-alabama-legislators-sometimes-still-cast-votes

Dougherty, Keith L. 2001. *Collective Action Under the Articles of Confederation*. New York, NY: Cambridge University Press.

Dougherty, Keith L., Michael S. Lynch, and Anthony J. Madonna 2014. "Partisan Agenda Control and the Dimensionality of Congress." *American Politics Research* 42(4): 600–627.

Douglass, Elisha. 1949. "Thomas Burke, Disillusioned Democrat." *North Carolina Historical Review* 26(2): 150–186.

Downs, Anthony. 1957. *An Economic Theory of Democracy*. New York, NY: HarperCollins.

Draper, Robert. 2012. *Do Not Ask What Good We Do: Inside the U.S. House of Representatives*. New York, NY: Simon & Schuster.

Drucker, David M. 2013. "GOP at Cross Purposes on 'Obamacare.'" *Roll Call*, April 25.

Drutman, Lee. 2015a. "The House Freedom Caucus Has Some Good Ideas on How the US House Should Operate." *Vox*, Polyarchy, October 20. http://www.vox.com/polyarchy/2015/10/20/9570747/house-freedom-caucus-process-demands

Drutman, Lee. 2015b. *The Business of America Is Lobbying: How Corporations Became Politicized and Politics Became More Corporate*. New York, NY: Oxford University Press.

Drutman, Lee. 2017. "House Leadership Has Been Writing Bills Behind Closed Doors for Years." *Vox*, March 3. https://www.vox.com/polyarchy/2017/3/3/14805112/house-bills-secretive-history

Dumain, Emma, and Matt Fuller. 2015. "McCarthy Shocks Conference by Dropping Speaker Bid." *Roll Call*, October 8. http://blogs.rollcall.com/218/mccarthy-shocks-conference-by-dropping-speaker-bid/

Eckman, Sarah J. 2017. *Congressional News Media and the House and Senate Galleries*. Congressional Research Service Report R44816, April 13.

Eddy, Mark. 2010. *Medical Marijuana: Review and Analysis of Federal and State Policies.* Congressional Research Service Report RL33211, April 2.

Egar, William T. 2016. "Tarnishing Opponents, Polarizing Congress: The House Minority Party and the Construction of the Roll-Call Record." *Legislative Studies Quarterly* 41(4): 935–964.

Eilperin, Juliet, Sean Sullivan, and Kelsey Snell. 2017. "Senate Rejects Measure to Partly Repeal Affordable Care Act, Dealing GOP Leaders a Major Setback." *Washington Post,* July 28. https://www.washingtonpost.com/powerpost/senate-gop-leaders-work-to-round-up-votes-for-modest-health-care-overhaul/2017/07/27/ac08fc40-72b7-11e7-8839-ec48ec4cae25_story.html?utm_term=.98e99bbcc15d

Elliot, Jonathan, ed. 1888. *The Debates in the Several State Conventions on the Adoption of the Federal Constitution as Recommended by the General Convention at Philadelphia in 1787.* 5 vols. Reprint. New York, NY: Burt Franklin.

Erikson, Robert S. 1978. "Constituency Opinion and Congressional Behavior: A Reexamination of the Miller-Stokes Representation Data." *American Journal of Political Science* 22(3): 511–535.

Erikson, Robert S., and Kent L. Tedin. 2015. *American Public Opinion: Its Origins, Content and Impact.* New York, NY: Routledge.

Erikson, Robert S., and Gerald C. Wright. 2000. "Representation of Constituency Ideology in Congress." In *Change and Continuity in House Elections,* ed. David W. Brady, John F. Cogan, and John F. Ferejohn, 149–177. Stanford, CA: Stanford University Press.

Ethridge, Emily. 2013a. "Club for Growth Opposes GOP-Backed Health Care Bill." *CQ Roll Call,* April 18.

Ethridge, Emily. 2013b. "House GOP Moves Forward with Health Bill Despite Conservative Opposition." *CQ Roll Call,* April 19.

Evans, C. Lawrence. 2018. *The Whips: Building Party Coalitions in Congress.* Ann Arbor, MI: University of Michigan Press.

Everett, Burgess. 2014. "Mark Begich Blasts Harry Reid on Amendments." *Politico,* June 30. http://www.politico.com/story/2014/07/mark-begich-harry-reid-amendments-109567

Everett, Burgess. 2015a. "Cruz Sternly Rebuked by GOP." *Politico,* September 28. http://www.politico.com/story/2015/09/ted-cruz-senate-rebuke-planned-parenthood-214183

Everett, Burgess. 2015b. "Cruz Calls McConnell a Democrat." *Politico,* October 29. http://www.politico.com/story/2015/10/cruz-mcconnell-democrat-215372

Everett, Burgess, and Manu Raju. 2014. "Senate Pushes Envelope on Gridlock." *Politico,* January 26. http://www.politico.com/story/2014/01/senate-pushes-envelope-on-gridlock-102627.html

Farenthold, David A. 2013. "The (86,000) Budget-Cutting Ideas That Got Away." *Washington Post,* March 27. https://www.washingtonpost.com/politics/the-85000-budget-cutting-ideas-that-got-away/2013/03/27/85a075a0-90a4-11e2-9c4d-798c073d7ec8_story.html?utm_term=.409d3d143325

Farrand, Max. 1966. *The Records of the Federal Convention of 1787*. Vol. 2. New Haven, CT: Yale University Press.

Fenno, Richard F. 1978. *Home Style: House Members in Their Districts*. Boston, MA: Little, Brown.

Fink, Evelyn C. 2000. "Representation by Deliberation: Changes in the Rules of Deliberation in the US House of Representatives, 1789–1844." *Journal of Politics* 62(4): 1109–1125.

Finke, Daniel. 2015. "Why Do European Political Groups Call the Roll?" *Party Politics* 21(5): 750–762.

Finocchiaro, Charles J., and David W. Rohde. 2008. "War for the Floor: Partisan Theory and Agenda Control in the U.S. House of Representatives." *Legislative Studies Quarterly* 33(1): 35–61.

Fishbein, Rebecca. 2018. "The Time the Word 'Damn' Almost Got a Man Kicked Out of Congress." *Vice*, July 19. https://www.vice.com/en/article/the-time-the-word-damn-almost-got-a-man-kicked-out-of-congress/

Fletcher, Michael A., and Ariana Eunjung Cha. 2011. "Wisconsin Assembly Approves Bill to Slash Union Rights for Public Workers." *Washington Post*, March 10. http://www.washingtonpost.com/wp-dyn/content/article/2011/03/10/AR2011031002020.html

Foran, Clare. 2017. "Why a Republican Senator Wanted a Vote on Single-Payer Health Care." *The Atlantic*, July 27. https://www.theatlantic.com/politics/archive/2017/07/congress-healthcare-single-payer-debate/535143/

Forgey, Quint. 2020. "Both Parties Pile on Massie after Effort to Force Recorded Vote Flops." *Politico*, March 27. https://www.politico.com/news/2020/03/27/trump-congressman-thomas-massie-coronavirus-vote-151523

French, Lauren, and Jake Sherman. 2015. "House Conservative Seeks Boehner's Ouster." *Politico*, July 28. https://www.politico.com/story/2015/07/house-conservative-john-boehner-ouster-120742

Friedman, Lisa, and Brad Plumer. 2022. "Surprise Deal Would Be Most Ambitious Climate Action Undertaken by U.S." *New York Times*, July 28. https://www.nytimes.com/2022/07/28/climate/climate-change-deal-manchin.html

Fuerbringer, Jonathan. 1987. "Tax Rise Is Passed by House: Partisan Strife Marks Attempt to Cut Deficit House Approves Tax Rise by One Vote." *New York Times*, October 30.

Gibson, Ginger. 2013. "Boehner: No Vote on Senate Immigration Bill." *Politico*, July 8. https://www.politico.com/story/2013/07/john-boehner-house-immigration-vote-093845

Gilbert, Michael D. 2006. "Single Subject Rules and the Legislative Process." *University of Pittsburgh Law Review* 67(4): 803–870.

Gillin, Joshua. 2016. "Patrick Murphy Has Voted Against 'Every' Zika Funding Bill, Marco Rubio Says." *PolitiFact*, September 14. http://www.politifact.com/florida/statements/2016/sep/14/marco-rubio/patrick-murphy-has-voted-against-every-zika-fundin/

Goldman, Lee. 2008. "False Campaigning Advertising and the `Actual Malice' Standard." *Tulane Law Review* 82(3): 889–928.

Goodnough, Abby, Robert Pear, and Thomas Kaplan. 2017. "Health Groups Denounce G.O.P. Bill as Its Backers Scramble." *New York Times*, March 8. https://www.nytimes.com/2017/03/08/us/politics/affordable-care-act-obama-care-health.html

Grose, Christian R., Neil Malhotra, and Robert Parks Van Houweling. 2015. "Explaining Explanations: How Legislators Explain Their Policy Positions and How Citizens React." *American Journal of Political Science* 59(3): 724–743.

Gross, Bertram. 1964. *The Managing of Organization:the Administrative Struggles*. New York, NY: Free Press of Glencoe.

Hall, Richard L., and Frank W. Wayman. 1990. "Buying Time: Moneyed Interests and the Mobilization of Bias in Congressional Committees." *American Political Science Review* 84(3): 797–820.

Hanson, Peter. 2014. *Too Weak to Govern: Omnibus Bills, Agenda Control and Weak Senate Majorities*. New York, NY: Cambridge University Press.

Harbridge, Laurel. 2015. *Is Bipartisanship Dead? Policy Agreement and Agenda-Setting in the House of Representatives*. New York, NY: Cambridge University Press.

Hawkings, David. 2015. "Scorched Senate Tactics Limiting Cruz's Options, Top Prize Excepted." *Roll Call*, October 5. http://www.rollcall.com/news/scorched-senate-tactics-limiting-cruzs-options-top-prize-excepted

Heath, Michelle, Leslie A. Roseanna, A. Schwindt-Bayer, and Michelle M. Taylor-Robinson. 2005. "Women on the Sidelines: Women's Representation on Committees in Latin American Legislatures." *American Journal of Political Science* 49(2): 420–436.

Heitshusen, Valerie. 2017. *Parties Leaders in the United States Congress, 1789–2017*. Congressional Research Service Report RL30567, January 5.

Hernandez, Raymond, and Christopher Drew. 2007. "Obama's Vote in Illinois Was Often Just 'Present.'" *New York Times*, December 20. https://www.nytimes.com/2007/12/20/us/politics/20cnd-obama.html

Herszenhorn, David. 2016. "Senate Votes to Advance Emergency Funding to Fight Zika Virus." *New York Times*, May 18. https://www.nytimes.com/2016/05/18/us/zika-senate-vote-emergency-funding.html

Hibbing, John R., and Elizabeth Thiess-Morse. 1995. *Congress as Public Enemy: Public Attitudes Toward American Political Institutions*. New York, NY: Cambridge University Press.

Higdon, James. 2018. "Washington's Most Powerful Anti-Pot Official Is Named Sessions. It's Not Who You Think." *Politico*, March 21. https://www.politico.com/magazine/story/2018/03/21/washingtons-most-powerful-anti-pot-official-is-named-sessions-its-not-who-you-think-217662/

Highton, Benjamin. 2019. "Issue Accountability in US House Elections." *Political Behavior* 41(2): 349–367.

Hillygus, D. Sunshine, and Todd G. Shields. 2009. *The Persuadable Voter: Wedge Issues in Presidential Campaigns*. Princeton, NJ: Princeton University Press.

Hinds, Asher C. 1907. *Hinds' Precedents of the House of Representatives*. Washington, DC: US Government Printing Office.

Hoffman, Daniel N. 1981. *Governmental Secrecy and the Founding Fathers: A Study in Constitutional Controls*. Westport CT: Greenwood Press.

Holan, Angie Drobnic. 2010. "Ed Perlmutter Voted for Viagra for Sex Offenders, Paid for by Health Care Bill? Nope." *PolitiFact*, October 26. http://www.politifact.com/truth-o-meter/statements/2010/oct/26/american-action-network/viagra-sex-offenders-paid-health-care-bill-nope/

Hooper, Molly K., Peter Schroeder, and Russell Berman. 2012. "Speaker Offered a Prayer Before Announcing the Defeat of Plan B." *The Hill*, December 21. https://thehill.com/policy/finance/137778-speaker-offered-a-prayer-before-announcing-the-defeat-of-plan-b/

Howell, William, Scott Adler, Charles Cameron, and Charles Riemann. 2000. "Divided Government and the Legislative Productivity of Congress, 1945–94." *Legislative Studies Quarterly* 25(2): 285–312.

Hudak, John. 2013. "Congress, the Affordable Care Act, and the Myth of the 'Exemption.'" *Brookings Blog*, October 4. http://www.brookings.edu/blogs/fixgov/posts/2013/10/04-aca-vitter-amendment-federal-workforce-hudak

Hudiburg, Jane A. 2018. *The House Journal: Origin, Purpose and Approval*. Congressional Research Service Report R45209, May 31.

Hug, Simon. 2010. "Selection Effects in Roll Call Votes." *British Journal of Political Science* 40(1): 225–235.

Hulse, Carl. 2014. "McConnell Vows a Senate in Working Order, If He Is Given Control." *New York Times*, March 3. http://www.nytimes.com/2014/03/04/us/if-given-gavel-mcconnell-vows-a-senate-in-working-order.html?_r=0

Hulse, Carl. 2019. "How Congress Is Weaponizing a Series of Hot-Button Votes." *New York Times*, March 9. https://www.nytimes.com/2019/03/09/us/politics/congress-symbolic-votes.html

Hunter, Marjorie. 1970. "Secrecy in Panels Upheld in House." *New York Times*, July 14.

Jacobson, Louis. 2010. "Sharon Angle Attacks Harry Reid over Giving Sex Offenders Taxpayer-subsidized Viagra." *PolitiFact*, October 8. https://www.politifact.com/factchecks/2010/oct/08/sharron-angle/sharron-angle-attacks-harry-reid-over-giving-sex-o/

Jacobson, Louis. 2014. "NRCC Says Rep. John Barrow, D-Ga., Voted with Barack Obama 85% of the Time." *PolitiFact*, September 15. http://www.politifact.com/truth-o-meter/statements/2014/sep/15/national-republican-congressional-committee/nrcc-says-rep-john-barrow-d-ga-voted-barack-obama-/

James, Frank. 2011. "Speaker Boehner Gets Gavel After Pelosi's Swan Song." *NPR*, January 5. https://www.npr.org/sections/itsallpolitics/2011/01/05/132682111/speaker-boehner-gets-gavel-after-pelosis-swan-song

Jenkins, Jeffrey A., and Nathan W. Monroe. 2012a. "Buying Negative Agenda Control in the U.S. House." *American Journal of Political Science* 56(4): 897–912.

Jenkins, Jeffrey A., and Nathan W. Monroe. 2012b. "Partisan Agenda Control in the US House: A Theoretical Exploration." *Journal of Theoretical Politics* 24(4): 555–570.

Jenkins, Jeffrey A., and Charles Stewart III. 2012. *Fighting for the Speakership: The House and the Rise of Party Government*. Princeton, NJ: Princeton University Press.

Jessee, Stephen A., and Sean M. Theriault. 2014. "The Two Faces of Congressional Roll-Call Voting." *Party Politics* 20(6): 836–848.

Jillson, Calvin C., and Rick K. Wilson. 1987. "A Social Choice Model of Politics: Insights into the Demise of the US Continental Congress." *Legislative Studies Quarterly* 12(1): 5–32.

Jillson, Calvin C., and Rick K. Wilson. 1994. *Congressional Dynamics: Structure, Coordination, and Choice in the First American Congress, 1774–1789*. Stanford, CA: Stanford University Press.

Jones, Charles O. 1968. "Joseph G. Cannon and Howard W. Smith: An Essay on the Limits of Leadership in the House of Representatives." *Journal of Politics* 30(3): 617–646.

Jones, Philip E. 2011. "Which Buck Stops Here? Accountability for Policy Positions and Policy Outcomes in Congress." *Journal of Politics* 73(3): 764–782.

Kane, Paul, and Matea Gold. 2013. "Boehner: Tea Party Groups Have 'Lost All Credibility.'" *Washington Post*, December 12. https://www.washingtonpost.com/news/post-politics/wp/2013/12/12/boehner-tea-party-groups-have-lost-all-credibility/?utm_term=.2f9d2c91d6a8

Kane, Paul, and Ed O'Keefe. 2013. "House Passes 2-Year Bipartisan Budget Deal." *Washington Post*, December 12. https://www.washingtonpost.com/politics/boehner-escalates-feud-with-conservative-groups-as-vote-on-budget-bill-looms/2013/12/12/3986871c-634f-11e3-91b3-f2bb96304e34_story.html?utm_term=.6a3c4b5616f5

Kaplan, Thomas. 2017. "Senate Soundly Rejects Repeal-Only Health Plan." *New York Times*, July 26. https://www.nytimes.com/2017/07/26/us/politics/senate-rejects-repealing-obamacare-without-replacement-trump.html

Kaplan, Thomas, and Robert Pear. 2017. "2 Senators Strike Deal on Health Subsidies That Trump Cut Off." *New York Times*, October 17. https://www.nytimes.com/2017/10/17/us/politics/alexander-murray-deal-obamacare-subsidies.html?_r=0

Kelly, Sean Q. 1993a. "Divided We Govern? A Reassessment." *Polity* 25(3): 473–484.

Kelly, Sean Q. 1993b. "Response: Let's Stick with the Larger Question." *Polity* 25(3): 489–490.

Kiely, Eugene. 2010. "Benton's Bogus Viagra Ad." *FactCheck.org*, May 11. https://www.factcheck.org/2010/05/bentons-bogus-viagra-ad/

Kim, Seung Min. 2013. "Harry Reid: David Vitter Trying to Get Elected Governor." *Politico*, September 24. http://www.politico.com/story/2013/09/senate-harry-reid-david-vitter-governor-97284.html

King, Aaron, David Rohde, and Frank Orlando. 2012. "Beyond Motions to Table: Exploring the Procedural Toolkit of the Majority Party in the United States Senate." In *Party and Procedure in the United States Congress*, ed. Jacob R. Straus, 173–194. New York, NY: Rowman & Littlefield.

Kingdon, John W. 1989. *Congressmen's Voting Decisions*. 3rd ed. Ann Arbor, MI: University of Michigan Press.

Klein, Ezra. 2012. "14 Reasons Why This Is the Worst Congress Ever." *Washington*

Post, July 13. https://www.washingtonpost.com/news/wonk/wp/2012/07/13/13-reasons-why-this-is-the-worst-congress-ever/?utm_term=.8b94db02b946

Klein, Ezra. 2013. "Goodbye and Good Riddance, 112th Congress." *Washington Post*, January 4. https://www.washingtonpost.com/news/wonk/wp/2013/01/04/goodbye-and-good-riddance-112th-congress/?utm_term=.d46f82146639

Koger, Gregory. 2010. *Filibustering: A Political History of Obstruction in the House and Senate*. Chicago, IL: University of Chicago Press.

Krehbiel, Keith. 1998. *Pivotal Politics: A Theory of U.S. Lawmaking*. Chicago, IL: University of Chicago Press.

Landers, Elizabeth. 2018. "Senate Democrats Force Vote to Reinstate Net Neutrality." *CNN*, May 9. https://www.cnn.com/2018/05/09/politics/democrats-net-neutrality-vote/index.html

Lawrence, John A. 2018. *The Class of '74*. Baltimore, MD: Johns Hopkins University Press.

Layton, Lyndsey. 2007. "House GOP Uses Procedural Tactic to Frustrate Democratic Majority." *Washington Post*, May 19. http://www.washingtonpost.com/wp-dyn/content/article/2007/05/18/AR2007051801697.html

Lee, Frances E. 2008a. "Agreeing to Disagree: Agenda Content and Senate Partisanship, 1981–2004." *Legislative Studies Quarterly* 33(2): 199–222.

Lee, Frances E. 2008b. "Dividers, Not Uniters: Presidential Leadership and Senate Partisanship, 1981–2004." *Journal of Politics* 70(4): 914–928.

Lee, Frances E. 2009. *Beyond Ideology: Politics, Principles, and Partisanship in the U.S. Senate*. Chicago, IL: University of Chicago Press.

Lee, Frances E. 2016. *Insecure Majorities: Congress and the Perpetual Campaign*. Chicago, IL: University of Chicago Press.

Lee, Frances E. 2018. "The 115th Congress and Questions of Party Unity in a Polarized Era." *Journal of Politics* 80(4): 1464–1473.

Lee, Mike. 2015. "Congress Needs Uber-Level Innovation." *The Federalist*, October 15. http://thefederalist.com/2015/10/15/congress-needs-uber-level-innovation/

Lesniewski, Niels. 2013. "Vitter Amendment Won't Go Away Quietly." *Roll Call*, September 30. https://www.rollcall.com/news/vitter-amendment-wont-go-away-quietly

Lesniewski, Niels. 2014a. "The Attack Ads Harry Reid Didn't Want You to See." *Roll Call*, October 30. http://blogs.rollcall.com/wgdb/10-attack-ads-harry-reid-strategy-senate-votes-2014/?dcz=

Lesniewski, Niels. 2014b. "Vulnerable Democrats Almost Always Voted with Obama." *Roll Call*, October 27. http://atr.rollcall.com/senate-votes-2014-cq-senate-democrats-obama/

Lesniewski, Niels. 2015a. "Senate Votes to Revive Export-Import Bank, Keep Obamacare." *Roll Call*, July 26. http://www.rollcall.com/news/home/senate-votes-to-revive-export-import-bank-keep-obamacare

Lesniewski, Niels. 2015b. "McConnell Show's He's the Boss." *Roll Call*, January 23. http://blogs.rollcall.com/wgdb/mcconnell-shows-hes-the-boss/?dcz

Levy, Gabrielle. 2015. "Speaker Ryan Pledges Return to Regular Order." *U.S. News*, October 29. https://www.usnews.com/news/articles/2015/10/29/paul-ryan-pledges-return-to-regular-order

Lieffring, Staci. 2013. "First Amendment and the Right to Lie: Regulating Knowingly False Campaign Speech after United States V. Alvarez." *Minnesota Law Review* 97(3): 1047–1078.

Lipinski, Daniel. 2001. "The Effect of Messages Communicated by Members of Congress: The Impact of Publicizing Votes." *Legislative Studies Quarterly* 26(1): 81–100.

LoGiurato, Brett. 2012. "Two Big Conservative Groups Come Out Against Boehner's 'Plan B.'" *Business Insider*, December 19. http://www.businessinsider.com/boehner-fiscal-cliff-plan-b-grover-norquist-heritage-club-for-growth-conservatives-obama-2012-12

LoGiurato, Brett, and Grace Wyler. 2012. "Boehner Disaster: Vote Delayed After Failure to Get Enough Support for Plan B." *Business Insider*, December 20. http://static.businessinsider.com/boehner-plan-b-vote-fiscal-cliff-obama-taxes-cuts-2012-12

Lott, Trent. 2005. *Herding Cats: A Life in Politics*. New York, NY: HarperCollins.

Luce, Robert. 1922. *Legislative Procedure: Parliamentary Practices and the Course of Business in the Framing of Statutes*. New York, NY: Houghton Mifflin.

Lynch, Michael S., and Anthony J. Madonna. 2013a. "Viva Voce: Implications from the Disappearing Voice Vote, 1807–1996." *Social Science Quarterly* 94(2): 530–550.

Lynch, Michael S., and Anthony J. Madonna. 2013b. "Partisan Brand Name Building and Deficit Politics: Examining the Role of Power Sharing on Party Issue Consistency." *Journal of Public Policy* 33(3): 319–344.

Lynch, Michael S., Anthony J. Madonna, Mark E. Owens, and Ryan Williamson. 2018. "The Vice President in the U.S. Senate: Examining the Consequences of Institutional Design." *Congress & the Presidency* 45(2): 145–165.

Lynch, Michael S., Anthony J. Madonna, and Jason M. Roberts. 2016. "The Cost of Majority Party Bias: Amending Activity under Structured Rules." *Legislative Studies Quarterly* 41(3): 633–655.

Madonna, Anthony J. 2011. "Institutions and Coalition Formation: Revisiting the Effects of Rule XXII on Winning Coalition Sizes in the U.S. Senate." *American Journal of Political Science* 55(2): 276–288.

Madonna, Anthony J., and Kevin R Kosar. 2015. "Could the Modern Senate Manage an Open-Amendment Process?" R Street Policy Study No. 42, October. http://www.rstreet.org/wp-content/uploads/2015/10/RSTREET42.pdf

Madonna, Anthony J., and Ian Ostrander. 2019. "A Congress of Cannibals: The Evolution of Professional Staff in Congress." Unpublished manuscript.

Mann, Thomas E., and Norman J. Ornstein. 2013. "Five Myths About the 112th Congress." *Brookings*, January 4. https://www.brookings.edu/opinions/five-myths-about-the-112th-congress/

Matthews, Donald R., and James Stimson. 1975. *Yeas and Nays: Normal Decision-Making in the U.S. House of Representatives*. New York, NY: John Wiley & Sons.

Matthews, Dylan. 2013. "It's Official: The 112th Congress Was the Most Polarized

Ever." *Washington Post*, January 17. https://www.washingtonpost.com/news/wonk/wp/2013/01/17/its-official-the-112th-congress-was-the-most-polarized-ever/?utm_term=.827e6afccbbe

Mayhew, David R. 1991. *Divided We Govern: Party Control, Lawmaking and Investigating: 1946–1990*. New Haven, CT: Yale University Press.

Mayhew, David R. 1993. "Reply: Let's Stick with the Longer List." *Polity* 25(3): 485–488.

Mayhew, David R. 2005. *Divided We Govern: Party Control, Lawmaking and Investigating: 1946–2002*. New Haven, CT: Yale University Press.

McCall, Samuel W. 1914. *The Life of Thomas B. Reed*. Boston, MA: Houghton Mifflin.

McCarty, Nolan M., Keith T. Poole, and Howard Rosenthal. 2008. *Polarized America: The Dance of Ideology and Unequal Riches*. Cambridge, MA: MIT Press.

McPherson, Lindsey. 2015. "Paul Ryan Talks Up Return to Regular Order." *Roll Call*, December 16. http://www.rollcall.com/news/home/paul-ryan-talks-return-regular-order

McPherson, Lindsey. 2016. "Huelskamp Forces House to Go on Record." *Roll Call*, September 21. https://www.rollcall.com/news/congress/we-are-either-a-team-or-were-not-democrats-struggle-with-republican-messaging-votes

McPherson, Lindsey. 2019. "'We Are Either a Team or We're Not'—Democrats Struggle with Republican Messaging Votes." *Roll Call*, March 1. https://www.rollcall.com/news/congress/we-are-either-a-team-or-were-not-democrats-struggle-with-republican-messaging-votes

McPherson, Lindsey. 2022. "How `Build Back Better' Started and How It's Going." *Roll Call*, July 21.

Meinke, Scott. 2016. *Leadership Organizations in the House of Representatives: Party Participation and Partisan Politics*. Ann Arbor, MI: University of Michigan Press.

Messerly, Megan, and Riley Snyder. 2017. "Senate Narrowly Votes to Approve Heller-Sponsored 'Cadillac Tax' Amendment: Cortez Masto 1 of 2 Democrats in Support." *Nevada Independent*, July 27. https://thenevadaindependent.com/article/senate-to-vote-on-heller-sponsored-amendment-to-repeal-cadillac-tax-on-certain-high-cost-health-plans

Miller, Gary, and Norman Schofield. 2003. "Activists and Party Realignment in the United States." *American Political Science Review* 97(2): 245–259.

Miller, John Chester. 1948. *Triumph of Freedom, 1775–1783*. Boston, MA: Little, Brown.

Miller, Warren E., and Donald S. Stokes. 1962. "Party Government and the Saliency of Congress." *Public Opinion Quarterly* 26(4): 531–546.

Mimms, Sarah. 2015. "McConnell's Majority-Leader Promises Sound Familiar." *The Atlantic*, January 4. https://www.theatlantic.com/politics/archive/2015/01/mcconnells-majority-leader-promises-sound-familiar/449637/

Monroe, Nathan W., and Gregory Robinson. 2008. "Do Restrictive Rules Produce Non-Median Outcomes? A Theory with Evidence from the 101st–108th Congresses." *Journal of Politics* 70(1): 217–231.

Morin, Rebecca. 2017. "McConnell Will Bring Up Bipartisan Health Care Bill If

Trump Says He Will Sign." *Politico*, October 22. https://www.politico.com/story/2017/10/22/mcconnell-trump-obamacare-health-care-244034

Morton, Rebecca B. 1999. *Methods and Models: A Guide to the Empirical Analysis of Formal Models in Political Science.* New York, NY: Cambridge University Press.

Nelson, Garrison. Committees in the U.S. Congress, 1947–1992, Senate/94–102nd Congresses, August 13, 2012. http://web.mit.edu/17.251/www/data_page.html#1

Nelson, Libby. 2009. "Detective's Name on New 9/11 Health Bill." *New York Times*, June 24. https://www.nytimes.com/2009/06/25/nyregion/25zadroga.html

Newhauser, Daniel and Matt Fuller. 2014. "Secret `Doc Fix' Deal Angers Rank and File." *Roll Call*, March 27. https://rollcall.com/2014/03/27/secret-doc-fix-deal-angers-rank-and-file-video/

Noel, Hans. 2013. *Political Ideologies and Political Parties in America*. New York, NY: Cambridge University Press.

Nyhan, Brendan, Eric McGhee, John Sides, Seth Masket, and Steven Greene. 2012. "One Vote Out of Step? The Effects of Salient Roll Call Votes in the 2012 Election." *American Politics Review* 40(5): 844–879.

O'Keefe, Ed. 2014. "The House Has Voted 54 Times in Four Years on Obamacare. Here's the Full List." *Washington Post*, March 21. https://www.washingtonpost.com/news/the-fix/wp/2014/03/21/the-house-has-voted-54-times-in-four-years-on-obamacare-heres-the-full-list/?utm_term=.4244134822f2

O'Keefe, Ed, Paige Winfield Cunningham, and Amy Goldstein. 2017. "House Republicans Claim a Major Victory with Passage of Health-Care Overhaul." *Washington Post*, May 4. https://www.washingtonpost.com/powerpost/republicans-plan-health-care-vote-on-thursday-capping-weeks-of-fits-and-starts/2017/05/03/e7dd7c28-306d-11e7-9dec-764dc781686f_story.html?utm_term=.896401d777cb

Oleszek, Mark J. and Walter J. Oleszek. 2012. "Legislative Sausage-Making: Health Care Reform in the 111th Congress." In *Party and Procedure in the United States Congress*, ed. Jacob R. Straus, 253–273. New York, NY: Rowman & Littlefield.

Oleszek, Walter J. 2014. "The Evolving Congress: Overview and Analysis of the Modern Era." In *The Evolving Congress*, prepared by the Congressional Research Service, 3–60. Washington, DC: US Government Printing Office.

Oleszek, Walter J., Mark J. Oleszek, Elizabeth Rybicki, and Bill Heniff Jr. 2016. *Congressional Procedures and the Policy Process*. 10th ed. Washington, DC: CQ Press.

Ornstein, Norman J. 2010. "The Motion to Recommit, Hijacked by Politics." *Roll Call*, May 19. https://rollcall.com/2010/05/18/the-motion-to-recommit-hijacked-by-politics/

Ornstein, Norman J., Thomas E. Mann, Michael J. Malbin, and Molly Reynolds. 2019. *Vital Statistics on Congress*. Washington, DC: Brookings Institution Press. https://www.brookings.edu/multi-chapter-report/vital-statistics-on-congress/

Osborn, George Coleman. 1943. *John Sharp Williams: Planter-Statesman of the Deep South*. Baton Rouge, LA: Louisiana State University Press.

Ota, Alan K. 2018. "With Only One Vote, McConnell Approves Treaty for the Blind." *Roll Call*, June 29. https://rollcall.com/2018/06/29/with-only-one-vote-mcconnell-approves-treaty-for-the-blind/

Palmer, Anna. 2013. "Shutdown Looms, Fundraising Zooms." *Politico*, September 28. https://www.politico.com/story/2013/09/government-shutdown-looms-fundraisi ng-zooms-097481

Palmer, Anna, and Lauren French. 2015. "Conservatives Give Ryan a Pass on Budget Deal They Despise." *Politico*, December 16. http://www.politico.com/story/2015 /12/budget-house-freedom-caucus-216876

Parlapiano, Alicia. 2021. "Biden's $4 Trillion Economic Plan, in One Chart." *New York Times*, April 28. https://www.nytimes.com/2021/04/28/upshot/biden-families-plan -american-rescue-infrastructure.html

Patty, John W. 2010. "Dilatory or Anticipatory? Voting on the Journal in the House of Representatives." *Public Choice* 143(1–2): 121–133.

Pear, Robert. 2010. "If Only Laws Were Like Sausages." *New York Times*, December 4. https://www.nytimes.com/2010/12/05/weekinreview/05pear.html

Pear, Robert, and Thomas Kaplan. 2017. "House Republicans Unveil Plan to Replace Health Law." *New York Times*, March 6. https://www.nytimes.com/2017/03/06/us /politics/affordable-care-act-obamacare-health.html

Person, Daniel. 2017. "The House Just Passed the Obamacare Repeal Bill. Here's How Washington's Delegation Voted." *Seattle Weekly*, May 4. https://www.seattleweek ly.com/news/as-health-care-vote-approaches-we-still-dont-know-where-reichert-s tands/

Petersen, R. Eric. 2001. "Is It Science Yet? Replicating and Validating the Divided We Govern List of Important Statutes." Paper presented at the Annual Meeting of the Midwest Political Science Association, Chicago.

Plautz, Jason. 2015. "Republicans Pull Vote on Confederate Flag Amendment." *The Atlantic*, July 9. https://www.theatlantic.com/politics/archive/2015/07/republicans -pull-vote-on-confederate-flag-amendment/452406/

Poole, Keith T. 2005. *Spatial Models of Parliamentary Voting*. New York, NY: Cambridge University Press.

Poole, Keith T., Jeffrey B. Lewis, James Lo, and Royce Carroll. 2011. "Scaling Roll Call Votes with wnominate in R." *Journal of Statistical Software* 42(14), 1–21.

Poole, Keith T., and Howard Rosenthal. 2007. *Ideology and Congress*. New Brunswick, NJ: Transaction Publishers.

Quirk, Paul J., and Joseph Hinchliffe. 1998. "The Rising Hegemony of Mass Opinion." *Journal of Policy History* 10(1): 19–50.

Raju, Manu. and John Bresnahan. 2013. "Will Democrats Haul Out Hookers in David Vitter Fight?" *Politico*, September 12. http://www.politico.com/story/2013/09/dav id-vitter-obamacare-democrats-secret-weapon-96744.html

Raju, Manu, and Burgess Everett. 2014. "Harry Reid's New Challenge: His Fellow Democrats." *Politico*, June 23. http://www.politico.com/story/2014/06/harry-reid -democrats-senate-gridlock-108212.html

Reed, Thomas B. 1889. "Obstruction in the National House." *North American Review* 149(395): 421–428.

Rice, Stuart A. 1925. "The Behavior of Legislative Groups: A Method of Measurement." *Political Science Quarterly* 40(1): 60–72.

Roberts, Jason M. 2005. "Minority Rights and Majority Power: Conditional Party Government and the Motion to Recommit in the House." *Legislative Studies Quarterly* 30(2): 219–234.

Roberts, Jason M. 2010. "The Development of Special Orders and Special Rules in the U.S. House, 1881–1937." *Legislative Studies Quarterly* 35(3): 307–336.

Roberts, Jason M., and Steven S. Smith. 2003. "Procedural Contexts, Party Strategy, and Conditional Party Voting in the U.S. House of Representatives, 1971–2000." *American Journal of Political Science* 47(2): 305–317.

Rogers, Steven. 2017. "Electoral Accountability for State Legislative Roll Calls and Ideological Representation." *American Political Science Review* 111(3): 555–571.

Rohde, David W. 1991. *Parties and Leaders in the Postreform House*. Chicago, IL: University of Chicago Press.

Rybicki, Elizabeth. 2017. *Availability of Legislative Measures in the House of Representatives (The "Three-Day Rule")*. Congressional Research Service Report RS22015, June 17.

Sala, Brian R. 2002. "Party Loyalty and Committee Leadership in the House, 1921–40." In *Party, Process, and Political Change in Congress: New Perspectives on the History of Congress*, ed. David W. Brady and Mathew D. McCubbins. Stanford, CA: Stanford University Press.

Sanchez, Humberto. 2016. "Fact Check: Was Scott Garrett the Only Member of the U.S. House New Jersey Delegation to Vote Against the Zadroga Act in 2010?" *Ballotpedia*, September 26. https://ballotpedia.org/Fact_check/Was_Scott_Garrett_the_only_member_of_the_U.S._House_New_Jersey_delegation_to_vote_against_the_Zadroga_Act_in_2010%3F

Saturno, James V. 2015. *Points of Order in the Congressional Budget Process*. Congressional Research Service Report 97-865, October 20.

Schickler, Eric. 2001. *Disjointed Pluralism: Institutional Innovation and the Development of the U.S. Congress*. Princeton, NJ: Princeton University Press.

Schneider, Elena. 2017. "Pelosi Plays Star Role in Georgia Special Election." *Politico*, June 16. https://www.politico.com/story/2017/06/16/nancy-pelosi-georgia-special-election-ossoff-handel-239615

Scholtes, Jennifer. 2010. "Bill to Create Ground Zero Health Program Blocked in House." *CQ*, July 29.

Severns, Maggie, Kimberly Hefling, and Jake Sherman. 2015. "House Leaders Muster Passage of Education Bill." *Politico*, July 8. https://www.politico.com/story/2015/07/house-gop-education-bill-votes-119839

Shapiro, Ari. 2010. "Jon Stewart's Latest Act: Sept. 11 Responders Bill." *NPR*, December 26. https://www.npr.org/2010/12/26/132310870/jon-stewarts-latest-act-sept-11-responders-bill

Shapiro, Fred R. 2008. "Quote . . . Misquote." *New York Times*, July 21. https://www.nytimes.com/2008/07/21/magazine/27wwwl-guestsafire-t.html

Sherman, Amy. 2014. "Democratic Group Says Ileana Ros-Lehtinen Voted Against VA Backlog Fixes." *PolitiFact*, June 6. https://www.politifact.com/florida/statements

/2014/jun/06/democratic-congressional-campaign-committee/ileana-ros-lehtinen-voted-against-va-backlog-fixes/

Sherman, Amy. 2016. “NARAL Misleads in Attack on Marco Rubio About Zika Funding.” *PolitiFact*, September 8. http://www.politifact.com/florida/statements/2016/sep/08/naral-pro-choice/naral-misleads-attack-marco-rubio-about-zika-fundi/

Sherman, Jake. 2014. “The Obsession of the House Freedom Caucus.” *Politico*, October 15. http://www.politico.com/story/2015/10/justin-amash-freedom-caucus-house-republicans-214819

Sherman, Jake. 2015. “GOP Stumbles over Abortion Bill.” *Politico*, January 21. https://www.politico.com/story/2015/01/house-gop-abortion-vote-114454

Sherman, Jake, and Heather Caygle. 2016. “Paul Ryan Proposes Blocking Amendments Could Kill Spending Bills.” *Politico*, June 8. http://www.politico.com/story/2016/06/paul-ryan-block-amendments-spending-bills-224061

Sherman, Jake, and Burgess Everett. 2015. “New Congress Stumbles Through Its First Month.” *Politico*, January 30. https://www.politico.com/story/2015/01/house-gop-abortion-vote-114454

Shiner, Meredith. 2013. “Enzi, Vitter Would Force Congress, Obama to Pay for Health Care.” *Roll Call*, August 27. http://blogs.rollcall.com/wgdb/enzi-vitter-bill-would-force-congress-obama-to-pay-for-health-care/

Shutt, Jennifer. 2016. “Zika Spending Stalemate in Congress Spills Over into Campaigns.” *Roll Call*, August 15. https://rollcall.com/2016/08/15/zika-spending-stalemate-in-congress-spills-over-into-campaigns/

Sievert, Joel. 2015. “The Electoral Connection in the U.S. Senate.” PhD dissertation, University of Georgia.

Simon, Jeff. 2010. “9/11 Responders Bill Fails, Parties Point Fingers.” *CNN*, July 30. http://www.cnn.com/2010/POLITICS/07/30/9.11.responders.bill/index.html, accessed April 29, 2019.

Sinclair, Barbara. 1989. *The Transformation of the U.S. Senate*. Baltimore: Johns Hopkins University Press.

Smith, Steven S. 1989. *Call to Order: Floor Politics in the House and Senate*. Washington, DC: Brookings Institution.

Smith, Steven S. 2007. *Party Influence in Congress*. New York, NY: Cambridge University Press.

Smith, Steven S. 2014. *The Senate Syndrome*. Norman, OK: University of Oklahoma Press.

Smith, Steven S., Ian Ostrander, and Christopher M. Pope. 2013. “Majority Party Power and Procedural Motions in the U.S. Senate.” *Legislative Studies Quarterly* 38(2): 205–236.

Soffen, Kim, and Kevin Schaul. 2017. “Which Health-Care Plans the Senate Rejected (and Who Voted ‘No’).” *Washington Post*, July 28. https://www.washingtonpost.com/powerpost/senate-gop-leaders-work-to-round-up-votes-for-modest-health-care-overhaul/2017/07/27/ac08fc40-72b7-11e7-8839-ec48ec4cae25_story.html?utm_term=.32de549d076d

Sotomayor, Marianna and Mike DeBonis. 2021. "Rep. Majorie Taylor Greene Has Been Gunking up the Works. She Says She's Not Backing Down." *Washington Post*, March 10. https://www.washingtonpost.com/powerpost/greene-adjourn-house-republicans/2021/03/10/e4a50854-80ec-11eb-ac37-4383f7709abe_story.html

Squire, Peverill, and Gary Moncrief. 2015. *State Legislatures Today: Politics Under the Domes*. Lanham, MD: Rowman & Littlefield.

Stanton, John. 2010. "CRS: Health Law May Allow Viagra Coverage for Sex Offenders." *Roll Call*, April 7. https://rollcall.com/2010/04/07/crs-health-law-may-allow-viagra-coverage-for-sex-offenders/

Stathis, Stephen W. 2003. *Landmark Legislation, 1774–2002: Major U.S. Acts and Treaties*. Washington, DC: CQ Press.

Stathis, Stephen W. 2014. *Landmark Legislation, 1774–2012: Major U.S. Acts and Treaties*. 2nd ed. Washington, DC: CQ Press.

Steinhauer, Jennifer. 2012. "The Formerly Routine Is Now the Tendentious." *New York Times*, March 24. https://www.nytimes.com/2012/03/24/us/politics/in-polarized-congress-routines-are-now-tendentious.html

Steinhauer, Jennifer. 2015. "John Boehner, House Speaker, Will Resign from Congress." *New York Times*, September 25. http://www.nytimes.com/2015/09/26/us/john-boehner-to-resign-from-congress.html?_r=0

Stern, Remy. 2011. "The Craigslist Congressman and the Crossdressing Prostitute." *Gawker*, February 25. https://web.archive.org/web/20121012092714/http:/gawker.com/5769037/the-craigslist-congressman-and-the-crossdressing-prostitute

Stevens, Robert D. 1982. "But Is the Record Complete? A Case of Censorship of the Congressional Record." *Government Publications Review* 9(1): 75–80.

Stewart, Charles, III, and Jonathan Woon. Congressional Committee Assignments, 103rd to 112th Congresses, 1993–2011: Senate, August 13, 2012. http://web.mit.edu/17.251/www/data_page.html#1

Stiglitz, Edward H. 2008. The House Rules Dataset: 98th to 109th Congress. Stanford University, Stanford, CA.

Story, Joseph. 1833. *Commentaries on the Constitution of the United States*. Boston, MA: Hilliard, Gray.

Stratmann, Thomas. 2002. "Can Special Interests Buy Congressional Votes? Evidence from Financial Services Legislation." *Journal of Law and Economics* 45(2): 345–373.

Straus, Jacob R. 2008. *Electronic Voting System in the House of Representatives: History and Evolution*. Congressional Research Service Report RL34366, November 25.

Straus, Jacob R. 2014. "Comparing Modern Congresses: Can Productivity Be Measured?" In *The Evolving Congress*, prepared by the Congressional Research Service, 217–241. Washington, DC: US Government Printing Office.

Sulkin, Tracy. 2009. "Campaign Appeals and Legislative Action." *Journal of Politics* 71(3): 1093–1108.

Tanden, Neera. 2014. "A Short History of Republican Attempts to Repeal Obamacare." *Politico*, January 30. https://www.politico.com/magazine/story/2014/01/house-republicans-obamacare-repeal-votes-102911

Taylor, Jessica. 2010. "Taylor: I Voted for McCain." *Politico*, October 15. https://www.politico.com/story/2010/10/taylor-i-voted-for-mccain-044119

Theriault, Sean M. 2003. "Patronage, the Pendleton Act, and the Power of the People." *Journal of Politics* 65(1): 50–68.

Theriault, Sean M. 2004. "Public Pressure and Punishment in the Politics of Congressional Pay Raises." *American Politics Research* 32(4): 444–464.

Theriault, Sean M. 2008. *Party Polarization in Congress*. New York, NY: Cambridge University Press.

Thierse, Stefan. 2016. "Going on Record: Revisiting the Logic of Roll-Call Vote Requests in the European Parliament." *European Union Politics* 17(2): 219–241.

Tiefer, Charles. 1989. *Congressional Practice and Procedure*. New York, NY: Greenwood Press.

Toffler, Alvin. 1970. *Future Shock*. New York, NY: Random House.

Truman, David B. 1951. *The Governmental Process: Political Interests and Public Opinion*. New York, NY: Alfred A Knopf.

Turman, Jack. 2017. "How Has the Health Care Debate Unfolded this Year?" *CBS*, July 27. https://www.cbsnews.com/news/as-senate-votes-continue-how-did-the-health-care-debate-unfold-this-year/

Ung, Jenny. 2016. "Fact Check: Sen. John McCain Mostly Right on Rep. Ann Kirkpatrick's Pay-Raise Vote." *AZ Central*, August 10. https://www.azcentral.com/story/news/politics/fact-check/2016/08/10/fact-check-john-mccain-ann-kirkpatrick-pay-raise-vote/87548336/

Vandoren, Peter M. 1990. "Can We Learn the Causes of Congressional Decisions from Roll-Call Data?" *Legislative Studies Quarterly* 15(3): 311–340.

Vermeule, Adrian. 2004. "The Constitutional Law of Congressional Procedure." *University of Chicago Law Review* 71(2): 361–437.

Walsh, Brian. 2013. "Conservatives Eat Their Own for Profit." *U.S. News*, September 12. https://www.usnews.com/opinion/blogs/brian-walsh/2013/09/12/the-senate-conservative-fund-and-the-heritage-foundation-profit-from-attacking-republicans

Warren, Mark. 2015. "Help! We're in a Living Hell and Don't Know How to Get Out." *Esquire*, October 15. http://www.esquire.com/news-politics/news/a23553/congress-living-hell-1114/

Wawro, Gregory. 2001. "A Panel Probit Analysis of Campaign Contributions and Roll-Call Votes." *American Journal of Political Science* 45(3): 563–579.

Wawro, Gregory, and Eric Schickler. 2004. "Where's the Pivot? Obstruction and Law-Making in the Pre-Cloture Senate." *American Journal of Political Science* 48(4): 758–774.

Wawro, Gregory, and Eric Schickler. 2006. *Filibuster: Obstruction and Lawmaking in the U.S. Senate*. Princeton, NJ: Princeton University Press.

Weigel, David. 2017. "Conservative Groups Keep Lobbying Against GOP's Health-Care Bill." *Washington Post*, March 22. https://www.washingtonpost.com/news/powerpost/wp/2017/03/22/conservative-groups-keep-lobbying-against-gops-health-care-bill/?utm_term=.fb7d319481cc

Weingast, Barry R. 1989. "Floor Behavior in Congress: Committee Power under the Open Rule." *American Political Science Review* 83(3): 795–815.

Weisman, Jonathan. 2012. "The Senate's Long Slide to Gridlock." *New York Times*, November 24.

Weisman, Jonathan. 2013a. "House Majority Leader's Quest to Soften G.O.P.'s Image Hits a Wall Within." *New York Times*, April 24.

Weisman, Jonathan. 2013b. "Boehner Retains Speaker's Post, but Dissidents Nip at His Heels." *New York Times*, January 3. https://www.nytimes.com/2013/01/04/us/politics/new-congress-begins-with-wishes-of-comity-but-battles-ahead.html

Wilcox, Clyde, and Aage Clausen. 1991. "The Dimensionality of Roll Call Voting Reconsidered." *Legislative Studies Quarterly* 16(3): 393–406.

Wilkerson, John, David Smith, and Nicholas Stramp. 2015. "Tracing the Flow of Policy Ideas in Legislatures: A Text Reuse Approach." *American Journal of Political Science* 59(4): 943–956.

Willis, Derek. 2019. "As Pelosi Takes Over, an Attempt to Revive the 'Lost Art' of Legislating." *New York Times*, January 2. https://www.nytimes.com/2019/01/02/upshot/will-pelosi-open-the-floor-to-bipartisan-ideas.html

Wilson, Rick K., and Calvin Jillson. 1989. "Leadership Patterns in the Continental Congress: 1774–1789." *Legislative Studies Quarterly* 14(1): 5–37.

Wolfensberger, Don. 2012. "Appropriations Process Wilts in the Sunshine." *Roll Call*, July 23. http://www.rollcall.com/news/Wolfensberger-Appropriations-Process-Wilts-in-the-Sunshine-216357-1.html

Wright, John R. 1985. "PACs, Contributions, and Roll Calls: An Organizational Perspective." *American Political Science Review* 79(2): 400–414.

Young, Garry, and Vicky Wilkins. 2007. "Vote Switchers and Party Influence in the US House." *Legislative Studies Quarterly* 32(1): 59–77.

Index

Note: Page numbers in italics refer to illustrations and tables.